Web Publishing with Microsoft FrontPage

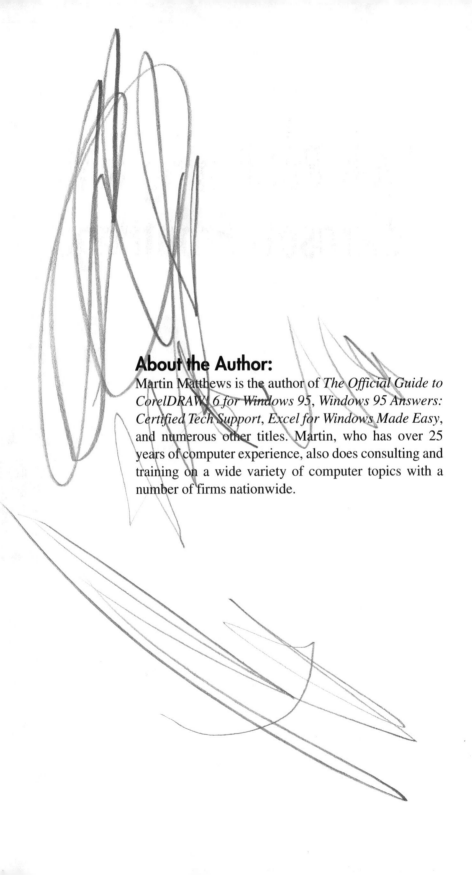

About the Author:

Martin Matthews is the author of *The Official Guide to CorelDRAW! 6 for Windows 95*, *Windows 95 Answers: Certified Tech Support*, *Excel for Windows Made Easy*, and numerous other titles. Martin, who has over 25 years of computer experience, also does consulting and training on a wide variety of computer topics with a number of firms nationwide.

Web Publishing with Microsoft FrontPage

Martin Matthews

Osborne **McGraw-Hill**

Berkeley   New York   St. Louis   San Francisco
Auckland   Bogotá   Hamburg   London   Madrid
Mexico City   Milan   Montreal   New Delhi   Panama City
Paris   São Paulo   Singapore   Sydney
Tokyo   Toronto

Osborne **McGraw-Hill**
2600 Tenth Street
Berkeley, California 94710
U.S.A.

For information on translations or book distributors outside the U.S.A., or to arrange bulk purchase discounts for sales promotions, premiums, or fundraisers, please contact Osborne **McGraw-Hill** at the above address.

Web Publishing with Microsoft FrontPage

1234567890 DOC 99876

ISBN 0-07-882224-6

Acquisitions Editor Wendy Rinaldi	**Indexer** David Heiret
Project Editor Janet Walden	**Computer Designer** Peter Hancik
Copy Editor Jan Jue	**Illustrator** Richard Whitaker
Proofreader Pat Mannion	**Quality Control Specialist** Joe Scuderi

Dedication:

Daniel G. Gestaut

Of all my friends, only a very few have been such for the better part of my life. Dan Gestaut is one. Quite simply, he is always there.

CONTENTS AT A GLANCE

Erik Paulsen, who is webmaster of his own site, (http://www.arcadiaweb.com) in Ojai, California, not only technically reviewed the entire book with great expertise, but also wrote much of Chapters 1, 11, and 12. And he did this while bringing up his new site and suffering the passing of his father. Erik not only knows the Web and the Internet, he knows what it takes to get a book out and he makes it happen. Thanks, Erik!

The job of Acquisitions Editor is largely defined by the person holding the position. To **Wendy Rinaldi**, the Acquisitions Editor on this book, it means being a partner with her authors, a partner who never tries to take over the authorship, but is always there with whatever support, encouragement, and gentle direction is needed. Wendy has put a lot of herself in this book and it is a much better book as a result. Thanks, Wendy!

Janet Walden is one of those people who are just fun to work with, who always have a smile in their voice, who are so competent at what they do that it always seems easy no matter how hard it is, and who have a caring respect for others that tells them they are valued. Janet is the Project Editor on this book and had the job of turning a very rough manuscript into a great book in an unbelievably short time—and throughout it all, it was fun to work with her. Thanks, Janet!

Jan Jue, the book's Copy Editor, is one of the best of her profession at finding those little inconsistencies that are so easy for the author to let slip by and yet can drive a reader crazy. In addition, Jan did a yeomen's job of removing all the grammatical, spelling, and stylistic errors that the author in his ignorance left in. Jan made a very major contribution to this book. Thanks, Jan!

George Ming, FrontPage product manager at Microsoft, always came back with answers to my seemingly endless questions. Thanks, George!

Dee Brown, of Freeland Travel, and **Donna White**, of Just Cruisin' & Travel, were most helpful in setting up the travel examples used in several chapters. Thanks, Dee and Donna.

George Henny, **Jeff Wallace**, and **Julie O'Brien** of WhidbeyNet, my Internet service provider, have been helpful in trying to set up the FrontPage server extensions and in answering my questions. Thanks, George, Jeff, and Julie.

Carole Boggs Matthews, life partner and sharer of our parenting thrills and spills, and an author in her own right, not only provided the all necessary support without which no project like this could ever get done, but also jumped in at the first sign of need to quickly and expertly turn out Appendix A. Thanks, my love!

ACKNOWLEDGMENTS

As the interest in the Internet and its World Wide Web has skyrocketed, so has the desire of both organizations and individuals to have a presence there, to put up their own web sites and be a part of the Internet phenomenon. At the same time, organizations are using the same technology to install intranets at a geometric rate, and therefore they have the need to create their own web sites to use internally. The problem has been that the tools to create both Internet and intranet web sites have been very crude and anything but easy to use. FrontPage has changed all of that. FrontPage provides a very easy-to-use, full-featured set of tools for the expert creation, delivery, and maintenance of web sites. And FrontPage does this in a WYSIWYG environment where you can see what you are doing as you are doing it.

Unfortunately, FrontPage comes with a slim 22-page manual that gives very brief instructions on installation and then tells you about online Help. *Web Publishing with Microsoft FrontPage* fills this void by giving you an easy-to-use, hands-on guide to this extremely powerful product.

About This Book

Web Publishing with Microsoft FrontPage leads you through the planning, creation, testing, deployment, and maintenance of both intranet and Internet web sites with FrontPage. It does this using substantial real-world examples and clear, step-by-step instructions. All of the major features of FrontPage are explained and demonstrated in such a way that you can follow along and see for yourself how each is used. In addition, *Web Publishing with Microsoft FrontPage* takes you beyond basic FrontPage web site creation and introduces you to HTML and how to use it with FrontPage, as well as how to set up an intranet site, and how to publish and promote your web site. *Web Publishing with Microsoft FrontPage* provides the one complete reference on how to make the most of FrontPage. If you are going to purchase FrontPage, or if you already use it, you need this book!

How This Book Is Organized

Web Publishing with Microsoft FrontPage is written the way most people learn. It starts by reviewing the basic concepts and then uses a learn-by-doing method to demonstrate the major features of the product. Throughout, the book uses detailed examples and clear explanations to give you the insight needed to make the fullest use of FrontPage.

Web Publishing with Microsoft FrontPage begins by introducing you to web sites and FrontPage. Chapter 1, "Designing and Creating Quality Web Pages," explores the world of the Internet and the intranet and looks at what makes for a good web page. Chapter 2, "Exploring FrontPage," takes you on a tour of the major FrontPage features, giving you a taste of the power inherent in this product.

In the next six chapters *Web Publishing with Microsoft FrontPage* demonstrates each of the major features of FrontPage by leading you through examples of their implementation. Chapter 3, "Using Wizards and Templates," shows you how to create webs and web pages with these powerful tools. Chapter 4, "Creating and Formatting a Web Page from Scratch," sets aside the wizards and templates and looks at the steps necessary to create a full-featured web on your own. Chapter 5, "Adding and Managing Hyperlinks and Hotspots," explores how to add interactivity and interconnectedness to your web. Chapter 6, "Using Tables and Frames," describes two completely different ways to segment a page and shows how you can make the best use of them. Chapter 7, "Working with Forms and WebBots," explains ways to let the web user communicate back to you, the web creator. Chapter 8, "Importing and Integrating Office and Other Files," shows you how to use existing or legacy files in your intranet and Internet webs.

The final four chapters of *Web Publishing with Microsoft FrontPage* cover ways of extending and enhancing what you can do with FrontPage. Chapter 9, "Working with HTML," provides an introduction to the HTML language and how to use it with FrontPage. Chapter 10, "Creating Your Own FrontPage Templates," shows you how to use your own templates to speed and standardize web creation. Chapter 11, "Setting Up an Intranet Web Site," leads you through the steps to create an intranet in your organization. Chapter 12, "Publishing and Promoting Webs on the Internet," looks at how to locate an Internet service provider, how to transfer your completed webs to their servers, and then how to promote your webs once they're online.

Web Publishing with Microsoft FrontPage concludes with two appendixes. Appendix A provides a detailed set of instructions on how to install FrontPage in different circumstances. Appendix B shows you four commercial web sites that have been largely created by FrontPage. You'll learn something about the organizations behind these sites, who have all been using FrontPage since early 1996, and what their experiences with FrontPage have been. These organizations have all done what you are setting out to do.

Conventions Used in This Book

Web Publishing with Microsoft FrontPage uses several conventions designed to make the book easier for you to follow. Among these are:

- **Bold type** is used for text that you are to type from the keyboard.

- *Italic type* is used for a word or phrase that is being defined or otherwise deserves special emphasis.

- The Courier typeface is used for the HTML code that is either produced by FrontPage or entered by the user.

- Small capital letters are used for keys on the keyboard such as ENTER and SHIFT.

- When you are expected to enter a command, you are told to press the key(s). If you are to enter text or numbers, you are told to type them.

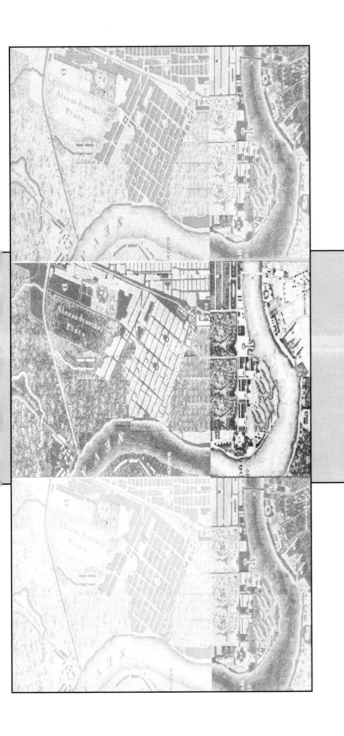

Designing and Creating Quality Web Pages

Communication, whether it be within a small group, throughout a large organization, or among many organizations, can almost always be improved—made faster, more easily received, and more easily responded to. One recent attempt at this improvement is the *web page*, a text and graphics form of communication transmitted by computers. While computers sit on the sending and receiving ends of web page communication, it is what *links* the computers that gives web pages one of their most important features—the ability of the sender and the receiver to operate independently, the ability of the sender to put the web page up on their schedule, and the ability of the receiver to get it anytime thereafter. The link used for the transmission of web pages is one of two forms of networking, either the public Internet using phone lines, or a private intranet using a local area network (LAN), generally within an organization.

The Internet and the World Wide Web

Not long ago, using "Information Superhighway," "the Internet," or "the Web" in everyday conversation might have produced blank looks. Now the Internet and the World Wide Web ("WWW" or simply "the Web") are talked about daily in the news, in schools, and in conversations among friends and coworkers. Many people still don't really understand what the Internet and the Web are, but they know they're out there and will affect how people live, work, and communicate.

Being able to access the resources of the Internet and having a presence on the World Wide Web are becoming as necessary as having a telephone. You could certainly get by without a telephone, but by doing so you would cut yourself off from communicating with the millions of people who do have telephones. As this is written (mid 1996) there are over 22 million sites on the World Wide Web. These range from personal pages, where individuals can share their opinions or interests with the world, to educational and corporate sites getting hundreds of thousands of *hits* (connections made to a web site) a day.

The Internet and the World Wide Web form the foundation of a global communications revolution that will change the way people communicate, work, and conduct business. They will make it easier and cheaper to exchange information, ideas, and products around the globe. Accessing a web site in Australia is as easy as accessing a web site across the street.

In this book you will learn how you can be part of this revolution. You will learn how you can use FrontPage to create and maintain a presence on the Web for your business, your organization, or for yourself. This book will take you through all the steps necessary to create your own web page—from initial design to placing your page on a web server where it can be accessed by anyone on the Web.

LANs and an Intranet

As important as the Internet has become to society, local area networks, or LANs, have become even more important to the exchange of information and communication within organizations. LANs started out as a means to share programs and data files among several people in an organization. This was then augmented with electronic mail (e-mail) for sending and receiving messages over the LAN. Recently, *intranets* have been added to LANs to provide a miniature version of the World Wide Web within an organization—a place for people to post and read text and graphics documents if and when they choose.

A good example of an intranet web page is a project report. Instead of e-mailing a weekly report to a long list of potentially interested people (and filling up everybody's in-basket in the process), a web page could be created and periodically updated that would not only give the current status, but also other, more static information, such as the people working on the project, its goals, and its funding. In this way, only those people who are truly interested can get the information and that group can change as they choose.

Except for possibly the content, there is no difference between a web page on the World Wide Web and a web page on an intranet. They are created the same way and can have the same features and components. The discussion and instructions throughout this book are aimed equally at the Web and an intranet and there are

examples of each. So in learning to create a web page, you can apply that knowledge to either form of dissemination.

IP: *Think of the Internet and a LAN as equivalent means of information transmission, one public and the other private; and think of the Web and an intranet as equivalent means of posting and reading information being transmitted over the Internet or a LAN respectively. The Web and an intranet are just advanced electronic bulletin boards and a web page is an electronic document posted on that bulletin board.*

What Is a Web Page?

Since the focus of this book is how to create web pages, look at a more detailed definition of what a web page is. A good starting place is that a *web page* is a text file containing HyperText Markup Language (HTML) formatting tags and links to graphics files and other web pages. The text file is stored on a *web server* and can be accessed by other computers connected to the server, via the Internet or a LAN, and using *web browsers*—programs that download the file to your computer, interpret the HTML tags and links, and display the results on your monitor. Another definition is that a web page is an interactive form of communication that uses a computer network.

There are two properties of web pages that make them unique: they are interactive and they can use multimedia. The term *multimedia* is used to describe text, audio, animation, and video files that are combined to present information—for example, in an interactive encyclopedia or a game. When those same types of files are distributed over the Internet or a LAN, you can use the term *hypermedia* to describe them. With the World Wide Web it is now possible to have true multimedia over the Internet. However, unless your clients have a high-speed service, such as the Integrated Services Digital Network's (ISDN) 128 Kbps service, downloading the large hypermedia files takes too long to routinely use them. On most LANs, which are considerably faster, this is much more doable, but there are still limitations and a potential need to keep the LAN open for high volume data traffic.

Web pages are interactive because the reader or user can send information or commands to a web site that will control an application running on the web server. For example, Figure 1-1 shows the home page of Digital's Alta Vista web index. The Alta Vista home page gives you access to an application that searches the Alta Vista index of web sites. You can use this and other search engines to locate sites on the Web. From this web page you can select which part of the Internet to search, how the results of the search will be displayed, and the keywords that the search will be based on. When you click on the Submit button, the information you've entered is sent to the Alta Vista web server. The database is then searched, and the results are used to create a new web page, which is displayed by your web browser. Figure 1-2 shows the results of a search using the keyword "origami."

Each web page has an address called the Uniform Resource Locator (URL). The URL for the Alta Vista home page is *http://www.altavista.digital.com.* The URL is displayed in the Address text box at the top of the screen (below the toolbar). A URL is the path on the Internet to a specific web page. It is used in the same way you use a path name to locate files on your computer. In this case, the URL tells you that the web page is located on a web server named *altavista.digital.com* connected to the World Wide Web (the *WWW*). The actual filename of the home page is either *default.htm* or *index.htm*; it is implied by being unstated. On a LAN the URL is similar, using the server name in a format like *http://servername/directory/homepage filename.* The home page file can also be be left off if it is index.htm or default.htm.

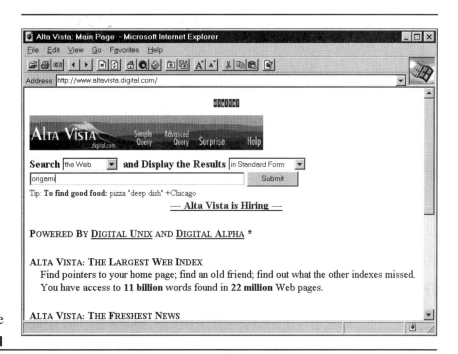

Alta Vista home page

■ FIGURE 1-1

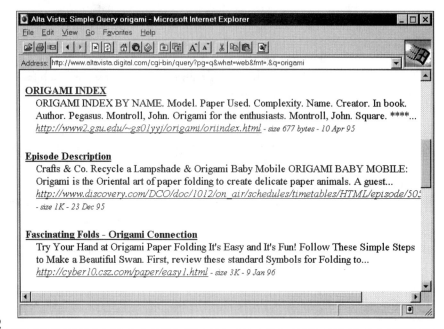

Alta Vista web page created to display results of search

FIGURE 1-2

Alta Vista found over 5,000 web pages containing the keyword "origami." The web page created by the Alta Vista server displays the title of each web page, an excerpt from the text on the page, and the URL for the page. Both the title of the page and the URL are displayed in a different color than the other text and are underlined. This indicates they are *hyperlinks.* Clicking on a hyperlink will cause your browser to load the location (web page) specified in the hyperlink. The hyperlink may take you to an actual location, or *bookmark,* within the same document, the way a bookmark works in a word processor file, or it may link you to a web site anywhere in the world. In fact, if a web page doesn't have an obvious identifier to its location, you may not even be aware of what country the web server you are connected to is in. You may start "surfing" the Web by clicking on hyperlinks on various pages to follow a train of thought and end up "traveling" around the world.

OTE: *Hyperlinks do not have to be underlined, although they will be displayed in a different color than the body text. With most web browsers you can use the Preferences option to control whether hyperlinks will be underlined, and you can also set the color they will be displayed in.*

When you submit keywords or other information to a web site, such as Alta Vista, you are actually running an application on the web server. Web servers can also download applications, for example, a Java applet, to your computer. *Java* is programming language that extends the flexibility and functions of the Web. *Applets* are small programs that are downloaded to your computer and then executed. An example of a Java applet is a currency-conversion program. When you click on the hyperlink to the applet, it is downloaded to your computer. You then enter the amount and type of currency you want to convert and the type of currency you want to convert it to, and the applet performs the conversion. You do not have to know how to program in Java in order to use a Java applet—a growing library of applets is already available on the Web. A good place to start is the Java home page (http://www.javasoft.com) or the Gamelan home page (http://www.gamelan.com).

As you can see, the World Wide Web is a flexible and powerful means of communication. How did this new medium come about?

The Birth of the Internet

The Internet is simply a set of computer hardware and software standards, or *protocols*, that allow computers to exchange data with other computers. The computers can be in the same room, or they can be located around the world from each other. They can use the same operating system software, such as Windows 95, or each can use a different computer operating system, such as Macintosh System 7.5 or UNIX. The standards that make up the Internet have become a modern *lingua franca*—a language enabling any computer connected to the Internet to exchange information with any other computer also connected to the Internet, regardless of the operating systems the computers use.

The birth of the Internet can be traced back to the launch of the first Sputnik by the Soviet Union in 1957. Concerned about losing the space race, the United States government created the Advanced Research Projects Agency (ARPA). By the late 1960s the use of computers by ARPA and other government agencies had expanded so much that a way for the computer systems to share data was needed. ARPANET, the predecessor to what we now know as the Internet, was created to meet this need.

The early growth of the Internet was funded by the government, but just as important as the money provided for research was the ability to impose standards on the computer industry. In the '60s computers made by different manufacturers were, for the most part, unable to exchange data because of differences in their software. As ARPA defined the standards that have become the foundation of the Internet, it required manufacturers to support those standards if they wanted to do

business with the government. This ensured that all computers would be able to exchange data with each other.

Another milestone in the history of the Internet came in the mid '80s, when the National Science Foundation (NSF) added its five supercomputing centers to the Internet. This gave educational centers, the military, and other NSF grantees access to the power of these supercomputers and, more importantly, created the *backbone* of today's Information Superhighway. This backbone is made up of all the high capacity (or *wide bandwidth)* phone lines and data links needed to effectively transfer all the information now on the Internet. Until this wide bandwidth infrastructure existed, the potential of ARPANET, NSFNET, and now the Internet couldn't be realized. By the end of the 1980s almost all the pieces were in place for a global telecommunications revolution.

The World Wide Web

Before 1990 the Internet had grown to be a highway linking computers across the United States and around the world, but it was still a character-based system. That is, what appeared on computer screens connected to the Internet was simply text. There were no graphics or hyperlinks. A graphical user interface (GUI) to the Internet needed to be developed. Tim Berners-Lee, a scientist working at the European Laboratory for Particle Physics (CERN) in Geneva, Switzerland, proposed a set of protocols for the transfer of graphical information over the Internet in 1989. Berners-Lee's proposals were adopted by other groups, and the World Wide Web was born.

The Internet is a wide area network (WAN), as compared with a local area network (LAN) among computers in proximity. For computers to share information over a WAN, there must be a physical connection (the communications infrastructure created by ARPA and the NSF and now maintained by private industry) and a common software standard that the computers use to transfer data. The physical connection depends on whether you use a modem to dial up to the Internet, or whether your computer is part of a LAN with an Internet connection. The physical layer includes the modem or network interface card in your computer. You also need a phone or dedicated network line that connects you to the Internet backbone. In either case, your computer, connected to the Internet either with a dialup or network connection, has the potential to share information with any other computer connected to the Internet anywhere in the world.

The Internet and World Wide Web, or simply the Web, are built upon several protocols:

- **Transmission Control Protocol/Internet Protocol (TCP/IP)** controls how information is packaged to be transferred between computers connected through the Internet.

- **HyperText Transfer Protocol (HTTP)** is the language the computers use to exchange information on the Web.

- **HyperText Markup Language (HTML)** is the programming language used to create the documents that are distributed on the Web and displayed on your monitor.

TCP/IP

To transfer information over the Internet or within a LAN, several requirements must be met. These include a way to assign each computer or site on the network a unique address (just like having a unique postal address) and "packaging" the information for transmission. These functions are handled by the Transmission Control Protocol and the Internet Protocol.

INTERNET PROTOCOL   The foundation of the system is the Internet Protocol (IP). The IP converts data into *packets* and provides an address for each site on the Internet. Packets are like the pages of a book. An entire book contains too much information to be printed on one page, so it is divided into multiple pages. This makes the information in the book much more manageable. The Internet Protocol does the same thing with the information in a file that is to be transmitted over the Internet or a LAN. It divides the information into packets that can be handled more easily by the network.

The other primary function of the IP is to provide addresses for the computers connected to the Internet. Each computer needs its own *IP address,* a group of four decimal numbers that provides a unique address for the computer. Examples of IP addresses are 198.68.191.10 and 204.250.144.70. These IP addresses are actually decimal representations of single 32-bit binary numbers. While a computer may be comfortable with 11000110 01000100 10111111 00001010 or 11001100 11111010 10010000 01000110 as an address, most people find decimal numbers easier to work with. This system of numbering allows for about 4.3 billion (2^{32}) possible combinations. If you are setting up a web server, you will need to get an IP address. These are assigned by the Internet Network Information Center (InterNIC). Your Internet service provider (ISP) can help you get an IP address. If you will be using an existing web server, the network administrator or *webmaster* will be able to tell you what the IP addresses are.

TRANSMISSION CONTROL PROTOCOL   While the Internet Protocol provides the basics for sharing information over the Internet, it leaves some things to be desired. The two most important are ensuring that all the packets reach their destination and that they arrive in the proper order. This is where the Transmission Control Protocol steps in. To understand how it works, assume you want to send a book to someone and you have to mail it one page (or packet) at a time. Also assume that there are no page numbers in the book.

How will recipients know that they received all the pages, and how will they know the proper order of the pages? TCP solves these problems by creating an "envelope" for each packet generated by the IP. Each envelope has a serialized number that identifies the packet inside it. As each packet is sent, the TCP assigns it a number that increases by 1 for each packet sent. When the packets are received, the numbers are checked for continuity and sequence. If any numbers are missing, the receiving computer requests that the missing packet be re-sent. If the packets are out of sequence, the receiving computer puts them back into the proper order. TCP also makes sure the information arrives in the same condition it was sent—that the data was not corrupted in transit.

TCP/IP provides the basic tools for transferring information over the Internet. The next layer up the ladder is the HyperText Transfer Protocol, the traffic director for the Web.

 OTE: *To set up an intranet on a LAN, you must add the TCP/IP protocols to the existing networking protocols (probably either IPX/SPX or NetBEUI) on both the server and all clients.*

HyperText Transfer Protocol

The HyperText Transfer Protocol (HTTP) is the heart of the World Wide Web and is also used with an intranet. HTTP composes the messages and handles the information that is sent between computers on the Internet using TCP/IP. To understand how HTTP works, you first need to understand the nature of client/server relationships.

CLIENT/SERVER RELATIONSHIPS   The basic function of the Internet or a LAN is to provide a means for transferring information between computers. To do this, one computer (the *server*) will contain information and another (the *client*) will request it. The server will process a client's request and transfer the information. The server may be required to process the request before it can be filled. For example, if the request is for information contained in a database, such as a request submitted to the Alta Vista web index, the server would first have to extract the information from the database before it could be sent to the client.

The passing of information between a client and a server has four basic steps:

1. A connection is made between the client and the server. This is handled by TCP/IP.

2. The client sends a request to the server. The request is in the form of an HTTP message.

3. The server processes the request and responds to the client. Again, this is in the form of an HTTP message.

4. The connection between the client and the server is terminated.

To access information on the Web or an intranet, you need an application that can send requests to a server and can process and display the server's response. This is the function of *web browsers*. The two most common web browsers are Microsoft's Internet Explorer and Netscape's Navigator.

HyperText Markup Language

The parts of the Web or an intranet covered so far, TCP/IP and HTTP, control how information is transferred over the network. HyperText Markup Language (HTML) is the component that controls how the information is displayed. The information sent from a web server is an HTML document. Here's what a simple HTML document looks like:

```
<HTML>
<HEAD>
<TITLE>A Simple HTML Document</TITLE>
</HEAD>
<BODY>
<H1>A Simple HTML Document</H1>
<B>This text is bold</B> and <I>this text is italic.</I>
</BODY>
</HTML>
```

Figure 1-3 shows how this HTML document is displayed by a web browser. Web browsers interpret the HTML document and display the results on your monitor. HTML files are simple ASCII text files that contain formatting tags which control how information (text and graphics) is displayed and how other file types are executed (audio and video files, for example).

HTML tags are usually used in pairs. An HTML document should begin with the <HTML> opening tag and end with the </HTML> closing tag. The <HEAD> </HEAD> tags enclose information about the web page, such as the title, which is defined by the <TITLE> </TITLE> tags and displayed in the title bar of the web browser. The body of the web page is enclosed by the <BODY> </BODY> tags. The <H1> </H1> tags define the enclosed text as a level 1 heading. The <B> </B> and <I> </I> tags respectively define text as bold or italic, as you can see in Figure 1-3.

 OTE: *HTML tags are not case-sensitive. They can be upper- or lowercase, or mixed case, such as <Body>.*

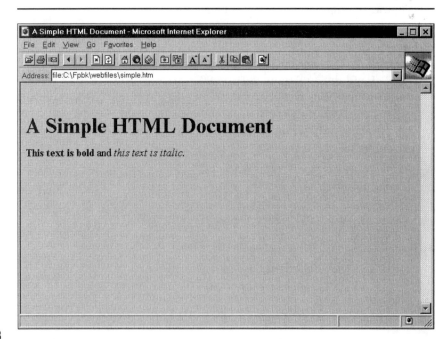

A simple HTML document

FIGURE 1-3

In the early days of the Web, these tags were typed in using a simple text editor to create web pages. This was time-consuming and not much fun. Today you can use FrontPage, a true WYSIWYG (what you see is what you get) HTML editor, to create your web pages. Gone are the days when you had to learn all the HTML tags and proper syntax. With FrontPage you design a page, and the proper HTML code is created automatically. It's never been easier to create your own web site.

In the next section you will learn what makes a good web site.

Designing for the Web

Like any other medium, the Web has idiosyncrasies that the good designer has to be aware of and compensate for. Because the Web is strictly a computer-based medium, the hardware your work will be displayed on (the video card, monitor, and settings) and the particular web browser used will have a tremendous impact on how your work appears.

Monitor Resolution

If you've designed works for paper, you are used to having a fixed-size "canvas" to work with. As you lay out the elements of the design, you know exactly how the design will appear when finished and viewed by the audience. This is not the case when you design for the Web. Your work may be displayed on a Macintosh with a 512×342 pixel monochrome display, or a PC with a 1024×768 pixel SVGA display. On the Web, graphics are displayed at a resolution chosen when they are added to a page. A graphic that fills the screen at a 640×480 resolution will only use a quarter of the screen at a 1024×768 resolution. Figure 1-4 shows a web page displayed at a 640×480 resolution. Figure 1-5 shows the same page at 800×600 resolution, and Figure 1-6 shows the page at 1024×768 resolution.

As you can see, the web page in Figures 1-4 through 1-6 was designed so that it would be a cohesive design at each possible resolution. The best way to tell how your design will appear is to view it on monitors at different resolutions as you work on it. Since this isn't always easy to do (your computer may need to be rebooted each time you change your video resolution), the next best thing is to work at 640×480 resolution and check your work at the different resolutions when you're done. In all probability, your work will be viewed at 640×480 resolution most of the time.

Web page at 640×480 resolution

FIGURE 1-4

Web page at 800×600 resolution

FIGURE 1-5

Web
page at
1024×768
resolution

FIGURE 1-6

IP: *If you are using Windows 95, you can often change your resolution
without rebooting by right-clicking on the desktop, choosing Properties,
selecting Settings, and changing the Desktop Area. Also, there is a free utility
available from Microsoft's Power Toys web page (http://www.microsoft.com /windows/
software/powertoy.htm) called QuickRes. This utility allows you to more often change
your video resolution without rebooting your system.*

Monitor Color Settings

On a PC, your monitor can display 16, 256, 64,000 (16-bit High Color), or 16 million
(24-bit True Color) colors. Again, you have no control over how many colors your
work will be displayed with, and it is inevitable that your work will be displayed on
monitors with only 16 colors.

The decision you have as a web page designer is whether to limit yourself to the
lowest common denominator (16-color, 640×480 resolution) or to work at a higher
standard. If you are designing a simple page with limited graphics, limiting your
design to 16 colors may make sense. It ensures compatibility with virtually all the

systems your work will be displayed on. (If someone is using a monochrome monitor to view your work, the point is moot, of course.)

However, if you limit yourself to 16 colors, you will not be able to effectively use scanned photographs or graphics with subtle shadings. In that case it would be better to use at least 256 colors. You cannot limit yourself to the lowest common denominator in every case. You simply have to accept that your work will not look its best on lower-end systems. The people with these systems hopefully will upgrade them as they discover that other people's systems look a lot better!

Another point to remember about color is that every monitor will display colors a little differently. There are many factors that affect how colors are displayed on a monitor, ranging from the age of the monitor to the light in the room. If you've worked with programs like Photoshop and have output to color printers, you know how difficult it can be to get the printed output to exactly match the colors you see on the monitor. If it's important that a particular color appear exactly the correct shade on a web page—when it's part of a logo, for example—you're simply out of luck. You can calibrate your own monitor and ensure the color is correct on a calibrated system, but once you turn it loose on the Web, you have no control over how it will appear.

If you design your web pages to be displayed on a 256-color, 640×480 resolution monitor and remember it will look different at other video resolutions, you can count on most people seeing your work the way you intended.

Data Throughput

Another factor that must be considered in the design of a web page is how long it will take the page to be downloaded and displayed. People tend to have short attention spans. If your page is taking too long to download, the user is likely to go on to another page without waiting for your page to finish loading. The two primary factors in the time it takes for a web page to be transferred are the size of the page, including graphics and other files, and the speed of the user's modem or network. You should remember that there are still quite a few 14,400 baud (14.4 Kbps) modems in use. (Anything slower, such as 2,400 or 9,600 baud modems, are almost useless for accessing the Web.) If everyone had ISDN (128 Kbps) lines, this would be less of a problem, but it will be awhile before that happens.

The text portion of a web page (the HTML code) is rarely large enough to cause long downloads; the usual culprits are graphic and multimedia files. There are several things you can do to minimize the problem. The first is to keep your graphic and multimedia files as small as possible. Some of the ways you can do that are

discussed later in the chapter in the section "Working with Graphics." You can also create several smaller pages, rather than one large page. You then use hyperlinks to connect the pages. This breaks up the loading time (the theory being that the user will tolerate several short delays better than one long delay).

IP: *FrontPage has a way of including the contents of one page on another (as you'll see in Chapter 2) that both makes repeated elements like headings easy to do and speeds loading.*

Another factor is the bandwidth of the web server where the page is located. If the server has a narrow bandwidth connection to the Internet (such as a 56 Kbps analog line), it can be easily overloaded when it's accessed by several users at the same time. If the server has a wide bandwidth connection—a full T1 (1.544 Mbps), for example—it is much less likely to be overloaded. However, the Internet has grown to the point where popular web servers are noticeably slower at peak times of the day and on weekends, even with wide bandwidth connections.

Web Browsers

All web browsers interpret and display HTML-encoded files. Currently, HTML 2.0 is the accepted standard, and HTML 3.2 is being developed (HTML 3.0 was never finalized). The manufacturers of web browsers, principally Microsoft and Netscape, chose not to wait for HTML 3.0 to be defined and implemented their own versions of HTML 3.0. This has been good for the Web to the extent that advances in browser capabilities have been made faster, but the compatibility of browsers has suffered. Some of the extensions offered by Microsoft and Netscape are compatible with each other, while others will only work with their own browser. Figure 1-7 shows a web page that uses some of the HTML tags introduced by Microsoft and Netscape displayed using Microsoft's Internet Explorer 2.0. Figure 1-8 shows the same page displayed with Netscape Navigator 2.01, Figure 1-9 shows the page displayed with Spry Mosaic 4.0, and Figure 1-10 shows the page in the FrontPage 1.1 Editor. As you can see, each browser, using its default settings, displays the HTML file differently.

At the top of the page are a level 1 heading followed by a level 2 heading. Below the heads are two tables separated by a horizontal rule. Tables were introduced in the draft specification of HTML 3.0. Both Microsoft and Netscape support tables

A simple
web page
displayed
with
Internet
Explorer
(v 2.0)

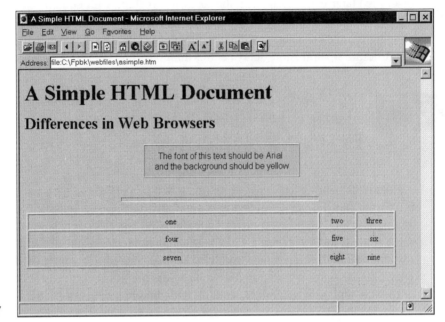

FIGURE 1-7

A simple
web page
displayed
with
Netscape
Navigator
(v 2.01)

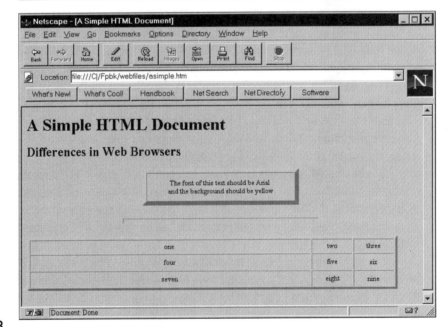

FIGURE 1-8

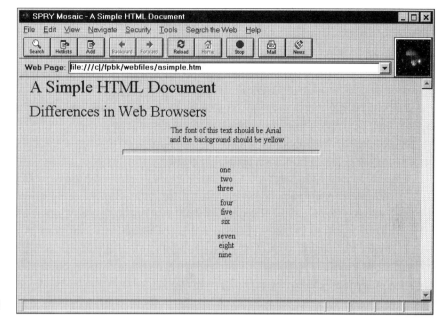

A simple
web page
displayed
with Spry
Mosaic
(v 4.0)

FIGURE 1-9

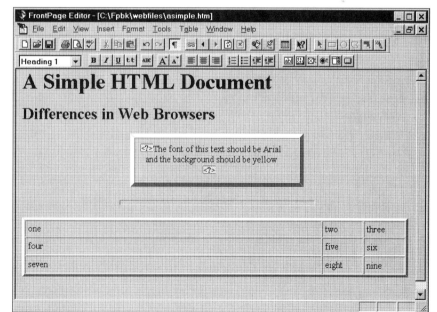

A simple
web page
displayed
with the
FrontPage
Editor
(v 1.1)

FIGURE 1-10

(with some differences), while Spry Mosaic does not (in version 4.0). The first table has one row and one column. The first table illustrates two important differences between Microsoft and Netscape's browsers. Microsoft's Internet Explorer allows you to change the background color of a cell in a table and the typeface of text, while Netscape Navigator does not. On the other hand, Navigator allows you to change the width of borders in tables, while Internet Explorer doesn't. (The FrontPage Editor does not display either the font or the background color, but does display a symbol, a question mark in a box, to tell you the font coding exists. If you look at the extended attributes for the cell, you'll see the background color.) Another difference is the amount of space inserted by the browser after a table or other element. Internet Explorer adds space between elements; Navigator does not.

Internet Explorer and Netscape Navigator interpret horizontal rules the same. In this example, the width of the rule is 50 percent of the window and the size (height) is 8 pixels. As you can see in Figure 1-9, Spry Mosaic also supports both width and height for horizontal rules. The final element of the page is a table with three rows and three columns. Internet Explorer and Navigator display the table in the same way, while Spry Mosaic simply ignores the HTML table tags.

 OTE: *This example web page was written to illustrate the differences between web browsers. By being careful it is possible to minimize many, but not all, of the differences between web browsers.*

Since you will have no control over which web browser your work will be displayed with, what HTML features should you use? Should you never use tables because some browsers don't support them? The short answer is no. HTML is actually a very limited language for page layout and design, and limiting yourself to the lowest common denominator will produce some very boring pages. Tables are one of the most powerful design tools HTML has to offer, and to produce visually interesting pages, you will have to use them. While Spry Mosaic does not support tables in version 4.0, you can be sure that table support will be added in future versions.

Both Internet Explorer and Netscape Navigator have features not supported by any other browser. If you decide that you want to use one of the unsupported features, you have to encourage the user to use the browser you tailored your design to. This is not as difficult as it may sound. Microsoft and Netscape together dominate the web browser market, and both offer free versions of their browsers on the Web for downloading. At the top of your web page you can simply create a hyperlink to either the Internet Explorer or Navigator download sites, and tell users they need one or the other. In fact, both companies provide graphics (shown here) that you can insert in your page to link to the downloadable files.

As a web designer, you need to use all the tools at your disposal. By checking how your work will appear with different web browsers, you can minimize many design problems. When you need to use an unsupported HTML element, you can make it easy for users to download the web browser they need. What you cannot do, if you really want to create good work, is limit yourself to the lowest common denominator.

Content

Good graphic design for your web pages is only half the battle. Your web pages also need to be interesting—there has to be a reason for people to visit your web site. The content of your web site is just as, if not more, important than the design.

First and foremost, your web site has to be rich in content, not hype. For example, if your site was created for marketing your line of kayaks, include the history of the sport, stories (with photos) of trips your users have taken, information for people new to the sport, hyperlinks to related sites (not necessarily your competitors), and anything else you can think of that might be interesting to kayakers. Just don't put up an online catalog and expect people to come back.

Next, be organized. Give people the tools they need to navigate your site. Before you start the graphic design for your site, plan the information flow. How will content areas be linked? How will users get around the site? Will they be able to get to any area in one hop, or will they have to traverse a convoluted series of links? Make it easy for your users. If they get frustrated trying to navigate your site, they won't be back. If people can download audio files from your site, make sure they can also download whatever player they need for the file. Don't make them search the Web, or even your site, for it.

Keep your site fresh. Update as often as you can. People are not going to come back to see the same old stuff. In the kayaking example, consider updating the trips featured every month. In winter (in the Northern Hemisphere) feature trips in New Zealand. Compare your web site to a magazine—no one would subscribe to a

magazine that was exactly the same every month, it would soon bore them. Your web site is no different.

Make sure your visitors know who you are. Identify every page in your site—don't rely on just the page title displayed in the web browser title bar. You don't have to have your name in a level 1 heading on each page, but make sure that if someone is following a link from another site, they know where they are.

Do it today. If you don't, someone else will. The Web is a fast moving, extremely competitive environment. You don't have time to rest on your laurels. With over 21 million web sites already in existence, you have plenty of competition for people's attention. You can create a world class web site, but it will take effort, planning, and creativity. Give people content and make it as easy as possible for them to get it.

Working with Graphics

Graphic images are an important element of your web site. On the Web, graphics come in two basic flavors: GIF and JPEG. Each format has its advantages and disadvantages.

 IP: *FrontPage allows you to bring in graphics in several standard formats such as .PCX, .TIF, and .EPS, and FrontPage will convert them to GIF and JPEG formats.*

GIF

The Graphic Interchange Format (GIF) was originally developed by CompuServe to minimize the size of graphics files. The smaller the file size, the less time needed to transfer the file. GIF was the first file type widely supported by web browsers. That is, GIF files could be displayed by the browser without using an accessory, or *helper,* application.

GIFs are indexed color bitmap files containing up to 256 colors (8-bit color). *Indexed color* simply means the graphic file uses a palette of up to 256 colors. The colors in the palette can be defined by the user, and the palette can contain fewer than the full 256 colors. When fewer colors are used, the file size is reduced. GIF files are compressed using a *lossless* compression algorithm. This means that no image data is removed by the compression process.

There are two versions of the GIF format currently in use: 87 and 89a. The 89a format has two features not found in the older 87 GIF or JPEG format—transparent backgrounds and interlaced images. Transparent backgrounds are created when one color in the GIF is replaced by the color of the background it is displayed on. This is a very useful feature for creating irregular-shaped images, such as text that you want to have floating over the background, rather than being in a rectangular box. You could create a similar look by using the same background color in the GIF as you use on your web page, but not all web browsers will display the colors exactly the same, and you may end up with an undesirable effect. You would also have to change the background color in the GIF if you changed the web page background. FrontPage has a graphics tool that allows you to make one color transparent (see Chapter 4).

When an image is interlaced, it is loaded and displayed at full size, but not all the information is used. The image appears "out of focus" and gets sharper in a series of passes. It takes four passes to display an interlaced GIF in its final form. Noninterlaced GIFs are displayed one stripe at a time, and each stripe is displayed at the final resolution. FrontPage has an option that allows you to make a .GIF file interlaced (see Chapter 4).

JPEG

The Joint Photographic Experts Group (JPEG) graphic format is a bitmap that can display up to 16.7 million colors (24-bit color). JPEG images are compressed using a *lossy* compression scheme. This makes the file smaller at the cost of some of the data in the image. Originally, web browsers used a helper application to display JPEG images, which meant that a separate window would be opened to display the image. Most current web browsers now display JPEG images without using a helper application.

GIF or JPEG?

Each format has its advantages and disadvantages. Which format you should use will depend on the specific use of the image.

GIF images are preferable when the image will contain fewer than 256 colors. For example, a graphic with only a few colors, like the "at work" graphic shown

here which contains only three colors, works best using GIF. This example also benefits from having a transparent background. This image is often used to indicate that a web page is "under construction." With a transparent background, it can be used

without modification on any web page, regardless of background color. On the other hand, if your image is a scanned color photograph, you would probably use JPEG, so it could have more than 256 colors.

OTE: *At one time it was common to find web pages that were "under construction." This is not recommended practice. Your web pages should be finished when they are put online.*

Whichever graphic format you use, you will need a good graphics program to work with and convert graphic images. Adobe Photoshop and Fractal Design Painter are good choices.

Multimedia Files

The Web is a rapidly evolving medium, and support for audio and video files is a major factor in that growth. Microsoft's Internet Explorer, for example, now includes support for .AVI files. These are multimedia (audio and video) files that can be played from within Internet Explorer without using a helper application. Internet Explorer will also play .WAV, .AU, and .MID audio files.

This is another area where the real world has left the Internet Engineering Task Force behind. Currently only Internet Explorer supports playing .AVI, .WAV, .AU, and .MID files without launching a helper application. This capability will eventually become standard in all Web browsers. It may not be implemented in the same way that Microsoft has chosen, or, by virtue of being first, Microsoft's tags may become the de facto standard of the industry.

The Motion Picture Experts Group (MPEG) has also developed standards for audio and video files that are used on the Internet. Currently, these files require helper applications to be played, but this will probably change in the future.

A number of other companies and organizations are developing products for utilizing the Internet for full multimedia broadcasting. Cornell University has developed CU-SeeMe (for information see http://www.wpine.com), a video conferencing application for the Internet. CU-SeeMe is capable of transmitting both audio and video. Video requires a 28.8 Kbps or faster modem, while audio can function well at 14.4 Kbps.

Progressive Networks' RealAudio (http://www.realaudio.com) provides higher-quality audio using the RealAudio player. NPR, ESPN, CNN, and ABC all provide RealAudio files of their news broadcasts on their Web sites. You can even hear a "live" simulcast of a Seattle classical music radio station on RealAudio's Web site. Xing Technology's StreamWorks (http://www.xingtech.com) is another program that provides audio and video feeds over the Internet.

The potential of the World Wide Web and an intranet seems almost limitless. It will affect society as fundamentally as the printing press, radio, and television. Your ability to use these facilities to create and maintain a presence for your organization, business, or just for yourself, will become an essential skill for the next millennium.

In the next chapter you will see the tools FrontPage provides to help you master the Web and an intranet.

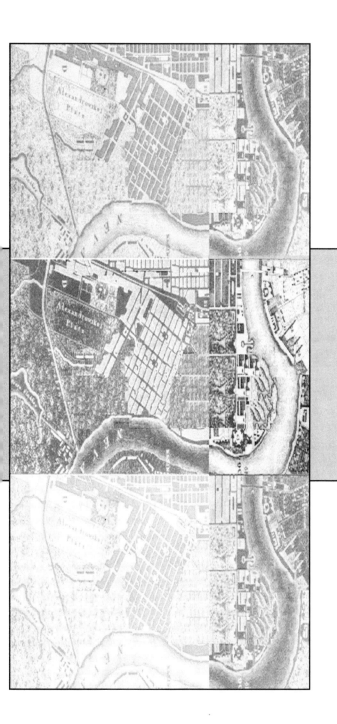

Exploring
FrontPage

Microsoft FrontPage is an authoring and publishing system for creating and delivering formatted content over the Internet or over a local area network (LAN). FrontPage provides the means to design, organize, and deliver an online publication, called a *web*, which may be one or more pages on the Internet's World Wide Web (the *Web*) or an intranet. FrontPage uses five major components to organize, create, manage, and deliver webs.

- The **FrontPage Explorer** allows you to organize your webs and their links by using several views of the pages in a web in a drag-and-drop environment. It is normally the place where you start a new web; use wizards and templates to create a structure; set permissions for end users, authors, and administrators; and copy a web from one server to another.

- The **FrontPage Editor** allows you to create, format, and lay out text; add graphics created outside of FrontPage; and establish hyperlinks with other areas of the same web or with other webs. It provides a WYSIWYG (what you see is what you get) editing environment where you can edit existing webs, including those created elsewhere on the Web, as well as new webs. In the FrontPage Editor you can use page wizards and page templates, apply *WebBots* for interactive functions, create forms and tables, add image maps with clickable hotspots, and convert popular image formats into GIF and JPEG formats used on the Web.

- The **To Do List** provides a means to manage the tasks required to create a web, who those tasks are assigned to, the task's priority, and the page in a web to which the task is assigned.

- The **Personal Web Server** allows you to directly deliver your webs to someone seeking them, as well as to provide file-management support for your webs.

- **FrontPage Server Extensions**, which are available for most popular Internet servers, add the functionality needed to implement the interactive parts of a FrontPage web.

Creating a Web

The FrontPage process of creating a web is unique and uses the following steps:

1. Plan the web. What are the goals; what text, graphics, forms, and hyperlinks will it contain; how will it flow; how will the user get around; and roughly what will the pages look like.

2. Start the FrontPage Personal Web Server and then the FrontPage Explorer.

3. In the Explorer create the structure of the new web by using a wizard and/or template, or simply by creating a blank page.

4. Also in the Explorer set the permissions—who can administer, author, and use the web you are about to create.

5. From the Explorer open the To Do List, and create the items you want on the list. If you used a wizard to create your structure, you will automatically have items in the To Do List that you can edit.

6. Back in the Explorer select the first page you want to work on, and open the FrontPage Editor with that page.

7. In the FrontPage Editor enter, format, and position the text you want to use. Insert the graphics, hyperlinks, frames, tables, and forms. If desired, import existing webs into yours.

8. As each page is complete, save it, mark the To Do task as complete, and from the FrontPage Explorer, select the next page you want to work on and reopen the FrontPage Editor.

9. Periodically open an Internet browser such as the Microsoft Internet Explorer or the Netscape Navigator, and look at the web you are creating. This allows you to test the full functionality of your web. You will be able to see and interact with the web as the user will. You can then revise the web by changing or updating the content, adjusting the page layouts, and reordering the pages and sections.

10. Verify the hyperlinks that you have placed in your web by using the Verify Links commands in the FrontPage Explorer.

11. When you are satisfied with your web, release it for use by copying it to the server from which you want to make it available. (That server must have the FrontPage Server Extensions installed on it to use many of the interactive features available in FrontPage, such as forms.)

12. Using your browser, download, view, and manipulate the web as the user would. Note the load times and the impression you are getting of the web. Ask others to view and use the web and give you their impressions and suggestions.

13. Revise and maintain the web as necessary, either by directly editing the copy on the server, or by editing your local copy and then replacing the server copy.

IP: *If someone other than you has permission to edit a web, you should copy the current version from the server and then edit it, rather than trusting the copy on your local machine. This avoids the "Twilight Zone Effect," where a web is edited by more than one person at one time.*

Creating a web with FrontPage gives you important advantages over other authoring systems. You can

■ Graphically visualize and organize a complex web with a number of pages, images, and other elements by using the FrontPage Explorer

■ Create and edit a complex web page in a WYSIWYG environment by using the FrontPage Editor without having to use or know HTML, the backbone of the Web

■ Easily manage the tasks that are required to build a web, who has responsibility for them, and their completion using the To Do List

■ Quickly create an entire web, page, or element on a page by using wizards or templates

■ Easily add interactive functions such as forms, text searches, and discussion forums without the use of programming, by using WebBots

■ Directly view and use a web on your hard disk with the FrontPage Personal Web Server

FrontPage Components

FrontPage is a true client/server application that provides all of the pieces necessary to create and deliver formatted text and graphical information over both a LAN and the Internet. From the client side, FrontPage provides

- The **FrontPage Explorer** to create, visualize, and manage an entire web with its many elements

- The **FrontPage Editor** to create and edit a web page by adding formatted text, graphics, frames, tables, forms, hyperlinks to other pages and webs, and other interactive elements

- The **To Do List** to track the tasks required to produce a web, identifying who is responsible for them, their priority, and status

From the server side, FrontPage provides

- The **Personal Web Server** to allow you and others on a LAN connected to you to use your webs from your hard disk

- The **FrontPage Server Extensions** to allow the implementation of the FrontPage interactive features on a commercial server

In the next several sections of this chapter you will further explore the FrontPage components. While it is not mandatory, it will be beneficial if you are looking at these components on your own computer. To do that, first start the Personal Web Server and then the FrontPage Explorer with these instructions:

1. Open the Start and then Programs menus, and select Microsoft FrontPage to open the FrontPage Programs menu shown here:

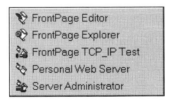

2. Click on Personal Web Server. You should see the Personal Web Server task appear in the task bar, as shown in the following illustration:

Ill 2-3

3. Again open the Start and Programs menus, select Microsoft FrontPage, and then click on FrontPage Explorer. The FrontPage Explorer window will open, as you will see in a moment.

FrontPage Explorer

The FrontPage Explorer is the normal starting place for creating a new web or editing an existing one. When you open an existing web in the FrontPage Explorer, you get a graphical view of the web, as you can see in Figure 2-1. The FrontPage Explorer is similar in a number of ways to the Windows 95 Explorer. The left pane displays a hierarchical structure of pages and objects (Outline view), while the right pane displays either the links to the page selected on the left (Link view, shown in Figure 2-1) or a list of the files supporting the web (Summary view) shown here:

Summary View:				
Title	File Name	Size	Type	Modified Date
images/bfeed.gif	bfeed.gif	1KB	gif	4/15/96 2:33:2
images/bhome.gif	bhome.gif	1KB	gif	4/15/96 2:33:2
images/bnews.gif	bnews.gif	1KB	gif	4/15/96 2:33:2
images/bprdsrv.gif	bprdsrv.gif	2KB	gif	4/15/96 2:33:2
images/brntxtr2.jpg	brntxtr2.jpg	1KB	jpg	4/15/96 2:33:2

By clicking on the plus and minus icons in the left pane, you can expand or collapse the view of the hierarchy. If you right-click on an object in either pane, its context menu will open, which, among other options, allows you to open the object's Properties dialog box. A final way that the FrontPage Explorer is like the Windows 95 Explorer is that in the Summary view you can sort the list of files by clicking on the field name immediately above the list, although you can only sort in ascending order.

A web contains one or more web pages with links among them. Web pages and their links create a hierarchical structure that is shown in the left pane of the FrontPage Explorer. You create this structure either by adding pages one at a time and then linking them, or by using one of the web wizards or templates to automatically create the desired pages and their links. You begin web wizards and templates, as well as custom webs with your own pages, by clicking on the New Web button in the toolbar, or by choosing New Web in the File menu. This opens the New Web dialog box that contains a list of web wizards and templates, as shown in the following illustration:

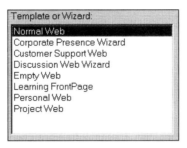

Web wizards and templates, both of which automatically create entire webs including a full set of pages, links, and other elements, differ only in the amount of interaction between you and the computer during the creation process. Templates create a ready-made web without any interaction with you. Wizards use one or more dialog boxes, such as the one shown in Figure 2-2, to ask you a series of questions during creation. Based on your answers to these questions, a customized web is created. In both cases, you can customize (or further customize, in the case of wizards) the resultant web pages and elements.

The web wizards and templates that are currently available in FrontPage are shown in Table 2-1.

Wizards and templates can create either new webs or additions to existing webs. Also, wizards and templates automatically create the tasks in the To Do List that support the pages that are created. As you'll see in a later chapter, you can build your

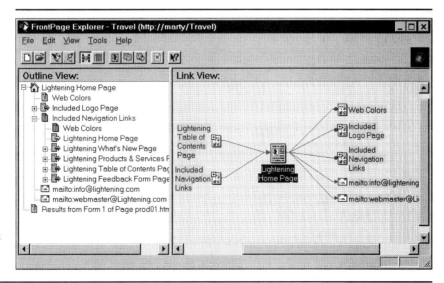

FrontPage
Explorer in
Link view

FIGURE 2-1

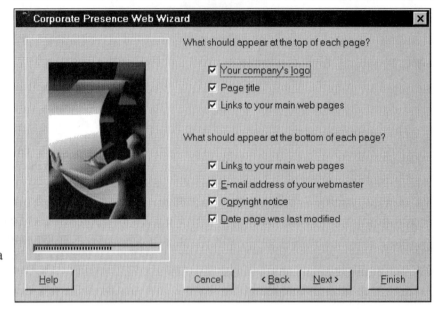

Wizards
use your
choices to
customize a
web they
build

FIGURE 2-2

own wizards and templates to, for example, create a standard look across all departments in a corporation.

 As you are working on your web, you can open the FrontPage Editor or the To Do List by using either the Show FrontPage Editor or Show To Do List option in the Tools menu (or the related buttons on the toolbar). You can also open the FrontPage Editor by double-clicking on the page you want to edit in the right-hand pane of the Explorer. When you are done creating a web, you can test all of the hyperlinks to external webs by selecting the Verify Links option of the Tools menu. Also, if you have edited a web and removed or changed some of the pages, use the Recalculate Links option of the Tools menu to update all of the internal links so there is not a reference to a nonexistent page. Finally, when everything is the way you want it, you can copy your web to the server, provided you weren't already working on the server, by using the Copy Web command in the File menu.

FrontPage Editor

The normal way that you get to the FrontPage Editor is to select a page in the FrontPage Explorer and then use one of the techniques discussed earlier to open the

Wizard or Template	What Is Created
Templates	
Normal Web	Single blank page, used in starting or adding to a custom web.
Customer Support Web	Web that tells customers how to contact you and provides a form where they can leave information so you can contact them. Includes an FTP download area, a frequently asked questions (FAQ) area, and a form for leaving suggestions and contact information.
Empty Web	Web without pages, so you can import pages from another web.
Personal Web	Single page with personal and professional information and ways to be contacted.
Project Web	Web that provides a way to communicate the status of a project including its schedule, who is working on it, and its accomplishments.
Wizards	
Corporate Presence Wizard	Web that provides information about a company, including what it does, what its products and services are, how to contact it, and a means to leave feedback for it.
Discussion Web Wizard	Page that is an electronic bulletin board where users can leave messages and others can reply to those messages.

Web
Wizards
and
Templates
Available
in the
FrontPage
Explorer

■ **TABLE 2-1**

FrontPage Editor. You can also open the FrontPage Editor directly from the Start | Programs | Microsoft FrontPage option and then use the File menu to open a particular page which is an HTML (.HTM) file. In any case, when you open the FrontPage Editor, you'll see a window that looks very much like most word processors, in particular, Microsoft Word for Windows, as you can see in Figure 2-3.

This is where you can enter and edit text. It is also where you can add graphics; frames; tables; forms; hyperlinks, including hotspots on graphics; and WebBots to your page, as you'll read about in a moment.

As you saw in Chapter 1, a web page is a lot of HTML (HyperText Markup Language) code and a little bit of text. If you use a normal word processor or text editor to create a web page, you must learn and use HTML. With the FrontPage Editor, you don't need to know HTML. You simply enter the text you want, format it the way you want using normal word processing formatting tools, and add graphics, forms, and other elements. When you are done, FrontPage will generate the HTML for you. It is no harder than creating and formatting any other document, and what you see on the screen is very close to what you would see in a web browser. Not only does the FrontPage Editor convert the text and formatting that you enter to HTML, you can import RFT and ASCII text files into the FrontPage Editor, and they will have the HTML added to them.

IP: *If you want to see the HTML behind a web page, choose HTML from the View menu.*

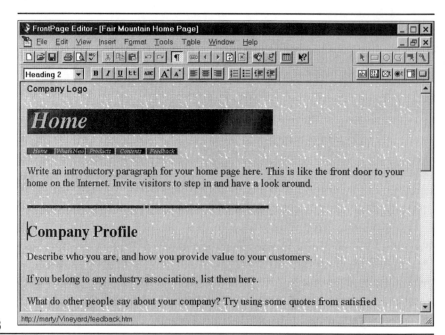

FrontPage
Editor
window

FIGURE 2-3

Formatting Text

The formatting that is available from the FrontPage Editor is quite extensive, but it is limited to the type of formatting that is available with HTML. For example, in most web browsers the end user, not the web author, can determine the font that is used for both proportional text and fixed-width text. Therefore, in web authoring you can determine whether to use proportional text or fixed-width text, but not which font to use—that will be determined by the user. Also, HTML predefines a number of formatting styles whose name and definition are unique to the Web. The paragraph styles supported in FrontPage are described in Table 2-2 and shown in Figure 2-4. They are applied either from the toolbar or the Format menu.

OTE: *Internet Explorer accepts a FONT tag that allows you to change the font (that is, <FONT FACE="Arial"></FONT>). This is not currently available in other browsers and is only supported in FrontPage through the Extended Attributes dialog box.*

OTE: *The Formatted paragraph style is the only tag that allows you to use multiple spaces in text. HTML throws out all but one space when it encounters multiple spaces, except when the Formatted style is used. This is what should be used for forms to get the labels to right-align and the text boxes to left-align.*

Paragraph Style	How It Looks
Normal	Displayed with the proportional font, normally Times Roman.
Formatted	Displayed with the fixed-width font, normally Courier.
Address	Displayed with the proportional font in an italic style. Named because it is often used to display information on how to contact the owner of the web.
Heading 1-6	Displayed with the proportional font in a bold style in six different sizes.

Paragraph
Styles

TABLE 2-2

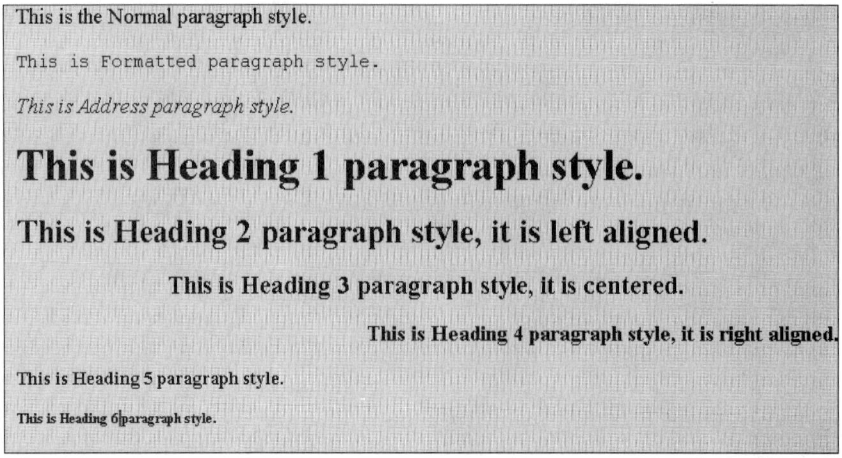

This is the Normal paragraph style.

This is Formatted paragraph style.

This is Address paragraph style.

This is Heading 1 paragraph style.

This is Heading 2 paragraph style, it is left aligned.

This is Heading 3 paragraph style, it is centered.

This is Heading 4 paragraph style, it is right aligned.

This is Heading 5 paragraph style.

This is Heading 6 paragraph style.

Examples of paragraph styles

FIGURE 2-4

Any of the paragraph styles can use left, center, or right paragraph alignment applied either from the Paragraph Format dialog box or with the alignment buttons in the toolbar.

Character styles, which are described in Table 2-3 and shown in Figure 2-5, are applied through either the drop-down list on the left of the formatting toolbar, or the Format menu, which opens the Character Style dialog box.

Strong, Emphasis, Citation, Sample, Definition, Code, Variable, and Keyboard are logical styles. The appearance of the text with these tags is determined by the browser. Strong, for example, could be defined as italic if the user wanted to. Older browsers allowed you to change the defaults for these tags, but this seems to be a feature that has disappeared. Bold, Italic, Underlined, Blink, Typewriter Font, Strike-Through, and Font Size are physical styles that are not changeable by the browser.

Characters in any style can be one of seven preset sizes from 8 points to 36 points, as shown in Figure 2-6, one of 48 preselected colors or a custom color, and either

Character Style	How It Looks
Bold (Strong)	Makes text bold
Italic (Emphasis)	Makes text italic
Underlined	Makes text underlined
Strike-Through	Puts a line through text
Typewriter Font	Puts text in the fixed-width font
Citation	Formats text in the Citation style, normally italic
Sample	Formats text in the Sample style, normally in a fixed-width font
Definition	Formats text in the Definition style, normally italic
Blink	Makes text blink (defined only in Netscape Navigator)
Code	Formats text in the Code style, normally the fixed-width font
Variable	Formats text in the Variable style, which is either italic (Netscape) or the fixed-width font (Microsoft)
Bold	Formats text in a bold style
Italic	Formats text in italic
Keyboard	Formats text in the Keyboard style, normally the fixed-width font with a bold style

Character
Styles

TABLE 2-3

superscript or subscript position. Character size and color can be changed with the respective toolbar buttons, shown here, or though the Character Style dialog box.

In addition to the paragraph style that you have already seen, HTML and FrontPage allow you to define several types of lists. Table 2-4 describes the available list styles, which are shown in Figure 2-7. Note that at this time there is no difference between bulleted, directory, and menu lists. It is possible that this will change in the future.

 IP: *You can end any list by pressing CTRL-ENTER.*

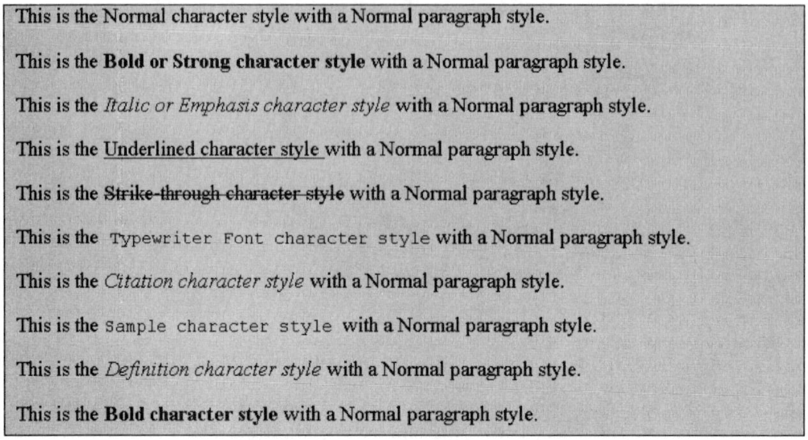

This is the Normal character style with a Normal paragraph style.

This is the **Bold or Strong character style** with a Normal paragraph style.

This is the *Italic or Emphasis character style* with a Normal paragraph style.

This is the <u>Underlined character style</u> with a Normal paragraph style.

This is the ~~Strike-through character style~~ with a Normal paragraph style.

This is the `Typewriter Font character style` with a Normal paragraph style.

This is the *Citation character style* with a Normal paragraph style.

This is the `Sample character style` with a Normal paragraph style.

This is the *Definition character style* with a Normal paragraph style.

This is the **Bold character style** with a Normal paragraph style.

Examples of some of the character styles

FIGURE 2-5

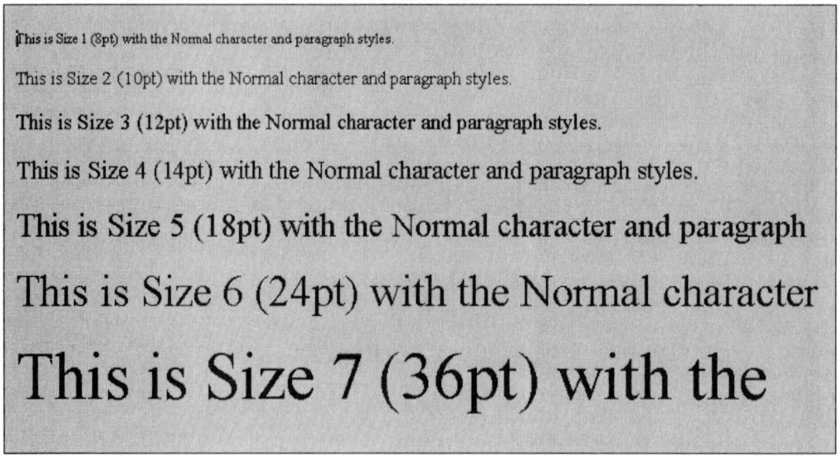

This is Size 1 (8pt) with the Normal character and paragraph styles.

This is Size 2 (10pt) with the Normal character and paragraph styles.

This is Size 3 (12pt) with the Normal character and paragraph styles.

This is Size 4 (14pt) with the Normal character and paragraph styles.

This is Size 5 (18pt) with the Normal character and paragraph

This is Size 6 (24pt) with the Normal character

This is Size 7 (36pt) with the

Examples of character sizes

FIGURE 2-6

List Style	How It Looks
Bulleted List	Series of paragraphs with a hanging indent and a bullet on the left
Numbered List	Series of paragraphs with a hanging indent and a number on the left
Directory List	Series of short (normally less than 20 characters) paragraphs
Menu List	Series of paragraphs, one line or less in length, in a vertically compact format
Definition List	Pairs of paragraphs as terms, which are left-aligned, and definitions, which are indented similar to dictionary definitions

List Styles

TABLE 2-4

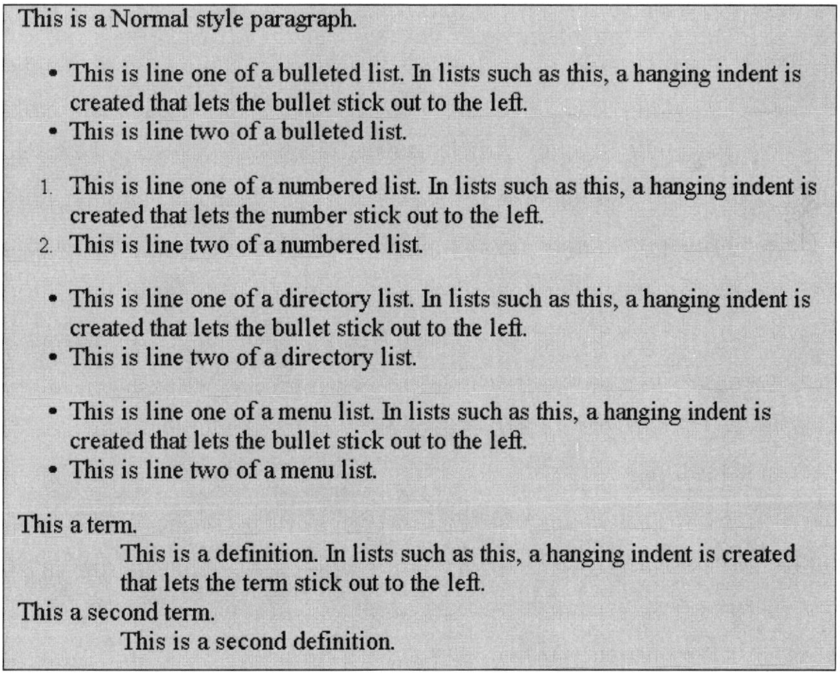

This is a Normal style paragraph.

- This is line one of a bulleted list. In lists such as this, a hanging indent is created that lets the bullet stick out to the left.
- This is line two of a bulleted list.

1. This is line one of a numbered list. In lists such as this, a hanging indent is created that lets the number stick out to the left.
2. This is line two of a numbered list.

- This is line one of a directory list. In lists such as this, a hanging indent is created that lets the bullet stick out to the left.
- This is line two of a directory list.

- This is line one of a menu list. In lists such as this, a hanging indent is created that lets the bullet stick out to the left.
- This is line two of a menu list.

This a term.
　　This is a definition. In lists such as this, a hanging indent is created that lets the term stick out to the left.
This a second term.
　　This is a second definition.

List style examples

FIGURE 2-7

Not all web browsers treat the formatting in a web the same; they may even ignore some formatting. Blink, in particular, is a style that is ignored by all but the Netscape Navigator. Also, several styles may produce exactly the same effect in many browsers. For example, in most instances, the Emphasis, Citation, Definition, and Italic styles often produce the same effect. If you are creating a web for a broad public audience, it is worthwhile to test it in recent versions of the two primary web browsers: Netscape Navigator and Microsoft Internet Explorer.

 IP: *Use only the physical styles excluding Blink to be assured of the widest usability.*

The Character Style dialog box or the Text Color button on the toolbar allows you to set the color of selected text. You can also set the color of text for an entire page through the Page Properties dialog box, which is opened from the File menu and shown in Figure 2-8. Colored text is useful on colored backgrounds, as you can see in Figure 2-9, and to create an unusual look on a page.

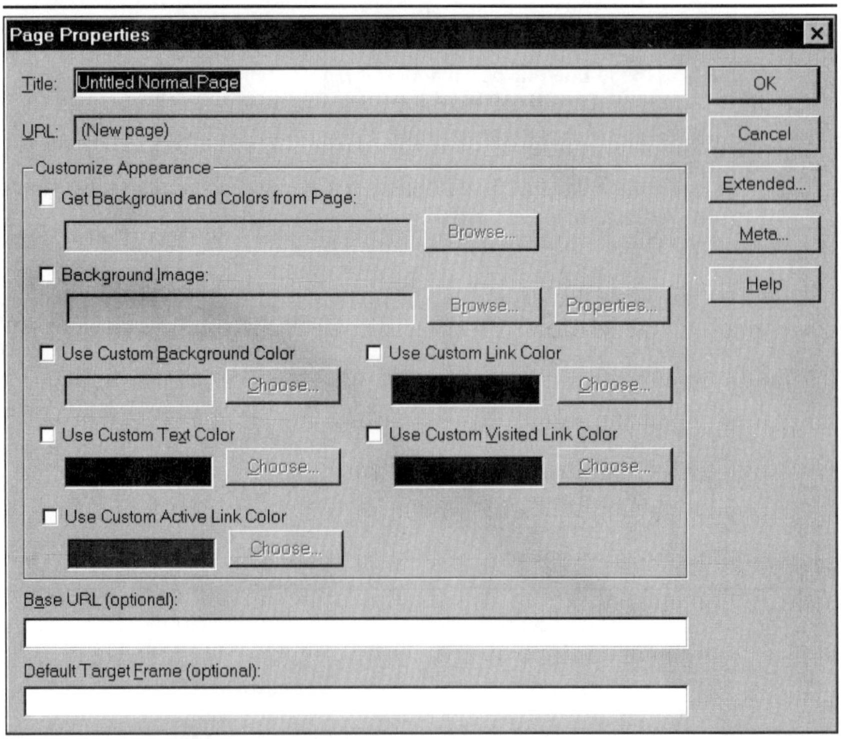

Page Properties ☒

Title: `Untitled Normal Page` [OK]

URL: `(New page)` [Cancel]

Customize Appearance
☐ Get Background and Colors from Page: [Extended...]
`_____` [Browse...] [Meta...]

☐ Background Image: [Help]
`_____` [Browse...] [Properties...]

☐ Use Custom Background Color   ☐ Use Custom Link Color
`_____` [Choose...]   `████████` [Choose...]

☐ Use Custom Text Color   ☐ Use Custom Visited Link Color
`████████` [Choose...]   `████████` [Choose...]

☐ Use Custom Active Link Color
`████████` [Choose...]

Base URL (optional):
`_____`

Default Target Frame (optional):
`_____`

Page Properties dialog box

■ FIGURE 2-8

Colored
text on
graphic
background

 FIGURE 2-9

Inserting Graphics

FrontPage allows you to add graphics to a web page in two ways:

■ You can add a background image that fills a page, which you can identify
in the Page Properties dialog box you saw earlier. By placing a graphic in
the background, you can enter text on top of it.

OTE: *A background graphic will be tiled if it doesn't fill the screen. Even
if it fills the screen at 640x480, it may be tiled at higher resolutions.*

■ You can add a stand-alone graphic image that you can identify in the
Insert Image dialog box opened from the Insert menu. The graphic should
be sized before you insert it. Once it is inserted, you can right-click on the
graphic and select Properties to open the Image Properties dialog box
shown in Figure 2-10. Here you can enter the alignment, the amount of
space to place on the top and to the left of a graphic, the thickness of a

Image Properties dialog box

FIGURE 2-10

border, if any, and the alternative text to display if the graphic is not displayed. You can also identify a hyperlink to follow if the user clicks on the graphic. Figure 2-11 shows the results of the settings in the dialog box shown in Figure 2-10.

 IP: *You can center or right-align a graphic by selecting it and clicking on the Center or Right Align button in the toolbar.*

Graphics that are included in web pages must be either GIF or JPEG format. This has presented a problem in the past, because most clipart and graphics programs use other formats. FrontPage has solved this problem by allowing you to import other file formats that FrontPage will convert to GIF or JPEG. The file formats that FrontPage can accept are

GIF (.GIF)
JPEG (.JPG or .JFF)
PCX (.PCX)
PostScript (.EPS)
SUN Raster (.RAS)
Targa (.TGA)
TIFF (.TIF)
Windows Metafile (.WMF)
Windows or OS/2 BMP (.BMP)
Windows Paint (.MSP)
WordPerfect (.WPG)

It's important to remember that graphics take a long time to download and therefore become frustrating for the user who has to wait for them. Even though a graphic may look really neat, if users have to wait several minutes for it to download, they probably are not going to appreciate it or stick around to look at it.

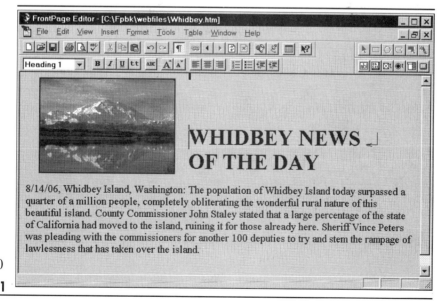

A graphic aligned with the settings shown in Figure 2-10

FIGURE 2-11

Adding Forms

So far you have seen how to display text and graphics on a web page—how to deliver information to the user. In the FrontPage Editor you can also add a form in which the user of your web can send you information. You can create a form either field-by-field or all at one time by using the Form Page Wizard. You'll see how the Form Page Wizard works in a later section. Here, look at the field-by-field approach. You can use either the Form Field option on the Insert menu, or more easily, the buttons in the Forms toolbar.

To use the Forms toolbar, described in Table 2-5, simply place the insertion point where you want the field, and then click on the button for the field you want. A dialog box will open and ask you to name the field and specify other aspects of it, such as the width of the box on the form and the number of characters that can be entered. Figure 2-12 shows one way a form can be built. In Chapter 7 you'll go through the detail steps of designing and building a form.

Button	Description	Example in Figure 2-12
abl	One-Line Text Box	Address
	Scrolling Text Box	Other Address
	Check Box	Using our products?
	Radio Button	Age
	Drop-Down Menu	Which products?
	Push Button	Send and Reset

Form Field Creation Buttons

TABLE 2-5

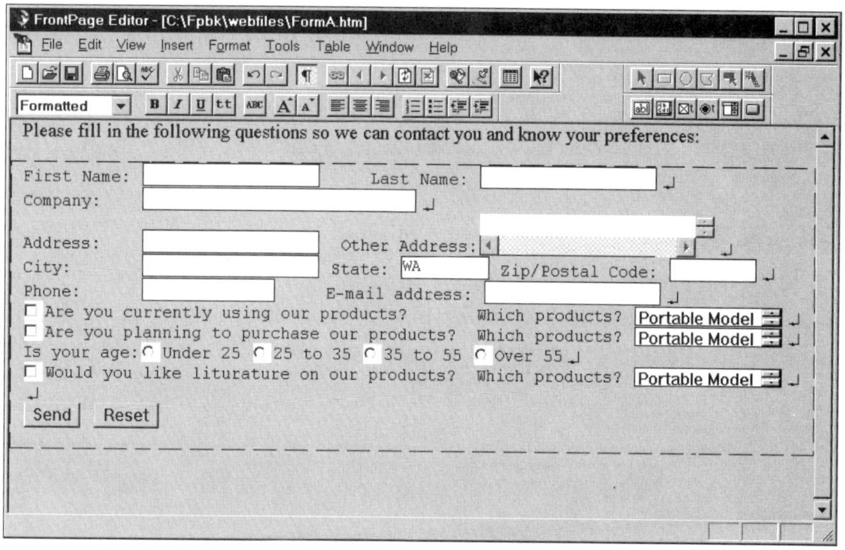

2

FrontPage Editor - [C:\Fpbk\webfiles\FormA.htm]

File Edit View Insert Format Tools Table Window Help

Formatted

Please fill in the following questions so we can contact you and know your preferences:

First Name: _____   Last Name: _____

Company: _____

Address: _____   Other Address: ◄ _____ ►
City: _____   State: WA   Zip/Postal Code: _____
Phone: _____   E-mail address: _____
□ Are you currently using our products?   Which products? Portable Model
□ Are you planning to purchase our products?   Which products? Portable Model
Is your age: ○ Under 25 ○ 25 to 35 ○ 35 to 55 ○ Over 55
□ Would you like liturature on our products?   Which products? Portable Model

[Send]   [Reset]

All form
fields are in
the same
form block
and use the
Formatted
paragraph
style

FIGURE 2-12

IP: *If you put form fields in the same form block (area enclosed by a dashed line) and use SHIFT-ENTER to create a new line, you can stack the fields closer together, and they will all have the same form properties.*

IP: *If you format form fields with the Formatted paragraph style, you can align the labels and text boxes using multiple spaces as shown in Figure 2-12.*

When you create a form field-by-field, you need to provide a means of gathering the data that is entered on it. With FrontPage the best way to do this is with the Save Results bot. This is a piece of code that is in the FrontPage Server Extensions residing on your web server. When the user fills out and submits your form, the Save Results bot accepts the information and stores it in a file that you can read. To activate the Save Results bot, right-click on the first field, choose Properties, and then click on the Form button. This opens the Form Properties dialog box where you can open the Form Handler drop-down list, and choose the Save Results bot. Then click on

Settings to open the Settings For Saving Results Of Form dialog box shown in Figure 2-13. Here you need to enter the filename and file format that you want to use to contain the information that is returned. You may or may not want to include the field names in the output or the additional information. You must do this for each field that is in a separate form block (the area enclosed with a dashed line).

Using Tables

 In webs, tables provide a means of dividing some or all of a page into rows and columns. Tables can be used to display tabular data as well as to simply position information on a page, perhaps with a border around it. In Chapter 1, you saw two

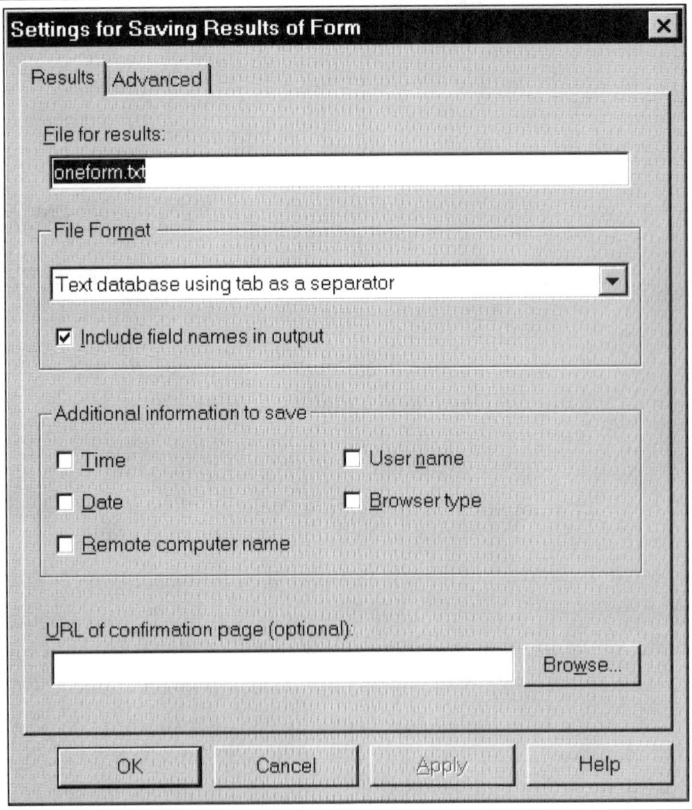

Settings
For Saving
Results Of
Form
dialog box

FIGURE 2-13

Table	Window	Help
Insert Table...		
Insert Rows or Columns...		
Insert Cell		
Insert Caption		
Merge Cells		
Split Cells...		
Select Cell		
Select Row		
Select Column		
Select Table		
Table Properties...		

examples of tables, and how three different web browsers displayed them (in Figures 1-7 through 1-9). FrontPage has an extensive capability for creating and working with tables such as the one shown in Figure 2-14. Tables are created using either the Insert Table button in the toolbar or the Insert Table option on the Table menu. In either case the Insert Table dialog box will open. This allows you to specify the size, layout, and width of the table you are creating. Once a table is created, you can modify it through the Table menu, you can right-click on the table and choose Table Properties to change the overall properties of the table, or you can choose Cell Properties to change the properties of a single cell. Chapter 6 will go in-depth into tables.

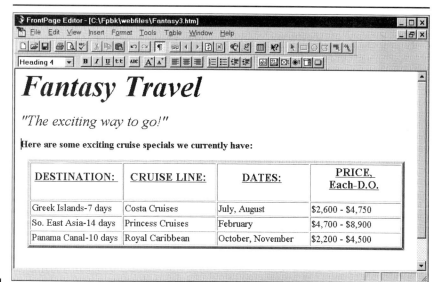

Table created in FrontPage

FIGURE 2-14

Working with Wizards and Templates

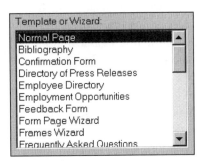

In the New Page dialog box, the FrontPage Editor provides a number of *page* wizards and templates (as distinct from the *web* wizards and templates available in the FrontPage Explorer) to help you create many specialized pages.

For example, to use a wizard to create a custom form similar to the one created earlier, you would select the Form Page Wizard from the New Page dialog box that is opened only from the File menu. This opens a series of dialog boxes that ask you questions about what you want on the form you want to build, an example of which is shown in Figure 2-15. When you are done, a form is automatically created such as that in Figure 2-16.

One of a series of questions leading to the creation of a form

FIGURE 2-15

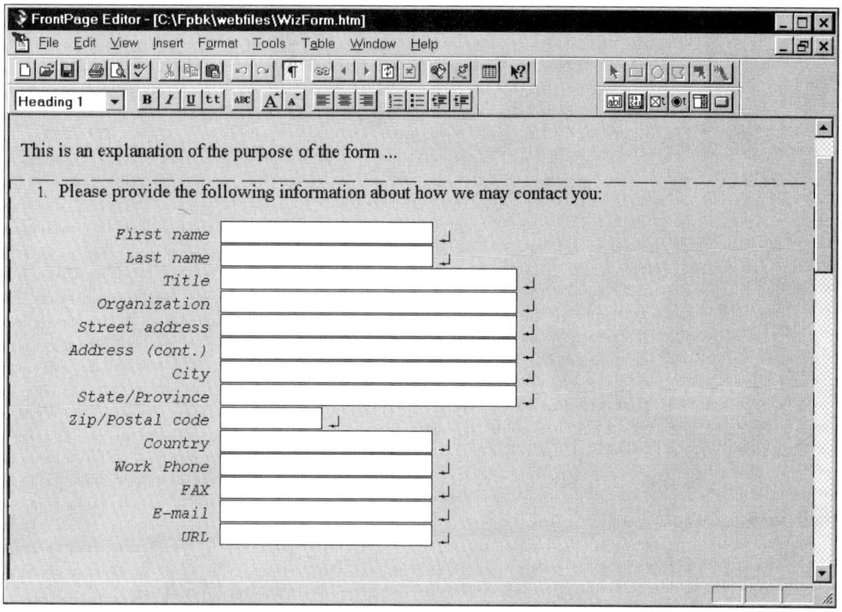

A form created by the Form Page Wizard

FIGURE 2-16

OTE: *The New Page button on the toolbar directly gives you a new page using the Normal Page template and does not open the New Page dialog box.*

The page templates, like their counterparts in the FrontPage Explorer, simply create a new formatted page for you without any input from you. With both wizards and templates, though, you can customize the resulting web page as you see fit. The wizards and template provide an excellent way to get a quick start on a large variety of web pages, as shown in Table 2-6.

IP: *Wizards and templates quickly get you over the "where do I start" hurdle and give you a "first cut" that you can customize.*

Frames are a powerful way to organize a web page by combining several pages on one page, each in a tile or *frame,* as you can see in Figure 2-17. FrontPage uses the Frames Wizard to create the several pages necessary for a given layout. With the

Wizard or Template	What Is Created on a New Page
Bibliography	List of references to other pages or works
Confirmation Form	Acknowledgment of the receipt of input from the user
Directory of Press Releases	Date-ordered list of hyperlinks to press releases
Employee Directory	Alphabetical list of employees with a table of contents containing hyperlinks to each employee
Employment Opportunities	Alphabetical list of job openings with a form for the user to ask for further information
Feedback Form	Form for a user to give you comments
Form Page Wizard	Custom form you have designed using this wizard
Frames Wizard	Page made up of other pages that are arranged in tiles or frames
Frequently Asked Questions	List of questions and their answers
Glossary of Terms	Alphabetical list of terms and their definitions
Guest Book	Form for users of your web to leave their identification and comments
Hot List	Categorized list of hyperlinks to other web sites
HyperDocument Page	List of document subsections meant to be hyperlink destinations
Lecture Abstract	Announcement of an upcoming seminar, lecture, or workshop
Meeting Agenda	Announcement of a meeting with a list of topics for discussion
Normal Page	Blank page
Office Directory	Geographical list of company offices with hyperlinks to countries and regions
Personal Home Page Wizard	Custom home page you have designed using this wizard

Wizards
and
Templates
Available
in the
FrontPage
Editor

TABLE 2-6

Wizard or Template	What Is Created on a New Page
Press Release	Normal press release format that can be linked to the Directory of Press Releases
Product Description	Description of a product including its features, benefits, and specifications
Product or Event Registration	Registration form for an event or for product support
Search Page	Search engine for finding keywords within the pages of a web
Seminar Schedule	Description of a seminar that is meant to be linked to a Lecture Abstract page
Software Data Sheet	Software product description including the features and benefits of the product
Survey Form	Form to collect information from users of your web
Table of Contents	List, in outline format, of hyperlinks to the other pages in your web
User Registration	Form for registering to use a secure web
What's New	List, in date order, of recent changes and announcements

Wizards and Templates Available in the FrontPage Editor (*continued*)

TABLE 2-6

Frames Wizard you can choose one of several canned layouts, as shown in Figure 2-18, or you can create a custom layout with the rows, columns, and dimensions that you want. When you use frames, you cannot see the finished product in FrontPage, you will only see and edit the individual pages (the example in Figure 2-17 uses three pages). You must open a browser, such as Netscape Navigator 2.0, to see the finished product. Frames will be discussed in-depth in Chapter 6.

 OTE: *As this is written, frames can only be viewed using Netscape Navigator, but Microsoft's Internet Explorer 3.0, due out in the second half of 1996, is supposed to have this capability.*

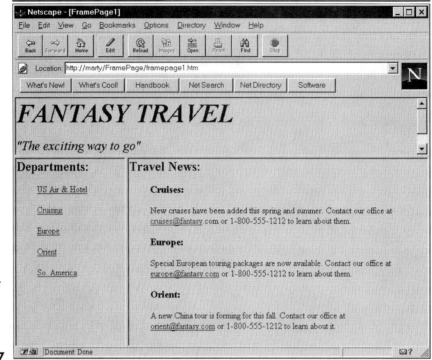

Example of a web page using frames

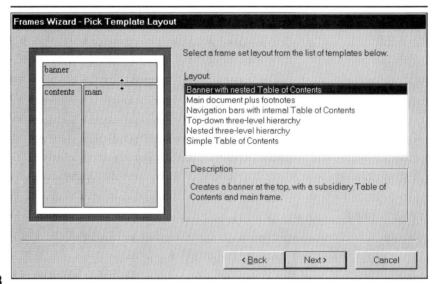

Canned layouts available in the Frames Wizard

Using WebBots

WebBots provide automation in a web—the ability to do more than just provide text and graphics on a page. For example, WebBots, or just "bots," let the users search a web, return information to you that has been entered on a form, and allow the users to participate in a discussion group. Most of FrontPage's bots, though, just make creating and maintaining a web easier. In other web-authoring packages, this same capability requires various levels of programming. In FrontPage you simply have to set up and enable a WebBot.

The Discussion WebBot is automatically enabled when you create a new web from the FrontPage Explorer by using the Discussion Web Wizard. The Save Results WebBot is automatically enabled when you use the Form Page Wizard in the FrontPage Editor or, as you saw earlier, you can enable it manually in the Forms Properties dialog box. All other bots are enabled through the Insert Bot dialog box (shown next) opened by choosing Bot from the Insert menu. The bots that you can place on a page are described in Table 2-7.

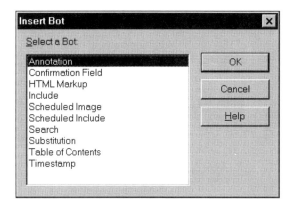

Adding Hyperlinks and Mapping Hotspots

In the FrontPage Editor you can add hyperlinks (or "links"), which allow the user of a web to quickly jump from one page to another, or to a particular element on the same or another page (called a "bookmark"), or to a different web or web site. You can make either text or a graphic be the element the user clicks on to make the link, and you can map certain areas of a graphic to be different links (called "hotspots"). You create a link by first selecting the object that you want the user to click on and

WebBot	Capability Added to a Web Page
Annotation	Allows the insertion of notes you want to see in the FrontPage Editor, but that you do not want the user to see in a web browser.
Confirmation Field	Echoes the information entered on a form by users, so you can show users what they entered.
HTML Markup	Allows the insertion of HTML commands in a FrontPage web page. If you find an HTML command that you want to use, and which is not supported in FrontPage, you can insert it in this manner.
Include	Allows you to include one web page on another. If you want to have a constant header on every page, you can put the header on a web page and then include that page on all others in the web.
Scheduled Image	Allows you to display an image in a web page for a given period. When the time expires, the image is not displayed.
Scheduled Include	Allows you to include one page on another for a given period. When the time expires, the included page is not displayed.
Search	Creates a form in which the user can enter a word or words to search for in the current web, carries out the search, and returns the elements matching the criteria.
Substitution	Substitutes a value on a web page with a configuration variable when the page is viewed by the user.
Table of Contents	Creates and maintains a Table of Contents page with links to all the other pages in the web.
Timestamp	Places on a page the date and time the page was last edited or updated.

WebBots That Can Be Inserted on a Page from FrontPage Editor

TABLE 2-7

then clicking on the Create or Edit Link button, or by choosing Link from the Edit menu. In either case, the Create Link dialog box will open as shown in Figure 2-19.

Within the Create Link dialog box, you can select a bookmark on any open page or just an open page without a bookmark, any page in the current web with or without a bookmark, any URL or address on the World Wide Web, or a new page yet to be defined in the current web. The address on the Web can be another web, or HTTP site, or an Ftp, Gopher, Mail, News, Telnet, or Wais site. When you have created a hyperlink, the object on which the user is to click changes to a different color and may become underlined as you can see in the words "Caribbean," "Alaska," and "Europe" in Figure 2-20.

A graphic can have its entire area defined as a link, or you can identify specific areas in a graphic as separate links while any unidentified areas are assigned a default link. For example, a travel agency could provide a map that allows the user to quickly

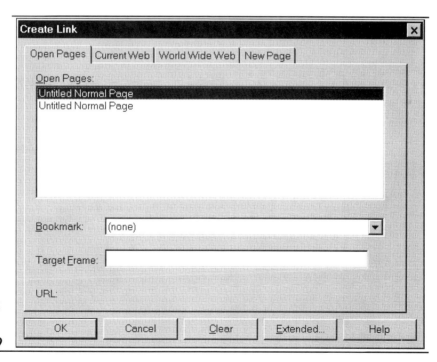

Create Link dialog box

FIGURE 2-19

Fantasy Travel

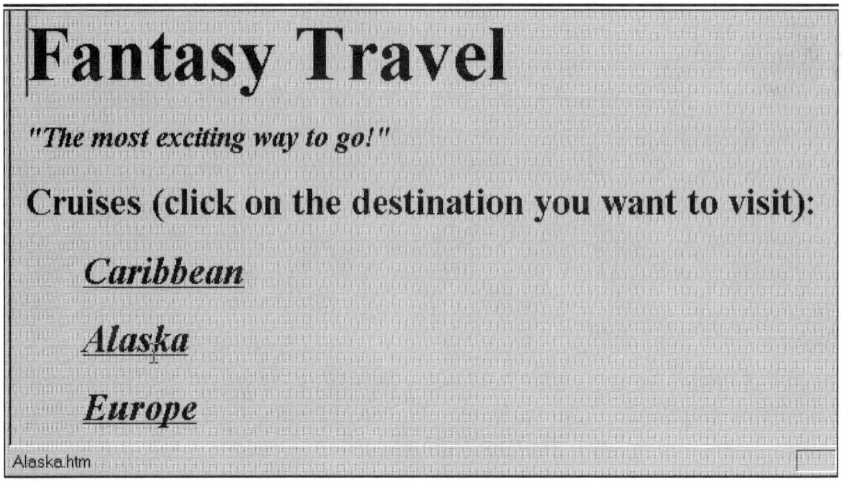

"The most exciting way to go!"

Cruises (click on the destination you want to visit):

<u>Caribbean</u>

<u>Alaska</u>

<u>Europe</u>

Hyperlinks
are
underlined
and a
different
color

Alaska.htm

FIGURE 2-20

get to information about a particular area of the world by simply clicking on that area, as you can see in Figure 2-21.

Fantasy Travel

"The exciting way to go!"

Click on the area of the world you want to visit.

Hawaii.htm

Selecting a
link within
a graphic

FIGURE 2-21

IP: *The left end of the status bar tells you the link under the mouse pointer,* Hawaii.htm, *in Figure 2-21.*

You identify hotspots on a graphic by using the drawing tools in the upper right  of the toolbar. First select the graphic, then select the rectangle, circle, or polygon tool. Use it to draw a border around the area of the graphic you want to be the hotspot. When you are done identifying all the hotspots, your graphic will look something like this (although users won't see the lines in a browser):

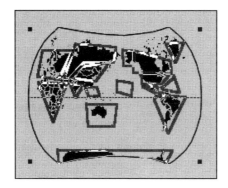

The rightmost pair of drawing tools provides two unique functions. The second from the right tool turns off the graphic and shows you just the hotspots, and the rightmost tool allows you to click on any color in the graphic and make it transparent, allowing the page background to show through.

 OTE: *Transparent backgrounds only work with GIF 89a files. If you try using a transparent background with a JPEG, you get a dialog box that says the JPEG will be converted to a GIF.*

To Do List

 To open the To Do List, you must have a web open. Then from either the FrontPage Explorer or the FrontPage Editor you can click on the To Do List button in the toolbar, or select Show To Do List from the Tools menu. In either case the To Do List window opens, as you can see in the following illustration:

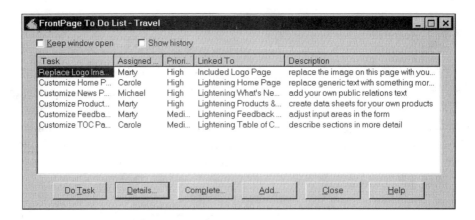

The items on the To Do List are placed there either by a web wizard or by you, which you can do with either the Add button in the To Do List window or by choosing Add To Do Task from the Edit menu in either the FrontPage Explorer or the FrontPage Editor. When you add a new task, you give it a name, assign it to an individual, give it a priority, and type in a description in the Add To Do Task dialog box shown in Figure 2-22.

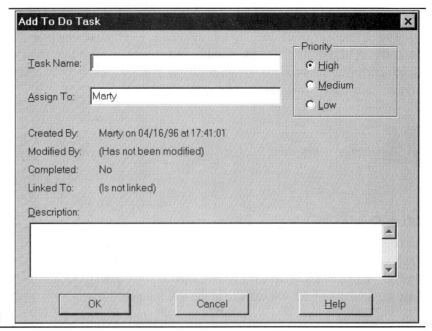

Add To Do
Task dialog
box

FIGURE 2-22

Once you have a complete To Do List, you can use it to go to the various sections of a web that still require work by selecting a task and clicking on the Do Task button. This will open the FrontPage Editor and display the page that needs work. When you have completed the task, you can return to the To Do List window and select Complete, where you can either mark the task as completed and leave it in the list, or delete the task from the list. By clicking on Details in the To Do List window, you can modify who the task is assigned to, its priority, and its description, but not the task name.

IP: *You can sort the tasks in the To Do List on any field by clicking on the field name at the top of the list.*

Personal Web Server

The Personal Web Server provides the file management for a web (as distinct from an individual page) in FrontPage. You need to have it running if you want to create or edit a web on your computer, unless you have some other Internet server software running along with the FrontPage Server Extensions for that server. The Personal Web Server simply sits in the background as a task on your task bar. When it is handling a task, you'll see the word "busy" in the task bar, otherwise it is idle. Other than by exiting or closing down the Personal Web Server, you have no control over it.

IP: *The Personal Web Server can be all the server you need for a small intranet linking six to ten workstations.*

FrontPage Server Extensions

The FrontPage Server Extensions must be installed on the server that is distributing a web that contains many of the advance features in FrontPage. Among these are

- Forms
- Hotspot image maps

- WebBots that are active while a web in being used in a browser, such as:

  - Confirmation field bot

  - Discussion bot

  - Registration bot

  - Save Results bot

  - Search bot

FrontPage Server Extensions are available from Microsoft for most of the popular Internet servers, both UNIX- and Windows NT-based systems, at *http://www.microsoft.com/frontpage/freestuff/fs_fp_extensions.htm.*

In the following chapters you will use all of the components of FrontPage and many of their features to build your own webs.

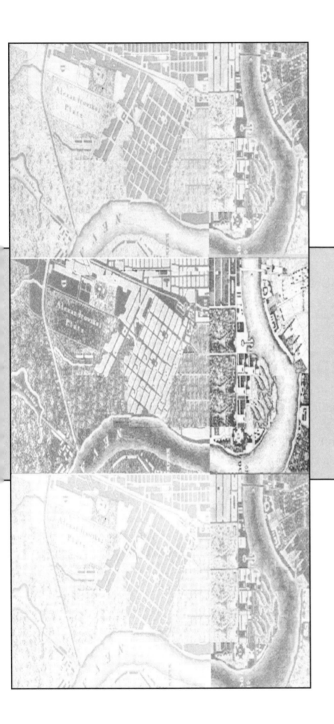

Using Wizards and Templates

As you saw in Chapter 2, the easiest way to create a web with FrontPage is by using a wizard or a template. You'll remember that *wizards* ask you questions about the web you want to create and then build a web based on your answers, whereas *templates* create a particular kind of web without input from you. In this chapter you'll see how to use wizards and templates in both webs and pages, and the results that they produce. The purpose of this is twofold: it gets you acquainted with the wizards and templates, and it demonstrates many of FrontPage's features, which have been included in the webs produced by the wizards and templates.

Web Wizards and Templates

FrontPage provides wizards and templates at both the web level and the page level. Begin looking at the web level by loading both the Personal Web Server and the FrontPage Explorer as you did in Chapter 2. When the program loading is complete, click on the New Web button in the toolbar, or open the File menu and choose New Web. The New Web dialog box will open and display a list of Templates and Wizards.

Applying the Normal Web Template

The starting place for creating a general-purpose web is with the Normal Web template. This template creates a single web page on which you can place anything. Do that now with these instructions (the New Web dialog box should be open on your screen):

1. Double-click on Normal Web in the New Web dialog box or, assuming that Normal Web is already selected, just click on OK. The New Web From Template dialog box will open, as you can see here:

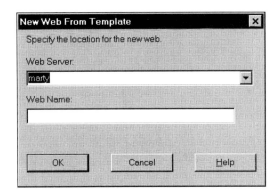

3

2. Select the web server that you want to use. The domain name of your web server should already be entered (probably the name of your computer, for example, "marty" in the preceding illustration—see the discussion of the Personal Web Server installation in Appendix A). If you do not have a server name entered, select or enter the domain name of the server where your web will reside.

3. Enter the name you want to give this web. This name cannot use spaces, but can be longer than eight characters. For this example, the web will be referred to as "Normal1," so if you do not have another name you want to use, enter **Normal1** for the Web Name and then click on OK.

OTE: *The terms Normal Web, Normal1, and Normal Page can get confusing, so here is how they relate to each other: a template named Normal Web was used to create a web which was named Normal1. This new web contains a single page (its home page) named Normal Page. You could rename Normal Page, but it isn't in this book.*

4. The Name and Password Required dialog box will then open as shown next. This dialog box is asking you for the administrator's name and password that was established when FrontPage was installed. Enter these now and click on OK. The Normal1 web will be created and displayed in the FrontPage Explorer.

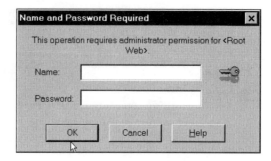

5. Right-click on the Normal Page representation in either the Outline or Link view and choose Properties from the pop-up or context menu that opens as a result of right-clicking. The Properties dialog box for the Normal1 web, similar to the one shown in Figure 3-1, will open. Here you can see the filename and URL that have been generated for the new web. In the Summary tab you can see when and by whom the web was created and modified. You can also add comments.

6. Close the Properties dialog box, and then double-click on the page in the right pane to open the page in the FrontPage Editor. The FrontPage Editor will open with a blank page.

On the blank page you can enter and format any text you want, insert graphics, and add forms, tables, and other elements as you saw in Chapter 2. In later chapters

The Properties dialog box for the Normal1 web

FIGURE 3-1

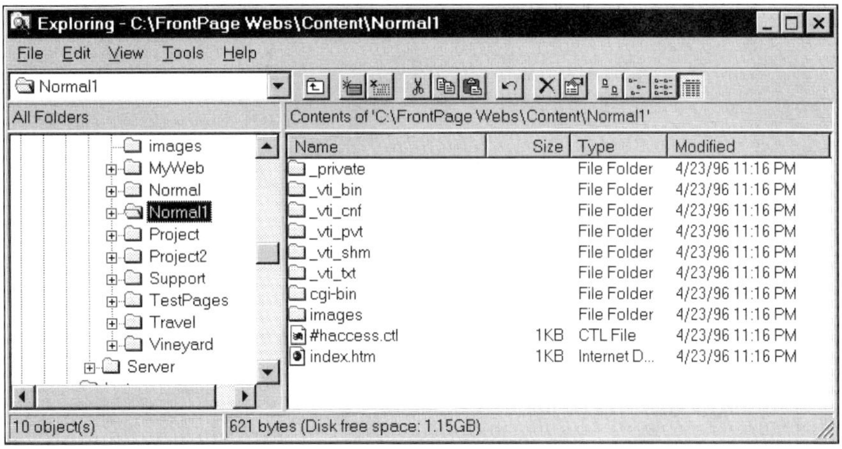

Windows
95 Explorer
view of the
structure
created for
a single
web page

FIGURE 3-2

you will do all of these tasks. The purpose here is simply to see that the Normal Web template does in fact create a single blank web page. It also creates all of the structure (shown in Figure 3-2 above) that is behind a web in FrontPage. (If you used the default directories when you installed FrontPage, your Normal1 web is stored under C:\FrontPage Webs\Content\Normal1.)

Why go to all this trouble for a single web page? FrontPage needs the structure to perform its functions. Since most webs have a number of pages and other functions such as forms, the structure is needed for organizing the web and making it easy to use and maintain.

Adding pages to a web created with the Normal Web template is done simply in the FrontPage Editor. Try the following instructions, and then go back to the FrontPage Explorer and see how the new page is automatically integrated into the web that was created.

1. Open the FrontPage Editor's File menu, and choose New to open the New Page dialog box. Normal Page should be selected as the template. Click on OK to create a new page in your Normal1 web.

2. Again open the File menu, and choose Save to open the Save As dialog box. Type **Second Page** as the Page Title. The Page URL should automatically change to "second.htm," as you can see:

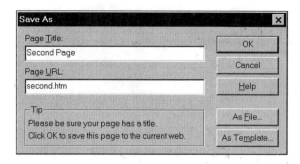

3. Click on OK to save the page, and then click on the FrontPage Editor's Close button, or open the File menu and choose Exit to leave the FrontPage Editor and return to the FrontPage Explorer. When the FrontPage Explorer opens, you'll see a new page, "Second Page" (shown in Figure 3-3), has been added to the web you created earlier.

4. Open the FrontPage Explorer's File menu and choose Delete Web. You'll be informed that deleting a web is a permanent action, and there is no undo for it. Click on Yes to delete the Normal1 web.

As you create your own webs, you'll probably use the Normal Web template often to create the small or custom webs that you'll need.

A second page integrated into the original web

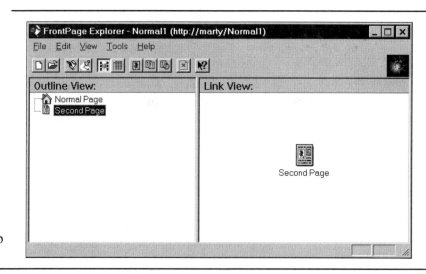

FIGURE 3-3

Creating a Personal Web

The Personal Web template available in FrontPage creates a basic single-page web to publicize a person or small organization. Build that next as your second project, with the following steps:

1. From the FrontPage Explorer, open the File menu, choose New Web, select Personal Web, and click on OK. Make sure the Web Server is correct, enter a name such as MyWeb, and click on OK. The new web appears with a number of hyperlinks that you can customize, as you can see in Figure 3-4.

2. Double-click on My Home Page in the right pane to open it in the FrontPage Editor.

The page that opens has a lot of features incorporated in it, some of which are shown in Figure 3-5. These features are only suggestions and can be customized.

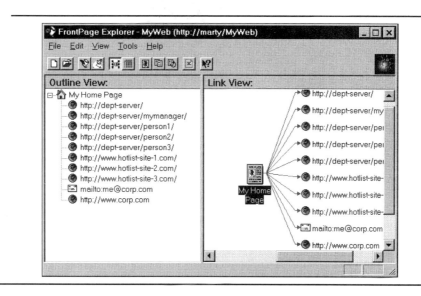

A personal web as created by the Personal Web template

FIGURE 3-4

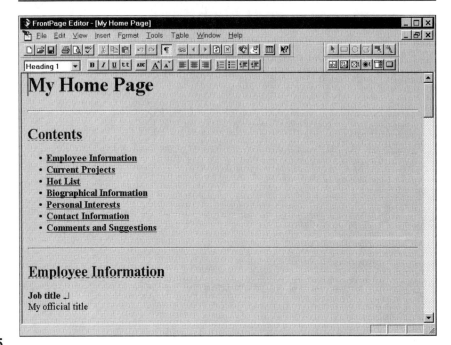

Page
created
with the
Personal
Web
template

FIGURE 3-5

They provide a starting place that you can use or delete depending on your needs, and you can add any other features that you want. Use the scroll bar and review the following features:

■ **Plain text** is text that you can replace with your own words. For example, Michael Smith might replace "My Home Page" with "Michael Smith's Page."

■ **Bookmarks**, text with a dashed underline, are references to which you can jump using a hyperlink. You can see the name of the bookmark by right-clicking on text that has a dashed underline and selecting Properties. For example, right-clicking on Contents and selecting Properties opens the Bookmark dialog box shown next, which tells you the bookmark attached to Contents is "top."

- **Hyperlinks**, text of a different color with a solid underline, are links to bookmarks or other pages in the current web, or to other webs. Again, you can open the Properties dialog box and see where the link is pointing. The "Employee Information" in the Contents list, for example, is pointing to a bookmark named "jobinfo" in the open page, as you can see in the dialog box in Figure 3-6, which was opened by right-clicking on "Employee Information" in the Contents list and then and selecting Properties.

 OTE: *Bookmarks and hyperlinks can be graphics as well as text.*

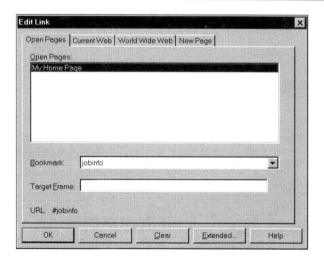

Edit Link
dialog box

FIGURE 3-6

■ **Annotation text**, which is in a third color and causes the mouse pointer to turn into a little robot, like the one shown here, does not appear when the web is viewed with a browser. This text is created with the Annotation WebBot. It is meant for notes to the web authors and editors.

> **Department or workgroup** ⏎
> My department's name ... with a link to its home page
>
> **Manager** ⏎
> My manager's name ... with a link to his or her home page
>
> **Direct reports**
>
> • A person who works for me
> • Another person who works for me
> • Yet another person who works for me

■ **URLs** or Internet addresses are just hyperlinks to that address but with a specific protocol such as mailto for e-mail or FTP for file transfer. The Properties dialog box for the link will show you the full address and protocol and let you change them.

■ **Forms** for entering comments and the reader's name or, preferably, e-mail address allow your reader to communicate with you. Note that responses from the form are stored in the file homeresp.txt. You can change this and other aspects of the form by opening the Properties dialog box and clicking on Form and then Settings.

■ **Timestamp**, at the bottom of the page, is created with the Timestamp WebBot. You can change its format and the way it is set through its Properties dialog box.

When you are done looking at the personal web page, close the FrontPage Editor and then delete MyWeb in the FrontPage Explorer. The "simple" personal web you can create with the Personal Web template is a good starting point for many webs and offers a number of useful features. Consider it as you create your own webs.

Using the Project Web Template

The Project Web template creates a multipage web, shown in Figure 3-7, that is used to keep people up to date on a project. It lists a project's staff members, schedule, and status, and provides independent page headers and footers, an archive, a search

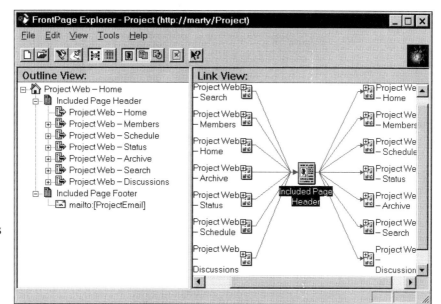

Project web, as it is created by the Project Web template

FIGURE 3-7

engine, and a discussion bulletin board. Follow these steps to look at some of the features that are unique to this template:

1. From the FrontPage Explorer open the New Web dialog box and select Project Web. A new web will be created and will appear in the FrontPage Explorer. Click on the plus sign on the left of the Included Page Header page to expand the directory tree so it looks like Figure 3-7.

2. Click on Project Web–Home in the left pane, and then double-click the same page in the right pane to open the FrontPage Editor with that page. The page shown in Figure 3-8 will be displayed.

Included Pages

FrontPage has a WebBot that allows you to include one page on another. Thus, if you want the same information or objects to be on several pages, you can put that information on one page and then include that page on all the others where you want

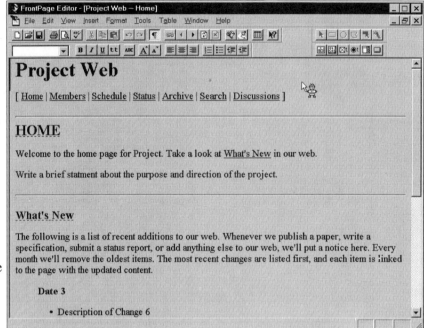

Project
Web—Home
page with
an included
header page

FIGURE 3-8

it. This is done with the Include WebBot (WebBots will be discussed in Chapter 7). This is how the included pages work:

1. Move the mouse pointer to the top of the page; the WebBot icon appears. That is because the top of the page is a separate header page (named header.htm in this case) applied to all pages in the web.

OTE: *You cannot edit the contents of a header page on a regular page. You must open the header page itself.*

2. Right-click on the top of the page and select Open header.htm. The header page will open as you can see next. Here you can edit the title and navigation bar (or "navbar") that will appear on every page of the web.

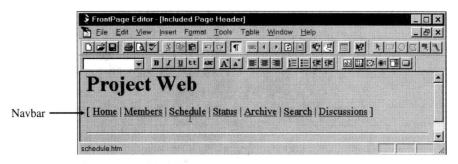

Navbar

3. Move the mouse pointer through the navbar, and in the lower-left corner of the window you'll see the pages to which the links will jump when they are clicked. In this case the navbar is just a series of words, each a hyperlink to a different page. You can also make a navbar out of a graphic or a series of graphics and use hotspots for the hyperlinks. You can edit both the words and the links—the words directly, and the links through the Properties dialog box.

4. In the Included Page Header you just opened, right-click on Members in the navbar and choose Properties. The Edit Link dialog box will open and show you the link to the Members.htm page. This is the link you would change if you wanted a different link. Click on Cancel to close the Edit Link dialog box.

5. Close the Included Page Header. Go to the bottom of the Home page, and you'll see a footer page that is also included on every web page. You can edit it as you can the header page.

6. Close the FrontPage Editor with the Home page, and return to the FrontPage Explorer.

7. Open and review the Members, Schedule, Status, and Archive pages. On each you'll see the header and footer placed there by the Include WebBot, as well as many features you saw on the Personal Web page.

Searches and Discussion Groups

The Project web that you created incorporates two other WebBot-created features—text searches and discussion groups—which add interactivity to the web. Look at these next:

1. Open the Project Web–Search page in the FrontPage Editor. Your screen should look like Figure 3-9. In the second section of this page is a one-field form that allows you to search the documents in the current web for a particular text string that you have entered in the form. This search form has been created by the Search bot. You can edit its characteristics by right-clicking in the search area and choosing Properties. The bottom part of the Search page contains instructions on how to structure a search query.

2. Close the Search page and open the Project Web–Discussions page, which contains links to two discussion groups. The discussion groups are separate webs and are created with the Discussion bot. These allow people to enter comments, and others to comment on their comments, thereby creating threads on a given subject. Most online forums follow this format.

3. Close the FrontPage Editor and delete the Project web in the FrontPage Explorer.

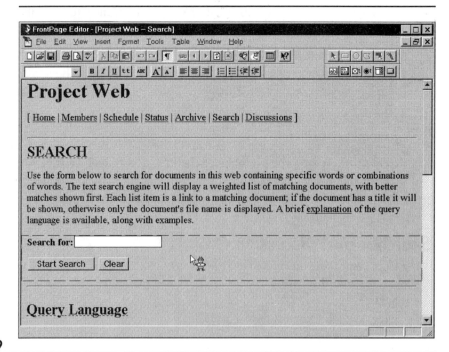

Search page for doing text searches

FIGURE 3-9

A web that has been created with the Project Web template provides an excellent communications tool, not only for projects, but also for any team, operation, or department. To get a better perspective of the Project web, open it next in a browser.

Looking at a Web in a Browser

Although FrontPage is WYSIWYG, you cannot fully use a web in FrontPage the way you can in a browser. For that reason it is always a good idea to look at your webs in a browser several times as you build them. The more interactive your web is, the more you need to do this. The only way to get a feel for how the interactive content is working is to use it. Do that with the Project web by using the following steps:

OTE: *To test many of the features of FrontPage, you need to use either Netscape's Navigator 2.0 or later, or Microsoft's Internet Explorer 2.0 or later, and actually you should have and use both. They are available free from http://home.netscape.com and http://www.microsoft.com, respectively.*

1. Open your browser as you normally do, and load the web you created from the Project Web template by typing your server or computer domain name and then the name of your project web. For example, using either the Microsoft Internet Explorer or the Netscape Navigator, the author typed "marty/project." The browser translated this into "http://marty/Project/" and opened the web as shown in Figure 3-10.

2. Click on the links in the navbar to see how that works and to look at the various pages.

3. When you get to the Search page, type **prototype** in the Search For text box, and then click on Start Search or press ENTER. In a few moments the search results will appear, as shown in Figure 3-11. This gives you two links to documents in the archive that contain the word "prototype."

OTE: *When you submit the search criteria or other information on forms, you may get a message cautioning you about the insecurity of the Web. You must decide if you care if someone sees what you are sending. In this case you probably won't care.*

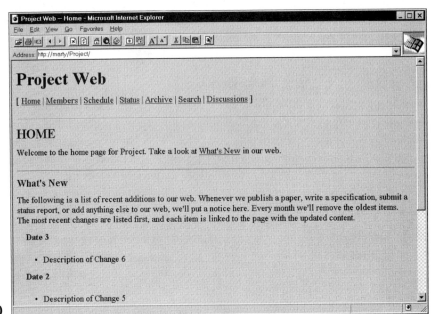

Project web
opened in
the Internet
Explorer

FIGURE 3-10

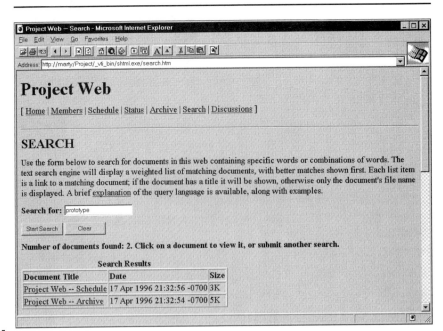

The results
of entering
a search
request

FIGURE 3-11

4. Open the Discussions page, click on Requirements Discussion, and then click on Post in the navbar. The Post Article form will open as you can see in Figure 3-12. Here you can enter a subject, which will be placed in the Table of Contents; your name; and then your comments. When others come to the discussion page, they will see your subject in the Table of Contents. By clicking on that entry, they can read your remarks and reply to them by clicking on Reply, which is added to the navbar. This reply will be added to the existing subject and will not create an additional entry to the Table of Contents.

5. When you are done looking at your project web in your browser, close the browser.

As you can see, the actual manipulation of the web, especially an interactive one, is a very important part of testing.

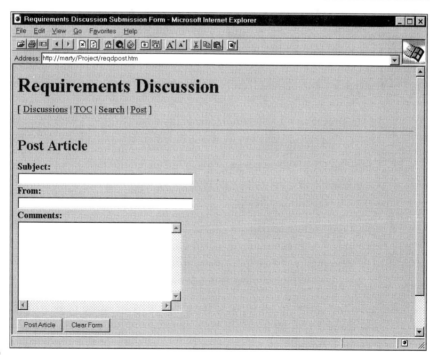

Form for adding comments to a discussion group

FIGURE 3-12

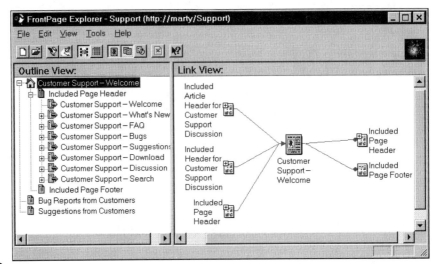

Customer
Support
Web
template

FIGURE 3-13

Applying the Customer Support Web Template

The Customer Support Web template, shown in Figure 3-13 above, makes a lot of information available to the user in several ways and allows the user to provide information to you in two ways. In doing this, the web uses FrontPage features you have already seen, but with different twists. Look at those differences now:

1. In the FrontPage Explorer create a Customer Support web from the New Web dialog box. Your result should look like Figure 3-13.

2. Open the Customer Support–Welcome page, the home page for this web. As you have seen before, this page has an included header and footer, with a navbar in the header.

3. Close the Welcome page and then open, look at, and close the What's New and FAQ (Frequently Asked Questions) pages. These pages, well-designed for their purposes, are simply combinations of text and hyperlinks with the included header and footer.

4. Open the Customer Support–Bugs page. If you scroll down the page, you'll see a special form for collecting errors in computer software ("bugs"). As with all other features in a wizard- or template-created web,

you can customize this, changing the text, size, and content of the fields. In the last case, right-click on the field and choose Properties. The field's Properties dialog box will open, as shown in Figure 3-14 for the second field. Here you can change the name of the field in the top text box and change the choices the field presents to the user by using the Add, Modify, and Remove buttons.

5. Close the Bugs page; open, look at, and close the Suggestions page, which contains another form; and then open the Download page. The purpose of the Download page is to allow users to transfer software or documents to their computers from your server. This is done with the FTP (file transfer protocol) Internet protocol.

6. If you scroll down the page and then move the mouse pointer over the links for these transfers, you'll see in the status bar the URL to effect the FTP transfer, like that shown in the lower-left corner of Figure 3-15.

7. Close the Download page and then open, look at, and close the Discussion and Search pages. These contain a discussion group and a search form similar to those you saw in the Project Web.

8. Open your Customer Support web in a browser and try its features, submitting a bug report and a suggestion. This will show you how these work.

9. When you are done, close the FrontPage Editor, and delete the Customer Support web.

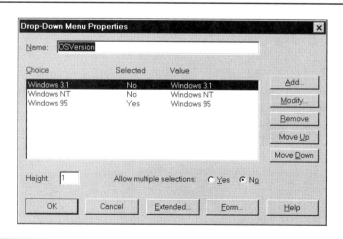

Drop-Down
Menu
Properties
dialog box

FIGURE 3-14

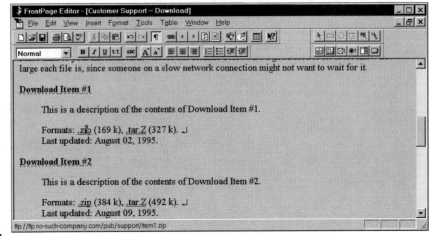

URL for
an FTP
transfer of
software or
a document

FIGURE 3-15

OTE: *The reason each of these webs is being deleted after you are done looking at them is that they take a fair amount of disk space. The Customer Support web, as it is created by the template, takes 360K, and the Project web takes 395K. Also, you can have only 13 webs in the FrontPage Explorer.*

Working with the Discussion Web Wizard

You have seen the discussion groups that were included in the Project and Customer Support webs. You can also create a separate discussion web or incorporate a discussion group in another web by using the Discussion Web wizard:

1. From the FrontPage Explorer, open the New Web dialog box and choose Discussion Web Wizard. Type the filename for the web, **DiscussionGroup,** and click on OK. The first Discussion Web Wizard dialog box will explain how a wizard works.

2. Click on Next. The second dialog box will ask you the features of a discussion group that you want to include, as you can see in Figure 3-16. Your choices include the following:

- **Submission Form** is the form used to submit comments to the discussion and is required to have a discussion group.

- **Table of Contents** provides a means of organizing and finding previously submitted comments by subject. If you want readers to read and comment on what previous contributors have submitted, then you need to include a table of contents.

- **Search Form** is an alternative way for readers to find previously contributed information. It allows a reader to find a contribution containing words other than those in the subject.

- **Threaded Replies** links multiple comments on the same subject. This allows the reader to directly go from one comment to the next on a given subject.

- **Confirmation Page** shows the person making a submission what the system has received.

3. Keep all of the options checked, so you can look at them, and click on Next. The third dialog box will open and ask for the title you want to use. Type **Discussion Group**.

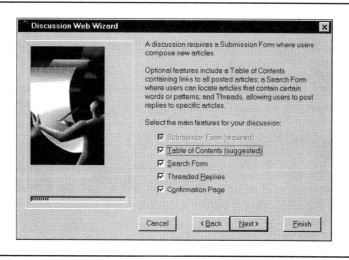

Choosing
the parts
of a
discussion
group

FIGURE 3-16

4. Again click on Next. The fourth Discussion Web Wizard dialog box will ask for the fields you want to start with on the submission form. You will be able to add more later with the FrontPage Editor.

5. Keep the default Subject and Comments and click on Next. The fifth dialog box will ask if you want to restrict the contributors to the discussion group.

6. Accept the default, Allow Anyone To Post, and click on Next. Also accept the defaults in the next five dialog boxes, clicking on Next in each of them, and then click on Finish in the final dialog box. The web will then be displayed in the FrontPage Explorer.

7. You can, of course, open the pages of the web in the FrontPage Editor and make any changes you desire. To really look at the Discussion web and try it, you need to look at it in a browser. Since one of the defaults chosen was to use frames, you need to use Netscape Navigator 2.0 or later to see the frames.

8. Open Netscape Navigator (or any browser) and load DiscussionGroup (type *your server name*/**discussiongroup**), and your Discussion Group web will appear as shown in Figure 3-17.

9. Click on Post A New Article (you should see a form similar to that shown in Figure 3-12), enter a subject, name, and some comments, and click on Post Article. (If you get a message saying you are about to send information over the Internet and it is insecure, click on Continue.) The confirmation should appear showing the subject you entered.

10. Click on Return To The Contents Page. Back at the Contents page you should again see the subject you entered under Contents. Click on your subject and you will see your name, the date and time you made the submission, and the comments you entered.

11. The navbar now has several new entries: Post To Start A New Thread, Reply To Add A Comment To Existing Thread, Next and Previous to go forward and backward in the current thread, and Up to go to the next thread.

12. Try these new navbar entries; make several submissions, both independent and in reply to another submission, so you can see how the navigation works. When you are done, close the browser and delete the web.

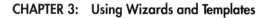

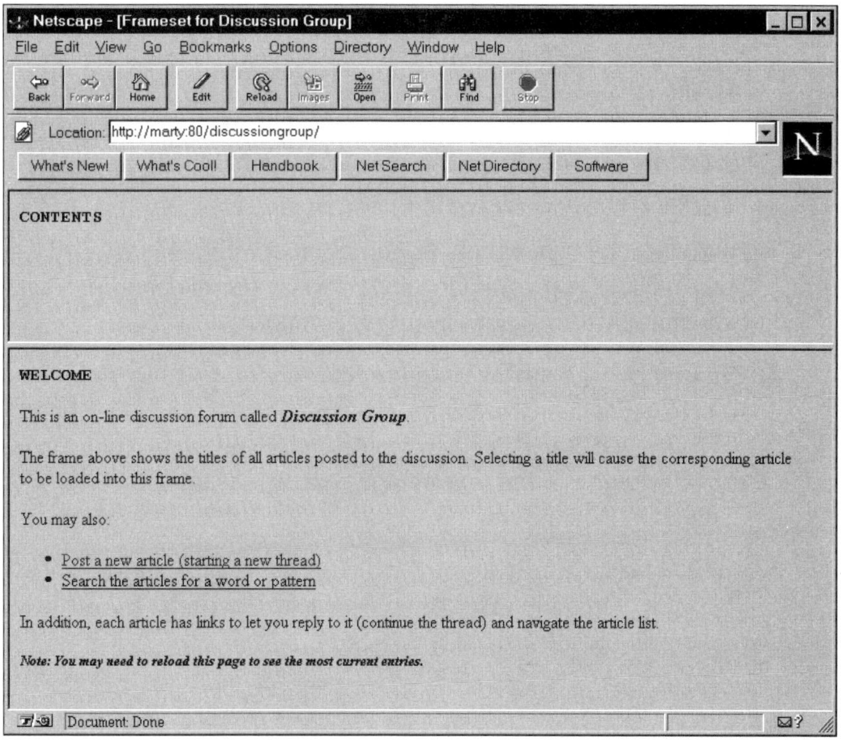

Discussion
Group web
opened in
Netscape
Navigator

FIGURE 3-17

A discussion group can be a powerful means to communicate among a group, and FrontPage offers an easy way to create one.

Using the Corporate Presence Wizard

The Corporate Presence web is one of the more sophisticated webs that FrontPage creates. By using a wizard, you get to do a lot of customizing as you build. Let's try it:

1. Choose Corporate Presence Wizard in the New Web dialog box, name it **Corporate**, click on OK, enter your Name and Password if necessary, and click on OK again. Click on Next in the first wizard dialog box, opening the list of pages that can be included in the web.

2. Select all of the options to include all the possible pages, and click on Next. This brings up a list of topics that can be included on the Home page. Accept the defaults for this and the next seven dialog boxes, which ask you what you want on each type of page, until you reach the dialog box (shown in Figure 3-18) that asks for the presentation style you want to use in your web. As you go through each of the dialog boxes, note the options; you have significant flexibility.

3. Look at each of the options—Plain, Conservative, Flashy, and Cool—that you have for the presentation style, and choose the one you want (Flashy is used in the illustrations later in this chapter).

4. Click on Next. You'll be asked for the background and text colors you want to use. This will create a web style sheet that will be applied to all the pages you create in this web. You can easily change it later, and thereby change all the pages in the web, by changing the Web Colors page in the FrontPage Editor.

5. Make the selections you want and click on Next. Then you are asked if you want to initially mark your pages with the Under Construction icon. Make your choice and click on Next.

Choosing the desired presentation style for a Corporate Presence web

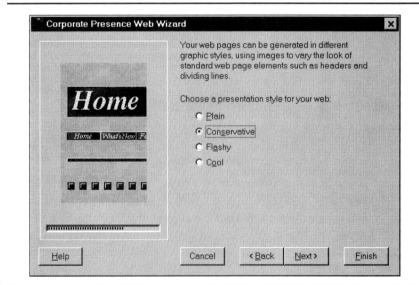

FIGURE 3-18

IP: *Using the Under Construction icon is generally not a good idea. If at all possible, finish the web before putting it on the server for public consumption.*

6. Enter the company name and address (any name and address is fine for this exercise), click on Next, enter the phone numbers and e-mail addresses to use, and again click on Next.

7. Make sure Show To Do List is checked and then click on Finish. The web will be created and displayed in both the FrontPage Explorer and the FrontPage To Do List. If necessary, open the To Do List by clicking on its button in the FrontPage Explorer's toolbar, so both the Explorer and the To Do List are visible, as you can see in Figure 3-19.

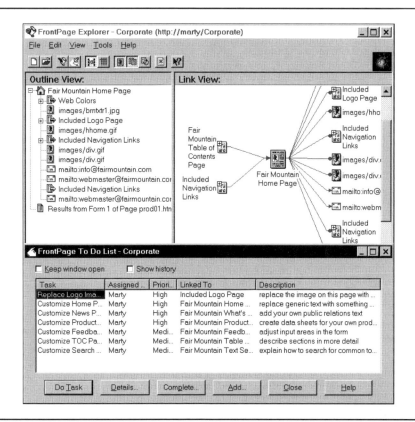

Corporate Presence web in both the FrontPage Explorer and FrontPage To Do List

FIGURE 3-19

8. Open the Home page in the FrontPage Editor, and then open each of the successive pages to see the many features that are incorporated in this web. Scroll each page to make sure you see everything. Right-click on the features to see their properties. Some of the features to note (see Figure 3-20 for the first five features):

- The "Company Logo" is an included page where you would put your company logo and name so they will appear on every page.

- The page title "Home" and its background are a graphic, hhome.gif. It is one of a series of graphics that are on each page. You can create such graphics in CorelDraw, Adobe Photoshop, or other graphics packages and then place them in FrontPage. Chapter 4 will further discuss placing graphics.

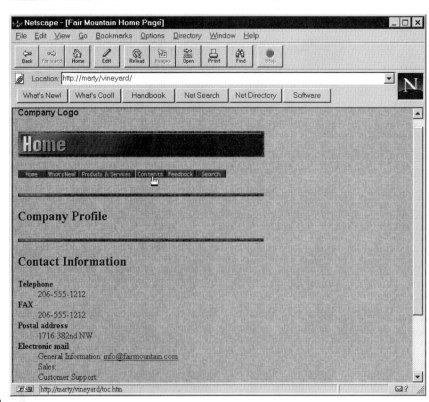

Corporate Presence web home page

FIGURE 3-20

- The navbar is a series of graphics, one for each of the hyperlinks, and is an included page that is used both at the top and at the bottom of each regular web page.

- The line above "Company Profile" is a graphic.

- The phone numbers, postal address, e-mail addresses, and company name are entered and maintained through the Substitution bot. WebBots are discussed in depth in Chapter 7.

- The small "new" on the What's New page is a graphic that you can use on your own pages. Search for the file Smallnew.gif.

- The "Table of Contents" is created by the Table of Contents bot. In the FrontPage Editor this does not look like much, but in a browser this is automatically expanded to include references to each page and each link on each page, as you can see in Figure 3-21. This table of contents is automatically updated when any page is changed.

9. When you are finished looking at all the pages in the FrontPage Editor, open your browser and try the features of the Corporate Presence web. In particular, try those noted earlier, especially the Table of Contents page.

10. When you finished with the browser, close it and then delete your Corporate Presence web.

Page Wizards and Templates

The web wizards are grand in their scope, with many different page types and many different features on each page. Sometimes, though, what you want is a single page or a single feature. For that purpose, FrontPage provides the page wizards and templates. In the remainder of this chapter you'll see some of the more useful page wizards and templates. Begin with these steps:

1. In the FrontPage Explorer create a new web using the Normal Web template; name it **TestPages**.

2. Double-click on the Normal Page in the right-hand pane of the Explorer to open the FrontPage Editor.

3. Open the File menu and choose New. The New Page dialog box appears.

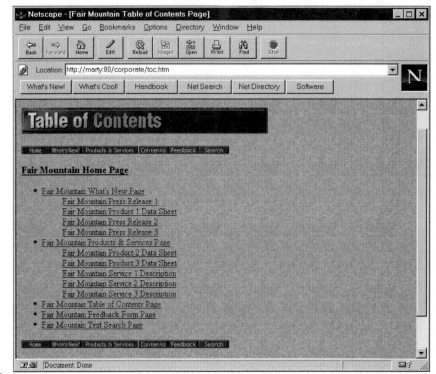

The expanded table of contents in a browser created with the Table of Contents bot

FIGURE 3-21

The 28 wizards and templates listed in the New Page dialog box represent a tremendous resource that you can use to build your own webs. Chapter 2 provided a brief description of all the page wizards and templates. Many are differentiated only by their layout and content. Let's look at six of the more general-purpose ones. Two general-purpose wizards that are not discussed here, Form Page Wizard and Frames Wizard, are left for in-depth discussion in Chapters 6 and 7. As each template or wizard is discussed, use the wizard or template to create a page and look at the results, at least in the FrontPage Editor, and possibly in your browser.

Confirmation Form Template

A confirmation page is used to show someone submitting information to you that their submission was received. When you create a submission form—for example, a feedback form or a registration form—a default confirmation page is automatically generated by FrontPage. You can create a custom confirmation page by using the Confirmation Form template, but you must specify that you want to use your confirmation page in the Form Properties dialog box of the submission form (from a form field's Properties dialog box, click on Form and then click again on Settings and fill in the URL of the confirmation page). In the FrontPage Explorer you can see the link between the submission form and the confirmation page it uses.

The Confirmation Form template creates a confirmation page using Confirmation Field bots as shown in Figure 3-22. These are used to place fields from the submission anywhere on the confirmation page. You can add additional fields to a confirmation page by using the Bot option on the Insert menu, as well as change the text and move the existing confirmation fields. Several submission forms can share the same confirmation page if the forms use the same field names.

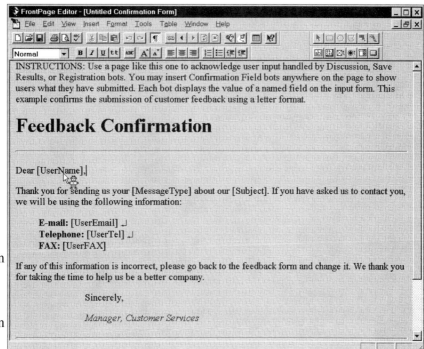

Confirmation Form template showing Confirmation Field bots

FIGURE 3-22

n **OTE:** *You must know the field names from the submission form when you are building the confirmation page, because the Confirmation Field bot, which requires the field name, does not allow you to browse for them.*

Feedback Form Template

The Feedback Form template creates a general-purpose form page that allows a user to send you comments, as you can see in Figure 3-23. The template creates several types of fields, gives them names that are also used in the Confirmation Form template, and activates the Save Results bot to capture the information submitted and to save it in the Feedback.txt file in the _Private subdirectory under the web's

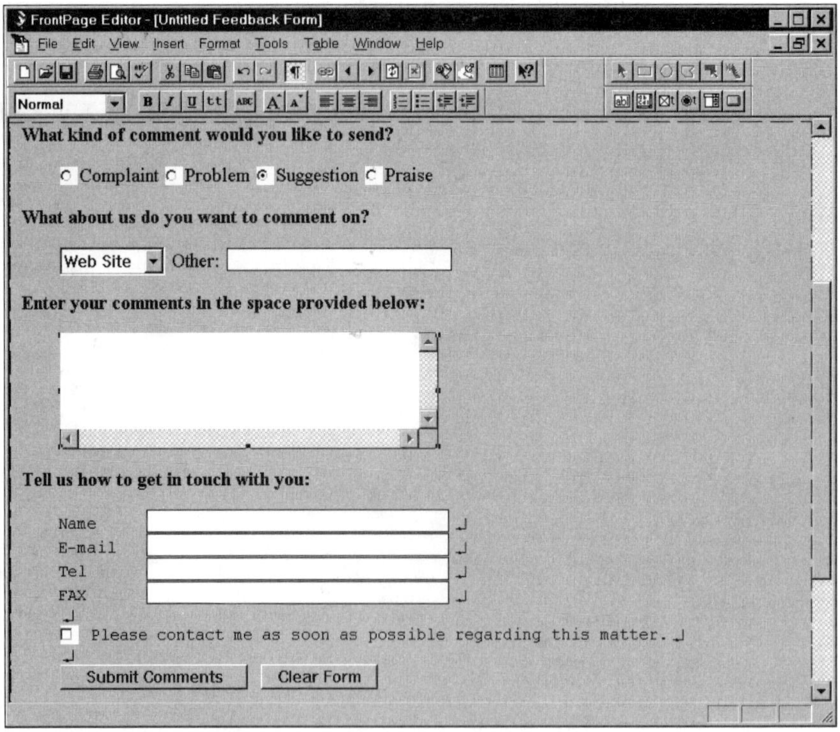

Form page created with Feedback Form template

FIGURE 3-23

directory. (If you use the default directory scheme and your web is named TestPages, then the full path for Feedback.txt is C:\FrontPage Webs\Content\TestPages_Private\ Feedback.txt.)

Glossary of Terms Template

The page that you see in Figure 3-24, created by the Glossary of Terms template, has an indexing scheme that is useful in many situations other than a glossary. This is particularly true for longer lists, such as lists of parts, employees, and publications. While it is very simple to create from scratch, the template still saves you from creating 27 bookmarks and 27 links.

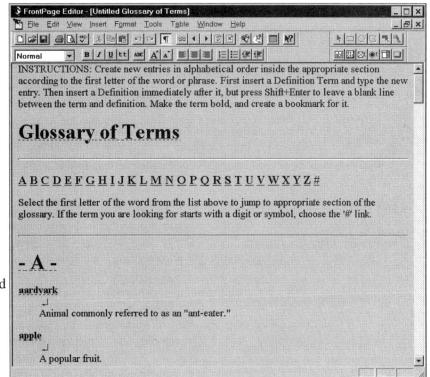

Alphabetized reference created by the Glossary of Terms template

FIGURE 3-24

Personal Home Page Wizard

Earlier in this chapter you saw how the Personal Web template created a single personal home page with all the supporting web files. The Personal Home Page wizard leads you through the creation of the same page without the web (you can create that with the Normal Web template), but giving you many options on what to include on the page as it is built, saving you time in customizing. In either case a personal home page can be used to promote you, a small organization, a product or service, or a concept. In the Personal Web template, the page just appears without you having any options. See the many options you have with the Personal Home Page wizard:

1. After selecting Personal Home Page Wizard from the New Page dialog box, you are asked to select the major sections that you want on this page. Select all of the suggested sections so you can see what they offer, and then click on Next.

2. In the second dialog box you are asked for the page URL (the page's filename) and the page title that will appear in the title bar of a browser. For this example, accept the defaults and click on Next.

3. The third dialog box asks you the information to include in the Employee Information section. Select all of the topics, and click on Next.

4. You are then asked to enter the name of the projects (could be anything) that you want to include on your page. Enter these, decide if you want them in a bulleted, numbered, or definition list, and then click on Next.

5. In the next several dialog boxes choose how you want a "Hot List" presented, the format of a biography section, a list of items for the Personal Interests section and how it is to be presented, your various addresses and phone numbers, and how you want to get the comments and suggestions that are submitted. In each case click on Next after making the necessary entries.

6. In the next to the last dialog box, you are asked the order of the sections on your page and are given a list of the sections. To change the order, click on a section you want to move, and then click on Up or Down the number of times it takes to move the section to where you want it.

7. When you have the sections in the order you want, click on Next, and
then click on Finish to create your home page. One possible result is
shown in Figure 3-25. Notice the many similarities with Figure 3-5.

There are many things that you can do to customize this page. One of the more
likely changes is to add additional pages to this home page and refer to them from
the home page. If you are going to do that, you'll need to first create a web in the
FrontPage Explorer, then create your home page, and finally create the additions,
all from within the web. As you are looking at this page, keep in mind that it has
many uses other than just for an individual.

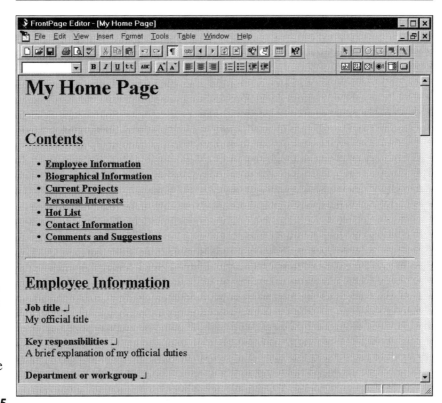

A personal
home page
created
with the
Personal
Home Page
wizard

■ **FIGURE 3-25**

OTE: *The page wizards and templates in FrontPage 1.1 do not incorporate tables, and in many cases tables would be superior to the way data is currently displayed. This probably will change in FrontPage 2.0.*

Search Page Template

The Search Page template provides all the text search features that you saw in the webs earlier in this chapter. It is completely self-contained, including the query language instructions, as you can see in Figure 3-26. When you include this page in a web, it will search all of the text in the web without any further effort on your part. (As you saw when looking at the Normal Web template at the beginning of this chapter, you can add a page like the Search Page to a web by opening the web in the

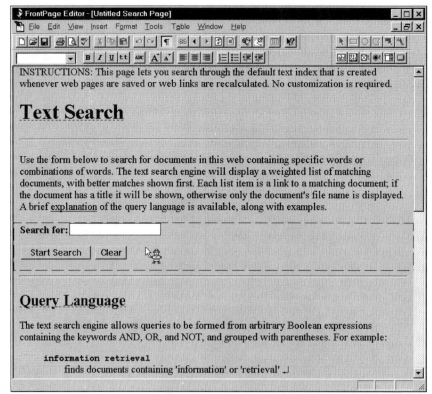

Text Search page created with the Search Page template

FIGURE 3-26

FrontPage Explorer, double-clicking on an existing page to open the FrontPage Editor, choosing New from the File menu, and then selecting the template or wizard you want to use to create the page.)

Table of Contents Template

The page, or more likely a portion thereof, created by the Table of Contents template is probably one of the more useful page templates. When you have finished adding all of the pages to a web, giving them each names, and creating links from a home page, add a table of contents page, or incorporate its contents on another page. This will not look like much in the FrontPage Editor (see Figure 3-27), but when you open the page in a browser, you'll have a complete table of contents of all the pages in the web. If there are links to the pages, they are shown in the hierarchical structure of their links. If the pages are not linked, they are listed after the linked pages, as you can see in Figure 3-28. The Table of Contents, then, creates a link to all the unlinked pages.

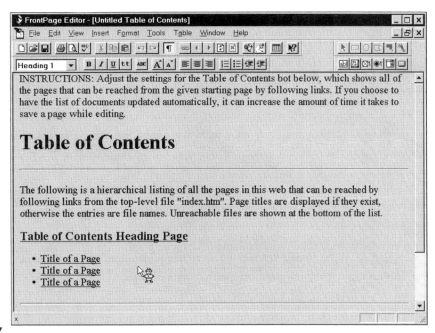

Table of Contents page in the FrontPage Editor

FIGURE 3-27

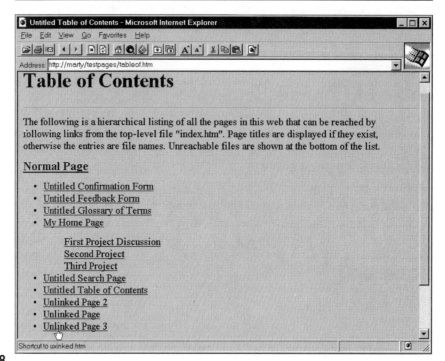

Table of
Contents
page in a
browser

FIGURE 3-28

 OTE: *Unlinked pages are listed in alphabetical order by their* URL or
filename, *not their title.*

Figure 3-28 was created from a web that contained the six pages created from
templates and wizards discussed here, plus a normal page used as the home page of
the web and containing the links in a custom navbar shown in Figure 3-29.
Additionally, three pages were created and linked to the projects area of the personal
home page, as well as three more pages that were unlinked. The creation, use, and
management of hyperlinks, including navbars, will be fully discussed in Chapter 5.

The templates and wizards available in FrontPage for both webs and pages are
an exceptionally valuable resource for creating the webs you want to build. If you
use your imagination as you build a web, you will find that the templates and wizards

A navigation bar (or navbar) used to link the six pages created here

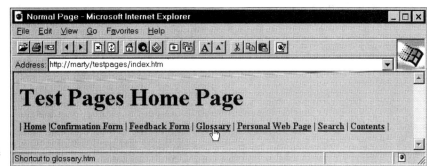

FIGURE 3-29

will save you a considerable amount of work. They also will give you a number of ideas on how to utilize the features of FrontPage in your webs. Look through the templates and wizards both before and as you are working on your web to get all you can out of them.

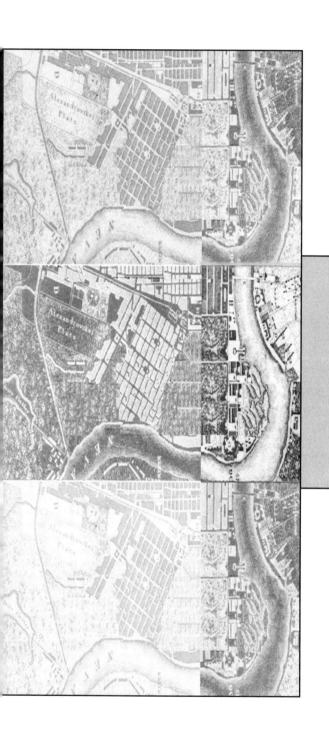

Creating and Formatting a Web Page from Scratch

In Chapter 3 you saw how to build a web and its pages by using a wizard or a template. You learned that using a wizard or template is the easiest way to create a web that uses many FrontPage features. Occasionally, you may want to build a web from scratch (and consequently increase your knowledge of the parts of a web). Let's create a web now, beginning with the planning.

Planning a Web

In Chapter 2 you were given a list of steps to build a web, starting with its planning. Planning is probably the most important step in making a good web—and the one most often shortchanged. Planning seeks to answer four questions:

- What are the goals of the web?

- What will its content be?

- How will it be organized?

- What do you want it to look like?

Suppose you work for a large travel agency named Fantasy Travel and have been given the task of creating an intranet web to communicate with the company's agents. Go through each of the four questions with that in mind. (With only small changes you could alternatively look at this as an Internet web to communicate to your potential clients.)

What Are Your Goals?

Setting the goals of a web is very important—if the goals are well thought out, you will probably end up with an effective web. Keep it simple. Having one or two obtainable goals for your web is better than having a number of goals that cannot all be met. Too many goals will scatter the focus of the web, making it much more difficult to accomplish any one of them.

For Fantasy Travel, there is one primary goal for their intranet web: to give their agents a competitive advantage by providing access to a consolidated list of the latest travel offerings. (An Internet web goal might be to get the user to call Fantasy and inquire about a possible trip.) There is a secondary and supporting goal: to keep the web frequently updated so the agents will look at it often.

What Is the Content?

To accomplish Fantasy Travel's goals, you'll need to include information about current travel specials over a broad range of travel options. The information needs to be complete enough to capture the agents' interest but concise enough for them to read quickly. Therefore, the content needs to include not only a brief description of current packages, but also general information the agents might need, such as the current exchange rates, climates, and current travel conditions.

How Is It Organized?

How well a web is organized determines how easily users can get the information they seek. This means that the desired information should be within one or two clicks of your home page, and the path should be clear—users won't have to guess how to get what they want. The home page mainly provides links to other pages. The pages behind the home page contain the desired information and are a single link away from the home page. The home page links to detailed information give relatively quick answers to those agents who are willing to take a couple of minutes, but following the links may not appeal to those who are in a hurry. For that quick answer, you need to have some low-priced specials briefly but prominently listed on the home page.

The structure of your web needs to be a simple and obvious tree structure, so that users always know where they are and how they got there. While a cross link between two third-level branches may seem like a quick way to get users from one place to another, it is also a quick way to confuse users about where they are. It is better to force users back up the tree and down another branch. If you never have more than two levels from your home page, it is not a big chore to backtrack. Besides, the previously visited pages are already on the users' disk, so they can quickly backtrack.

What Will It Look Like?

With all the concepts just discussed, what will this web look like? The best approach is to sketch the primary types of pages that you will be using. Figure 4-1 shows one way that the information in this web could be laid out to satisfy the desired points brought out in the plan. To keep to the desired three levels, there will be three types of pages:

- A home page with a list of interesting specials and links to all the different types of travel

- A second-level page for a type of travel with links to the details for a particular offering

- A third-level page for the details of a travel offering

All three pages will have the same footer, which will have a copyright notice, the date last updated, a postal address, and information on how to contact the webmaster (the person responsible for maintaining the web). The second- and third-level pages, of which there will be many, will share the same heading, which will have company and contact information as well as links to other pages. The home page will have a unique header and larger, separate links sections.

The web will begin with major travel options such as Alaskan cruises, China tours, and African safaris, which will be located on the home page. The web will flow to a list of specific offerings for a travel option, such as a list of Alaskan cruises, on the second-level pages. These will lead to the details of a specific offering, such as the specifics of a particular cruise, on the third-level pages. The "Current Specials" on the home page will link directly to the third-level details of those offerings.

This gives you a general view of what your web will look like, which is enough for the planning process. As you actually create the pages, you will fine-tune that look with the placing of graphics and the positioning of text.

Starting a Web

The Fantasy Travel web will be created over this and the following three chapters. This chapter will look at working with text and graphics. Chapter 5 will deal with hyperlinks and hotspots, Chapter 6 will add tables and frames, and Chapter 7 will work with forms and WebBots. The reason for this approach is to focus on one topic at a time. As a result, you'll see areas, especially in this chapter, that may be better

handled with, for example, a table or a WebBot. That discussion will be put off until the appropriate chapter, so each topic can be fully developed without interfering with others.

Developing all but the simplest webs is a long and tedious chore. Look at this proposed travel web—there will be a second-level page for each type of travel, of which there are probably six to ten types. There are then probably six to ten offerings

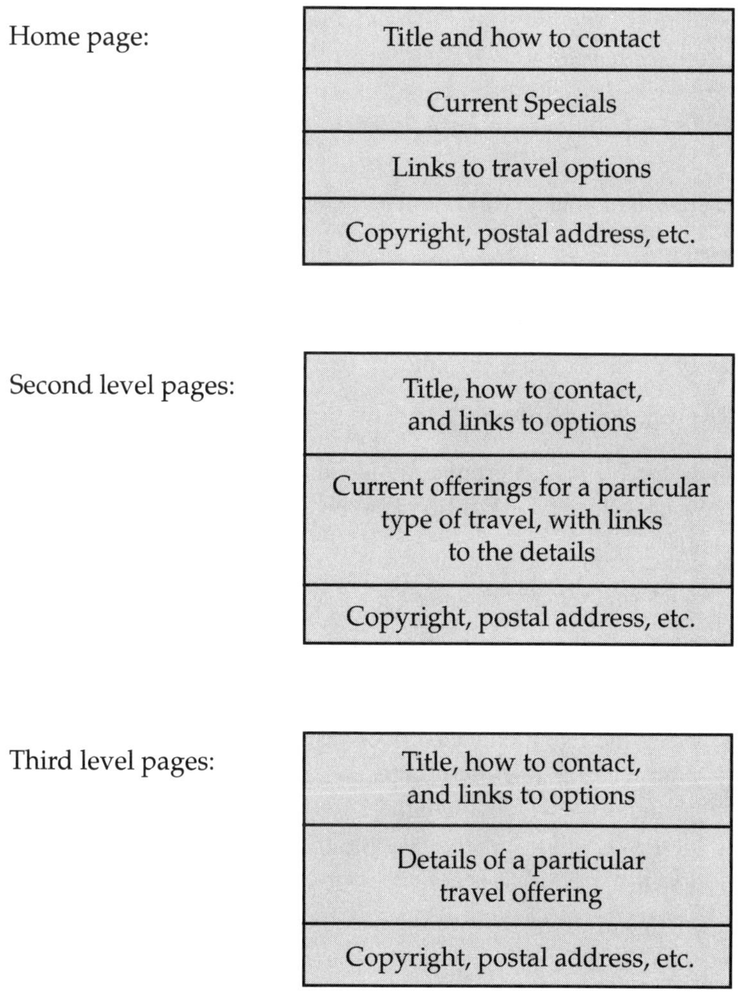

4

Home page:

| Title and how to contact |
| Current Specials |
| Links to travel options |
| Copyright, postal address, etc. |

Second level pages:

| Title, how to contact, and links to options |
| Current offerings for a particular type of travel, with links to the details |
| Copyright, postal address, etc. |

Third level pages:

| Title, how to contact, and links to options |
| Details of a particular travel offering |
| Copyright, postal address, etc. |

One way to lay out the Fantasy Travel web

FIGURE 4-1

for each type. That means at a minimum that there will be 36 third-level pages (not counting those that may be referred to directly from the home page), six second-level pages, and a home page—a total of at least 43 pages! You can let out your breath; in this chapter you'll only do one of each type of page. It is important to consider, though, how the page count explodes as you develop a web and how adding levels makes the web grow geometrically.

IP: *Leave enough time to complete the development of a web. One way to speed the process is to scan literature that you want incorporated (like travel brochures for the details of a travel offering) and then use optical character recognition (OCR) to convert them to text. Be sure to carefully edit any OCR-generated text (the process is less than perfect), and make sure you have written permission to reproduce other people's copyrighted material.*

To start the Fantasy Travel web:

1. Start the FrontPage Personal Web Server, and then load the FrontPage Explorer.

2. From the FrontPage Explorer, open the File menu and choose New Web.

3. From the New Web dialog box, select Normal Web, and click on OK.

4. In the New Web From Template dialog box, select the web server you want to use, type **FantasyTravel** as the Web Name, and click on OK.

5. Enter the Name and Password of the administrator for your web site, and click on OK.

6. In the right pane of the FrontPage Explorer, double-click on the Normal Page icon to open the FrontPage Editor.

7. Open the File menu and choose Page Properties. Change the Title from Normal Page to **Home Page**, and observe that the URL for this page includes the page's filename of Index.htm, as shown next. The home page of a web will normally have the filename Index.htm or default.htm. While this is expected, it is not necessary.

Page Properties

Title: Home Page

URL: http://marty/FantasyTravel/index.htm

8. Click on OK to close the Page Properties dialog box. Click on Save in the toolbar. Open the File menu, choose New, select Normal Page from the New Page dialog box, and click on OK.

9. Open the Page Properties dialog box, change the Title to **Second Level Page** (ignore the fact that the URL is not filled in), and click on OK to close the Page Properties dialog box.

10. Open the File menu and choose Save. You'll see that the Page Title has been picked up and the Page URL has been automatically filled in, like this:

Save As ✕

Page Title:

Second Level Page

Page URL:

second.htm

OK

Cancel

Help

Tip
Please be sure your page has a title.
Click OK to save this page to the current web.

As File...

As Template...

11. Click on OK to close the Save As dialog box. Open the File menu, choose New, select Normal Page from the New Page dialog box, and click on OK.

12. Open the Save As dialog box, change the Title to **Third Level Page** (note that the URL automatically changes as you type), and click on OK.

13. If you open the Window menu, you'll see three open pages appropriately named. If you open the FrontPage Explorer, you'll see that your web now incorporates three pages, as shown in Figure 4-2.

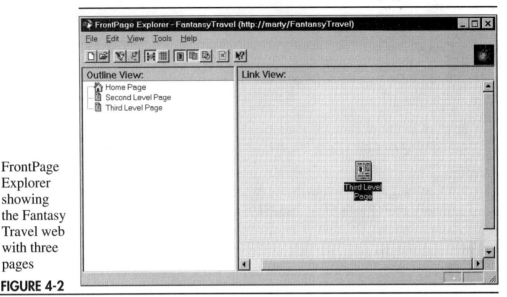

FrontPage
Explorer
showing
the Fantasy
Travel web
with three
pages

FIGURE 4-2

14. Back in the FrontPage Editor, open the Window menu, and choose Home Page to prepare for the addition of text.

Adding and Formatting Text

The text will be entered in sections corresponding to the bands on the sketches in Figure 4-1, for example, the title, the footer, and the current specials. Where applicable, this information will be entered and formatted on the home page and then copied to other pages. Begin by entering the footer.

Entering the Footer

The footer goes at the bottom of all the pages and contains the copyright notice, the postal address, phone numbers, information on how to contact the webmaster, and the date last revised. To create the footer:

1. On the Home Page in the FrontPage Editor, press ENTER several times to leave some room at the top of the page for the other information to be

entered. (The other information will take more than several lines, but this will get you started.)

2. Type the following information, just as it is shown here. Press SHIFT-ENTER (new line) at the ends of each of the first two lines.

> **Copyright 1996, Fantasy Travel, Inc. All rights reserved.**
> **1234 West Bayside Drive, Seattle, WA 98123, (206) 555-1234 or**
> **(800) 555-1234**
> **Send comments on this web site to webmaster@fantasytravel.com.**
> **Last revised 5/1/96.**

 OTE: *Using SHIFT-ENTER instead of ENTER reduces the amount of space between lines and helps group related material.*

3. If you look at the paragraph style in the Formatting toolbar, it should be Normal. This is a little large for the footer, so click on the down arrow in the Style list box, and select Heading 5. This reduces the size, but it is still easy to read, as you can see in Figure 4-3.

4. Click on the Save button in the toolbar or press CTRL-S to save your home page with its new footer.

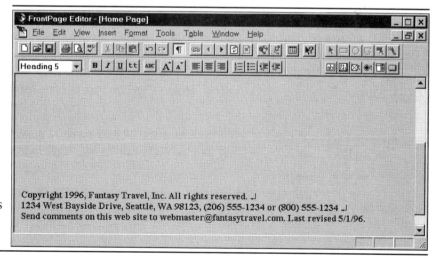

Footer text formatted as Heading 5

FIGURE 4-3

5. Drag across the text you just entered so all of it is highlighted. Click on the Copy button in the toolbar or press CTRL-C to copy the footer to the Clipboard.

6. Open the Window menu and choose the Second Level Page.

7. Click on the page, press ENTER several times, and then click on the Paste button in the toolbar or press CTRL-V to paste the footer onto the second page.

8. You can see that the paragraph style has reverted to Normal, so open the drop-down list and choose Heading 5, and then click on the Save button in the toolbar or press CTRL-S to save the second page.

9. Open the Window menu, choose Third Level Page, click on the page, press ENTER several times, click on Paste in the toolbar or press CTRL-V, select the Heading 5 style, and click on Save in the toolbar or press CTRL-S.

You now have the footer entered and correctly formatted on each page. Next work on the home page title.

Creating the Home Page Title

The home page title is the introduction to this web. It needs to be inviting and to reflect the company. It also needs to communicate how certain people can be reached. That is a big order and one that you'll revisit again in this chapter and in later chapters. To use text only:

1. Open the Window menu, choose Home Page, and press CTRL-HOME to return to the top of the home page in preparation for creating the title.

2. Type the following text, pressing SHIFT-ENTER at the end of the first and third lines, and pressing ENTER at the end of the second and fourth lines:

FANTASY TRAVEL
"The exciting way to go!"

> **For the latest fares, contact Julie Bergan at 555-1234 or John Donald at 555-1235**
> **or through e-mail at julieb@fantasytravel.com or jmd@fantasytravel.com**

3. Drag across all the text to select it, and then click on the Center align paragraph button. If the paragraph style isn't Normal, open the Style drop-down list box and select Normal.

4. Drag across the first two lines, open the Paragraph Style drop-down list box, select Heading 1, and then click on the Italic Text button in the Formatting toolbar.

5. Drag across just the first line, and click on the Increase Text Size button in the Formatting toolbar to increase the size of the first line to the 36-point maximum.

6. Click on the Save button to protect your work. Your final product should look like Figure 4-4.

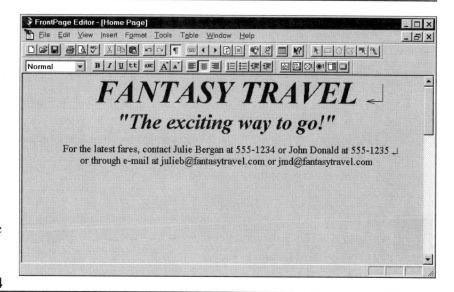

The completed home page title in its text form

FIGURE 4-4

Listing the Current Specials

The current specials are promotional fares for a particular week. Listing them gives agents immediate access to the latest and lowest fares.

IP: *It is very important to keep the list of specials updated. First, it provides a reason for people to come back and look at the page. Second, it prevents information in the list from getting out of date.*

To create the list of current specials:

1. With the blinking insertion point on the line immediately following the fourth line of the title text, press ENTER once to leave a blank line, and make sure that the paragraph style is Normal.

2. Type the following text as it is shown. Press ENTER at the end of each line.

> **CURRENT SPECIALS**
> **Super airfares to San Francisco: $75, LA: $175, New York: $275, & Miami: $375**
> **Hawaii, on the Kona beach, 1-bedroom deluxe condo, all amenities, $100 / night**
> **Fiji, air plus 6 nights in beautiful beach front bungalow with breakfast, $850**
> **Disneyland, air, 1 day Disneyland pass, 2 nights hotel, rental car, and more, $285**
> **London, air, 5 nights first-class hotel, breakfast, 2 city tours, and more, $750**
> **(Some restrictions may apply to the above fares.)**

OTE: *A single paragraph cannot have more than one paragraph style, nor can a single paragraph contain more than one bulleted or numbered line. For that reason, all of the lines in both the Current Specials and Travel Options sections have ENTER placed at the end of each line, even though it takes more space.*

3. Drag across and select line 1, and from the Paragraph Style drop-down list box, choose Heading 2.

4. Drag across lines 2 through 6, and click on the Bulleted List button in the Formatting toolbar.

5. Drag over the last line, click on the Decrease Text Size button and then click on the Increase Indent button twice (both buttons are in the Formatting toolbar).

6. Click on the Save button in the toolbar. Your Current Specials section should look like Figure 4-5.

Adding the Travel Options

The Travel Options section provides a list, really an index, of the travel options that are available from this travel agency. In Chapter 5, you'll come back and make these links to the second-level pages.

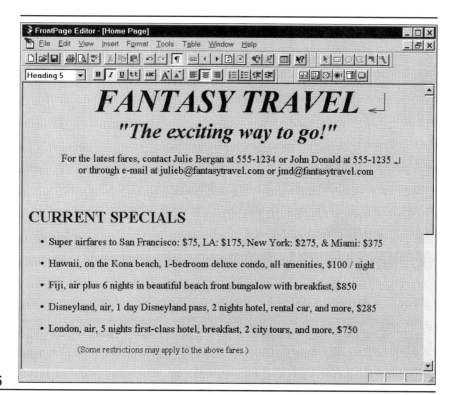

The completed Current Specials section

FIGURE 4-5

To create the Travel Options section:

1. With the blinking insertion point on the line immediately below the last line typed, type the following text. Press ENTER at the end of each line. You can copy the list of options on line 2 and use it on lines 4 through 7.

   AVAILABLE TRAVEL OPTIONS
   AIR TRAVEL: Domestic, Canada, Europe, So. America, Africa, Asia, So. Pacific
   CRUISES: Alaska, Panama Canal, Caribbean, Europe, So. America, Asia, So. Pacific
   TOURS: Domestic, Canada, Europe, So. America, Africa, Asia, So. Pacific
   HOTELS: Domestic, Canada, Europe, So. America, Africa, Asia, So. Pacific
   AUTO: Domestic, Canada, Europe, So. America, Africa, Asia, So. Pacific
   RAIL: Domestic, Canada, Europe, So. America, Africa, Asia, So. Pacific

2. Select line 1 and choose the Heading 2 style.

3. Select lines 2 through 7, and click on the Numbered List button in the Formatting toolbar.

4. Delete all but one blank line between the last line of the travel options and the beginning of the footer.

5. Save the home page. The bottom of your home page should look like Figure 4-6.

This completes the text that you will need on the home page.

Building the Title for Pages 2 and 3

On all but the home page, you want to have a brief title or heading with the ways to contact the specialists and the links to other pages. This keeps the contacts in front of the agents and gives them the primary way to navigate or get around the web. Use the next set of instructions to enter the text related to these items on page 2 and copy them to page 3. Later in this chapter you'll do some graphics work on this, and in Chapter 5 you'll establish the actual links to implement the navigation.

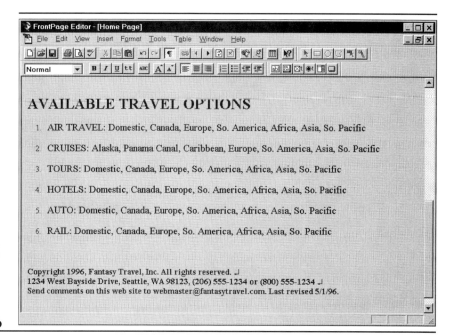

The completed Travel Options section

FIGURE 4-6

1. On the home page, drag over the first four lines of text that represent the title of the web, and click on the Copy button in the toolbar.

2. Open the Windows menu and choose Second Level Page. After the page opens, click in the top left corner to place the insertion point there, and click on the Paste button in the toolbar. The title appears on page 2.

3. If you have an extra blank line above the just-pasted title, press CTRL-HOME to move the insertion point to the very top of the page, and then press DEL to delete the leading paragraph mark.

4. Select the words "Fantasy Travel," and choose Heading 2 as the paragraph style. The size doesn't change, because you applied the special character size to these words.

5. Open the Format menu, choose Characters, select Normal for the Font Size to change the first line to the actual Heading 2 size, as you can see next, and then click on OK to close the Characters dialog box.

> *FANTASY TRAVEL* ⏎
> ## *"The exciting way to go!"*

OTE: *"Normal" font size is not a particular size, but rather allows the default size of a given paragraph style to take precedence.*

6. Select the second line and press DEL twice to delete the line as well as the paragraph mark. This also changes the phone numbers and e-mail addresses to Heading 2.

7. Select the words "For the latest fares, c" (include the comma, the space following it, and the letter "c" from the word "contact") and type an uppercase **C**.

8. After the first phone number, type a space and (**julieb**). After the second phone number, add another space and type (**jmd**) to add the e-mail addresses.

9. Delete the new-line symbol and the remainder of the contact information.

10. Select all of the words in the title *except* "Fantasy Travel," and click on the Decrease Text Size button once so all of the contact information fits on one line like this:

> ### *FANTASY TRAVEL* ↵
> **Contact Julie Bergan at 555-1234 (julieb) or John Donald at 555-1235 (jmd)**

11. Click on the Align Left button to left-align the title, and then move the insertion point to the first line after the title.

12. Type the following text, which in Chapter 5 will become a navbar with links to the rest of the web. (Note that there is a space, a vertical bar, and a space between each option.)

   | Home | Air Travel | Cruises | Tours | Hotels | Auto | Rail |

13. With the insertion point still in the future navbar, choose Heading 3 for the paragraph style. Your second page heading should now look like Figure 4-7. Click on the Save button to save the changes to page 2.

14. Select all three lines of the heading, and click on the Copy button in the toolbar.

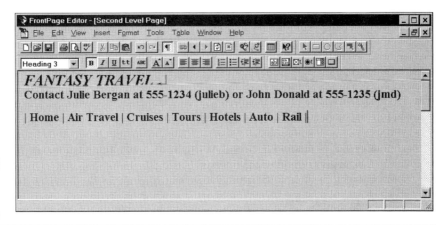

The completed second and third page headings

FIGURE 4-7

15. Open the Window menu, choose Third Level Page, click in the top left corner of the page to place the insertion point there, and click on the Paste button in the toolbar. The heading appears on page 3.

16. If you have an extra blank line above the just-pasted title, press CTRL-HOME to move the insertion point to the top of the page. Then press DEL to delete the leading invisible paragraph mark.

17. Click on the Save button to save page 3.

Entering the Offerings for a Travel Option

The body of information on the second-level pages is a listing of specific offerings for a particular type of travel—for example, a geographically ordered listing of the cruises. That is, of course, a long list. For this example, to keep the typing to a minimum, you'll work on the page for cruises, with only a couple of geographic areas and a couple of cruises in each.

1. Open the Window menu and choose Second Level Page. When the page opens, place the insertion point at the end of the navbar, and press ENTER twice to leave a blank line.

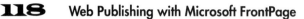

2. Type **CRUISES**, choose Heading 1, click on Center, and press ENTER.

3. Type **ALASKA**, choose Heading 3, click on Align Left, and press ENTER.

4. Choose Heading 5 and click on the Increase Indent button in the Formatting toolbar to format and indent the list of cruises.

5. Type the following cruise list, pressing SHIFT-ENTER after each of the first two lines and ENTER after the third line.

> **Royal Caribbean, Legend of the Seas, 7 nights, Vancouver to Skagway & rtn, May-Sept**
> **Princess Cruises, Sun Princess, 7 nights, Vancouver to Skagway & rtn, May-Sept**
> **Holland American, Nieuw Amsterdam, 7 nights, Vancouver to Sitka & rtn, May-Sept**

6. Click on the Decrease Indent button, choose Heading 3, type **SOUTH PACIFIC**, and press ENTER.

7. Choose Heading 5, click on the Increase Indent button, and type the following cruise list, pressing SHIFT-ENTER after the first line and ENTER after the last line

> **Princess Cruises, Pacific Princess, 16 days, Los Angeles-Hawaii-Papeete, Jan. 7 only**
> **Royal Caribbean, Legend of the Seas, 10 nights, Vancouver to Honolulu, Sept 15 only**

8. Choose Heading 4, and type the following notice:

> **Note: Excellent prices are available on these cruises, call for the latest ones.**

When you are done, your second-level page should look like Figure 4-8.

9. Delete all but one blank line between the last line entered and the beginning of the footer, and then save the page.

Importing the Details of a Travel Offering

The third-level pages contain the detailed description of one particular travel option. Since this is often better described by the travel provider, it may be helpful to use

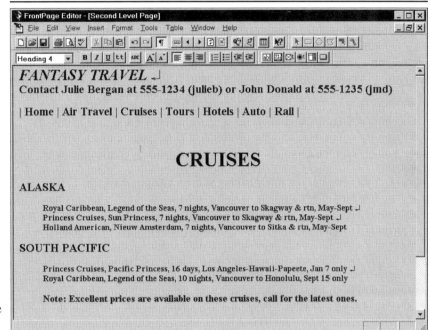

Completed
second page

their material if you have permission to do so (check with your legal department or advisor on the need for this). You can do this by typing in the material, or in some cases it might be faster to scan it in.

OTE: *Scanning text from brochures and other promotional pieces and then using optical character recognition (OCR) has a much lower success rate than if the text were on plain white paper. For small amounts of text, it is often easier to type it.*

In the following exercise you will use a combination of scanned and typed text to enter the information for the third page. If you have a scanner with OCR capability, you are encouraged to use it with something like a brochure or catalog—anything that is on slick paper with a mixture of text and pictures, and possibly with the text printed on a background image (the material can be about anything; it does not have to be related to travel). You'll then get an understanding of how that works. Of

course, if you do not have access to a scanner, then you can import any text in place of that used here. That will at least give you experience importing.

The trip used for this detailed description is a cruise from Los Angeles to Papeete, Tahiti, offered by Princess Cruises in their Fall '95–Spring '96 catalog (and is used by permission of Princess Cruises, A P&O Company). Several segments of text from this catalog will be scanned into Microsoft Word for Windows 95 and then inserted into the Fantasy Travel web.

 EMEMBER: *You may use any text to replace that used here. If possible, use a scanner as directed, but if that is unavailable, import any text you have.*

To build the body of the third page using scanned and typed text:

1. Using your scanner and its software in the normal manner, scan an article of approximately 100 words. Use your OCR program (most scanners come with an OCR program) to convert the text so that it can be read by Microsoft Word for Windows 95 or your word processing program.

2. Similarly scan and convert to text a table of approximately four columns and ten rows, and then scan and convert to text two articles of 20 to 30 words each.

3. In Microsoft Word for Windows 95 or your word processing program, edit the articles and table for scanning errors and any changes that you want to make. Then export the articles as .RTF files.

4. From the second page of the Fantasy Travel web in the FrontPage Editor, open the Window menu and choose Third Level Page.

5. On the second line below the navbar (leaving a blank line below the navbar), type the following text. Use SHIFT-ENTER at the end of the first line and ENTER on the second. Format these lines with Heading 2.

   Princess Cruises' Pacific Princess
   16 Days, Los Angeles to Papeete via Hawaii, 1/7/96 Departure

6. From the Insert menu, choose File. In the Insert dialog box, shown in the following illustration, open the Files Of Type drop-down list box, and choose RTF Files (*.rtf).

Insert ? ✕

Look in: 📁 Images

File name: *.htm   Open

Files of type: HTML Files (*.htm;*.html)   Cancel

HTML Files (*.htm;*.html)
RTF Files (*.rtf)
Text Files (*.txt)
All Files (*.*)

7. Select the name of your 100-word article and click on Open. The article will appear on your page, as you can see in Figure 4-9.

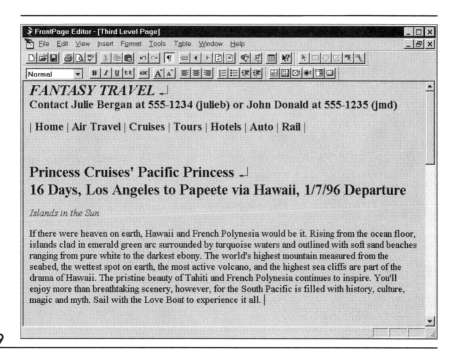

Imported article

FIGURE 4-9

8. In a similar way, import your table and then the two short articles.

Your table probably does not look very good, because it will have lost all of its horizontal alignment, as shown in Figure 4-10. FrontPage does not allow you to use tabs, and you cannot add additional spaces in a normal paragraph format. In Chapter 6 you'll see how to create FrontPage tables, but here's another way:

1. Select all of the lines of the table and choose Formatted from the Paragraph Style drop-down list box.

OTE: *The Formatted paragraph style uses a fixed-spaced font and allows you to add extra space between words.*

2. Insert spaces and replace paragraph endings with new-line endings (SHIFT-ENTER) on each line so your table looks more like it originally did, similar to the table in Figure 4-11.

3. If necessary, add or remove lines so that there is a single blank line before and after your two short articles.

4. On the second line after your short articles type the following text:

Material on this page originated from and is used with the permission of Princess Cruises.

enjoy more than breathtaking scenery, however, for the South Pacific is filled with history, culture, magic and myth. Sail with the Love Boat to experience it all.

DAY PORT ARRIVE DEPART

1 Los Angeles 5 PM 2-6 At Sea

7 OAHU (Honolulu), HAWAII 8AM 5PM

8 MAUI (Lahaina) 8AM 5PM

HAWAII

9 HAWAII (Hilo) 8AM 5PM

10-11 At Sea

12 CHRISTMAS ISLAND 9AM 1PM

A table as it is originally imported into FrontPage

 FIGURE 4-10

A text table using the Formatted paragraph style and using spaces to separate columns

FIGURE 4-11

enjoy more than breathtaking scenery, however, for the South Pacific is filled with history, culture, magic and myth. Sail with the Love Boat to experience it all.

DAY	PORT	ARRIVE	DEPART ⏎
1	Los Angeles		5 PM ⏎
2-6	At Sea ⏎		
7	OAHU (Honolulu), HAWAII	8 AM	5 PM ⏎
8	MAUI (Lahaina), HAWAII	8 AM	5 PM ⏎
9	HAWAII (Hilo)	8 AM	5 PM ⏎
10-11	At Sea ⏎		
12	CHRISTMAS ISLAND	9 AM	1 PM ⏎
13-14	At Sea ⏎		
15	BORA BORA, FRENCH POLYNESIA	9 AM	5 PM ⏎
16	MOOREA, FRENCH POLYNESIA	8 AM	4 PM ⏎
17	PAPEETE, TAHITI	Disembark AM	

IP: *Getting permission to use other people's work generally depends on whether it is to the advantage of the originator. For example, permission for the material used here from Princess Cruises was easy to get because it publicizes them and one of their cruises.*

5. Eliminate all but one line between the line you just typed and the page footer, and then save the page. The bottom of the page should look like Figure 4-12.

This completes the entry of all the text you need in this web. Now look at sprucing up the text with graphics.

Obtaining and Working with Graphics

There are three sources of graphics for a web: you can create them with programs like CorelDraw, Windows Paint, or Adobe Illustrator; you can import clipart, which is available in most places software is sold and with many packages, especially CorelDraw; and you can use a scanner to scan existing printed art. All of these have advantages and disadvantages. Using clipart is fast and easy, but it is often difficult to find exactly what you want. Scanned art gives you a lot of versatility, but you must have access to a scanner, and you must get permission from the art's creator to copy it. Creating your own art has the ultimate versatility, but it takes time and skill. Next, you'll look at all three types of graphics.

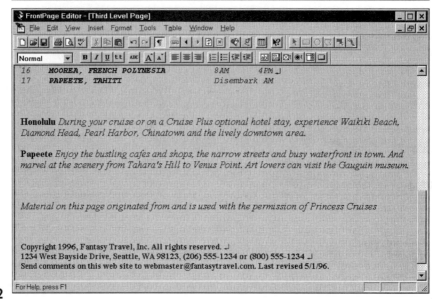

Text at the bottom of page 3

Adding graphics to an intranet page for internal consumption is only slightly different from doing that to an Internet page for external consumption. You are doing more selling externally and more information-providing internally. Also, since graphics take time to load, you may want to weight that factor more heavily internally. But don't err either by reducing graphics too much internally or by not paying attention to the loading time externally. Graphics can communicate a lot very quickly, and to some people graphics are far better at communicating than text. Therefore, make graphics an important part of your web, whether it is on the Internet or an intranet. Just keep in mind the time graphics take to load and the objectives of your web.

Creating and Inserting Graphics

In creating graphics for your web pages, you are limited only by your skill, imagination, and time. One type of graphic that is fairly easy to do with a number of programs is *word art*—a graphic created out of one or more words. To use word art for the web's title (CorelDraw is described here, but you can use any program you wish):

1. Open CorelDraw or your graphics program. Select the Text tool and set the defaults for artistic text to be Garamond, 48-point, and bold. Type **Fantasy Travel**.

2. Select the Extrude effect, set the depth to 1 with the vanishing point to the back and down. Also set the color to be a gray with the depth shading from gray to black, and then apply the extrusion. Your result should look like this:

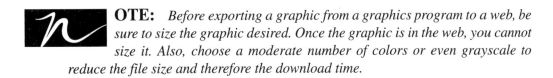

3. Save your image in its native file format, and then export it as a .TIF file. Size the graphic to 615 pixels wide by 100 pixels high, and set the number of colors to 256 shades of gray. Save the file as **Title.tif**.

OTE: *Before exporting a graphic from a graphics program to a web, be sure to size the graphic desired. Once the graphic is in the web, you cannot size it. Also, choose a moderate number of colors or even grayscale to reduce the file size and therefore the download time.*

4. Open the FrontPage Editor with the Fantasy Travel web, choose the Home Page from the Window menu, select the two words in the first line of the title (leaving the new-line symbol), and press DEL.

5. From the Insert menu, choose Image, select From File, identify your file (**Title.tif** if you followed the above instructions), and click on Open. The new title will come in, as you can see in Figure 4-13.

6. One problem with the graphic as imported is that it has a white background. Suppose you wanted it to be the same as the rest of the background. FrontPage has a Make Transparent tool at the far right of the toolbar that will remove any one color in a graphic. Click on the graphic

to select it, click on the Make Transparent tool, and then click on the white background. The result looks like this:

7. Save the changes to the home page. You'll be asked if you want to save the images you are using in this web (the title, in this case) with the web files; click on Yes even though that will begin copying your files.

The word art title as initially imported

FIGURE 4-13

AUTION: *Always save your images with your web files, because when you copy the web to a server, they will all be together and the FrontPage Explorer can do the copying for you.*

Adding Horizontal Lines

Horizontal lines help separate sections of a web page. FrontPage provides an easy way to add such lines through the Insert menu, and you can add your own lines by placing them as graphics. Try both techniques now with these steps:

1. With the Fantasy Travel home page displayed in the FrontPage Editor, place the insertion point on the blank line just above "Current Specials."

2. Open the Insert menu and choose Horizontal line. A horizontal line will appear on your page.

3. Delete the original blank line (the horizontal line creates its own line ending). You now have a line separating the top two sections on your home page, like this:

> For the latest fares, contact Julie Bergan at 555-1234 or John Donald at 555-1235 ↵
> or through e-mail at julieb@fantasytravel.com or jmd@fantasytravel.com
>
> ---
>
> **CURRENT SPECIALS**
>
> • Super airfare to San Francisco: $75, LA: $175, New York: $275, & Miami: $375

4. Move the insertion point down to the blank line just above "Available Travel Options." Here you'll add a horizontal line graphic that comes with FrontPage.

5. Open the Insert menu, choose Image, select From File, and if you installed FrontPage in the default directories, select the C:\Program Files\Microsoft FrontPage\webs\vtitut1.tem\images\hrule.gif directory.

6. Click on Center, to center the rule, so that it looks like this:

• London, air, 5 nights first-class hotel, breakfast, 2 city tours, and more, $750

(Some restrictions may apply to the above fares.)

AVAILABLE TRAVEL OPTIONS

1. AIR TRAVEL: Domestic, Canada, Europe, So. America, Africa, Asia, So. Pacific

---

7. Save your home page.

Placing Clipart

Clipart gives you that quick little something to jazz up a page. There are many sources of clipart, and some are bundled with Microsoft Office, Corel WordPerfect, and CorelDraw. To add a firecracker next to the Current Specials heading by using art from the CorelDraw clipart collection or any other piece of clipart you have available:

1. Open your graphics package such as CorelDraw, and import a firecracker-like piece of clipart (the \Clipart\Celebrat\Crack032.cmx file on the fourth CorelDraw 6 CD was used here).

2. While still in your graphics package, export your firecracker as a .TIF file, sizing it quite small (I used 59×53 pixels) and with 256 colors.

3. Open the FrontPage Editor with the Fantasy Travel home page, and move the insertion point to the left edge of the Current Specials heading.

4. From the Insert menu, choose Image, select From File, and then double-click on your firecracker. It should appear as you see here:

5. Remove the background by using the Make Transparent tool as you did earlier.

6. Save the home page.

It's easy to get carried away with adding small clipart images. They are neat and don't use much memory (the firecracker image you see here is only 2K compared with the title, which is over 10K), so people think that they add little to the load time. But if you put a bunch of them on a page, such as one for every paragraph, all of a sudden you have a problem.

Adding a Background

The default background used by FrontPage is the gray that you have seen in all the figures and illustrations so far in this chapter. You can change this to any color you wish or to a background image using the Page Properties dialog box. Again, you have to be aware of the load time impact as your background gets more sophisticated. Next, several possibilities for a background will be discussed.

Creating a Solid Color Background

Begin by looking at solid color backgrounds:

IP: *If you keep to black for your text—and there is no reason you must—then your backgrounds should be very light colors. In any case you should maintain a very high contrast between the background and text colors so they are easy to read.*

1. With the Fantasy Travel home page in the FrontPage Editor, open the File menu and choose Page Properties. The Page Properties dialog box will open as shown in Figure 4-14.

2. Click on Use Custom Background Color and then on Choose. The Color dialog box will open. Note the default color is the third from the right in the bottom row, as you see next. You can use any of the predefined 48 colors, or you can define up to 16 additional colors and use one of them.

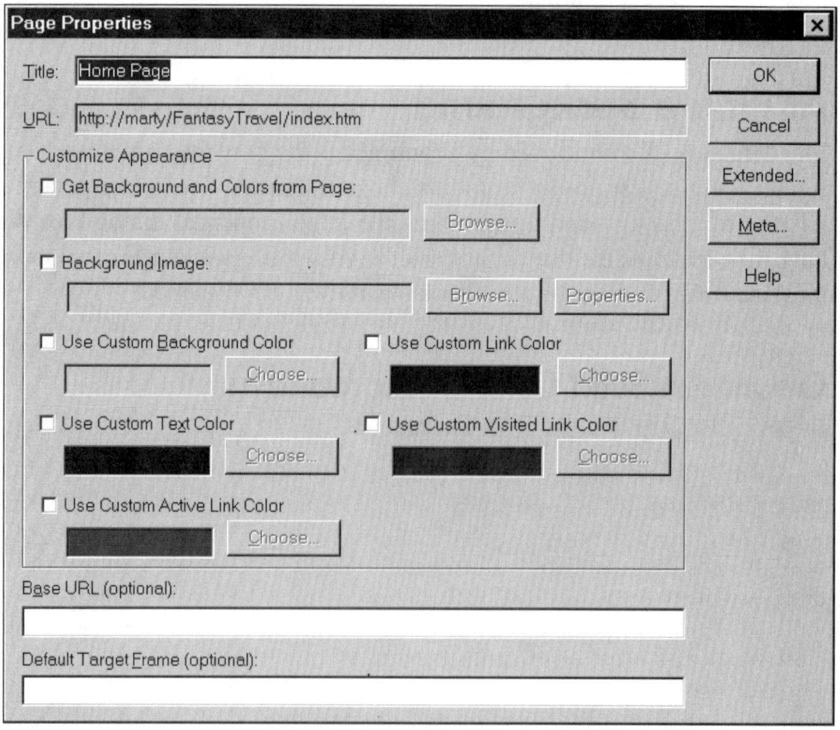

Page Properties			✕
Title: Home Page			OK
URL: http://marty/FantasyTravel/index.htm			Cancel
Customize Appearance			Extended...
☐ Get Background and Colors from Page:	Browse...		Meta...
☐ Background Image:	Browse...	Properties...	Help
☐ Use Custom Background Color	☐ Use Custom Link Color		
Choose...	Choose...		
☐ Use Custom Text Color	☐ Use Custom Visited Link Color		
Choose...	Choose...		
☐ Use Custom Active Link Color			
Choose...			
Base URL (optional):			
Default Target Frame (optional):			

The Page
Properties
dialog box

FIGURE 4-14

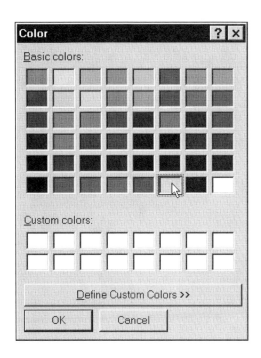

4

3. Click on Define Custom Colors, and the Color dialog box expands to what you see in Figure 4-15. You can create your own colors by either of two numerical schemes, or more simply by clicking on a color in the color selector and then adjusting the brightness on the right. One such color is a very light beige, which you can see being selected in Figure 4-15. Create a color of your own, and then click on Add To Custom Colors. You will see the color added to the Custom Colors on the left.

4. Click on your new color in the Custom Colors on the left and then click on OK. The color appears in the Page Properties dialog box; click on OK. The color appears on the web page. A light color can be quite attractive.

 IP: *Be sure and check how both the Netscape Navigator and Microsoft Internet Explorer display any custom color you create. Some colors may end up being dithered and won't look right.*

5. Save your home page.

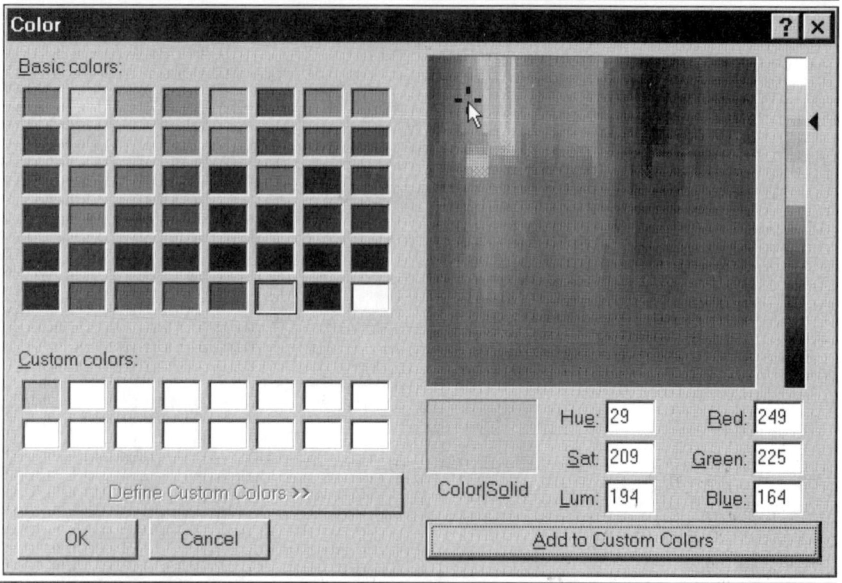

Defining a custom color in the Color dialog box

FIGURE 4-15

IP: *If you want to make the background the same on several pages in a web, then, after getting the first page the way you want it, open the second page, open its Page Properties dialog box, click on Get Background And Colors From Page, and select the first page.*

Using a Textured Background

Another choice for a background is one of the many textured backgrounds available on the Internet and from other sources. Within FrontPage there are 13 choices for a textured background in the C:\Program Files\Microsoft FrontPage\webs\vtdisc.wiz directory (if you used the default directory scheme). These textured backgrounds are used in some of the web wizards.

OTE: *Most textured backgrounds are made by tiling a small graphic. You can make your own with any small image, optimally 96x96 pixels. If the image has a repeatable pattern, it is possible to get it to be reasonably seamless, as FrontPage has done in its samples.*

To add a textured background:

1. Select the Second Level Page from the Window menu of the FrontPage Editor.

2. Open the File menu, choose Page Properties, and click on Background Image.

3. Click on Browse, select From File, open the C:\Program Files\Microsoft FrontPage\webs\vtdisc.wiz directory (if you used the default directory scheme), select the .JPG file type, and double-click on Blutxtr1.jpg.

4. Click on OK in the Page Properties dialog box, and the background appears as shown in Figure 4-16.

5. Save page 2 and answer Yes that you want the background image saved with your web.

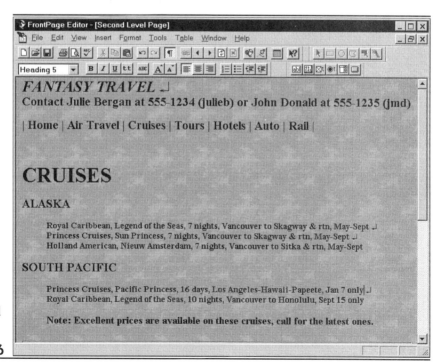

A textured background on page 2

FIGURE 4-16

Using a Single Background Image

You can also use a single background image to cover a page. In most circumstances this is not advised, because the image is quite large (the image used in this example is over 650K) and therefore will take a long time to download. Also, it is hard to get a single text color that shows up well against a multicolored image. Nevertheless, if you know that all your readers have high-speed connections, as they might in an intranet, a single background image can be quite striking. Try it:

1. Select the Third Level Page from the Window menu of the FrontPage Editor.

2. Open the Page Properties dialog box, click on Background Image, and browse to locate a large photographic image. (The image I've used was scanned out of the Princess Cruises catalog.)

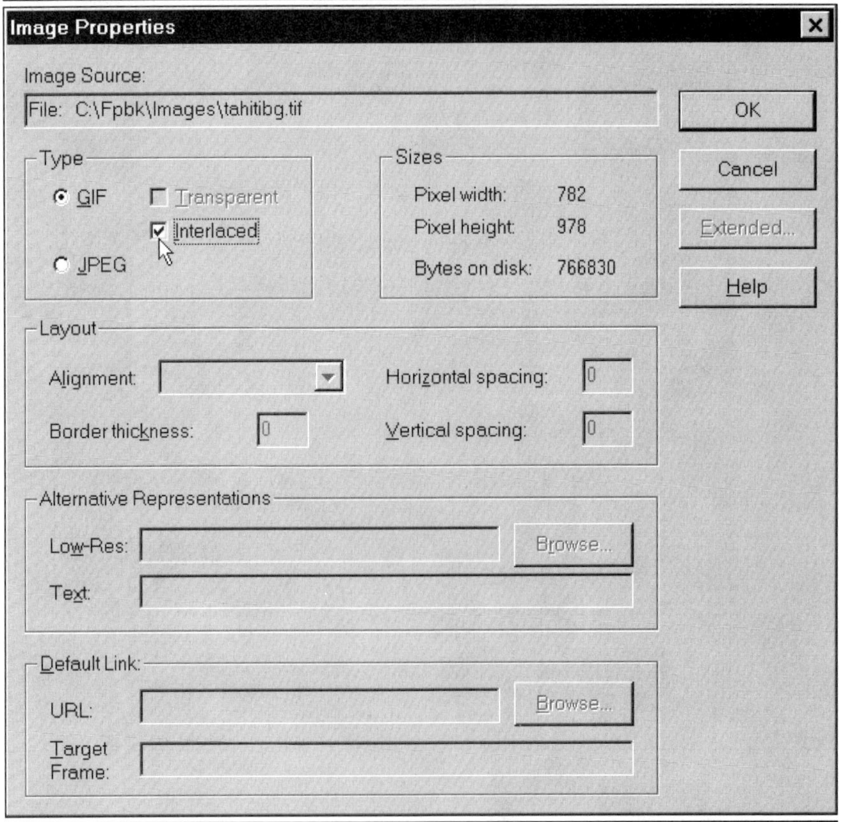

Image Properties	✕

Image Source:

File: C:\Fpbk\Images\tahitibg.tif

OK

Type
- ⦿ GIF ☐ Transparent
- ☑ Interlaced
- ○ JPEG

Cancel

Sizes
- Pixel width: 782
- Pixel height: 978
- Bytes on disk: 766830

Extended...

Help

Layout
- Alignment: [▼]
- Border thickness: 0
- Horizontal spacing: 0
- Vertical spacing: 0

Alternative Representations
- Low-Res: [   ] Browse...
- Text: [   ]

Default Link:
- URL: [   ] Browse...
- Target Frame: [   ]

Image
Properties
dialog box

FIGURE 4-17

3. After you have selected an image, click on Properties to open the Image Properties dialog box. Under Type, click on Interlaced, as shown in Figure 4-17 (on previous page), which allows the image to be progressively downloaded. People seem better able to wait for an image downloaded this way.

4. Click on OK to close the Image Properties dialog box, click on Use Custom Text Color, and then click on Choose. In the Color dialog box click on white in the lower-right corner.

5. Click on OK to close the Color dialog box, and then click on OK to close the Page Properties dialog box. Your background image with white text over it will appear as shown in Figure 4-18.

6. Save your page 3, answering Yes to saving the image with the web.

A single image used as a background image

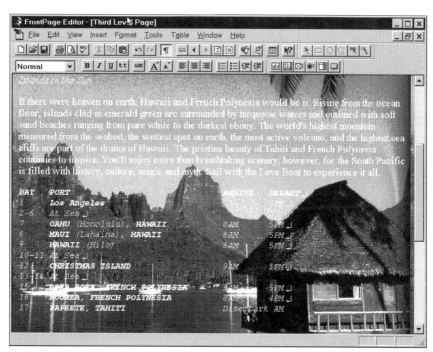

Scanned image used by permission of Princess Cruises.

FIGURE 4-18

Using Scanned Images

Using scanned images on web pages is very similar to using other graphics, except for what you may do to the image before bringing it into FrontPage. For example, you can scan an image into Adobe Photoshop, where you can crop it or otherwise edit it. To try that:

1. Using your scanner and its software in the normal manner, scan a picture that you want to bring into your web (I used an image of the Pacific Princess from the Princess Cruises catalog). This will create a .TIF or other bitmap file.

2. Open Adobe Photoshop or another program that can edit bitmap files, and crop the image to the size you want. Do any other editing and then resave the file.

3. In the FrontPage Editor, use the Windows menu to choose the Second Level Page.

4. Place the insertion point to the left of the word "Cruises." Open the Insert menu, choose Image, select From File, choose the type of file you are bringing in, and then click on the file you want to import. Your result will look something like Figure 4-19.

5. Save page 2, answering Yes that you do want to save the new image with the current web. Also, close the FrontPage Editor and the FrontPage Explorer.

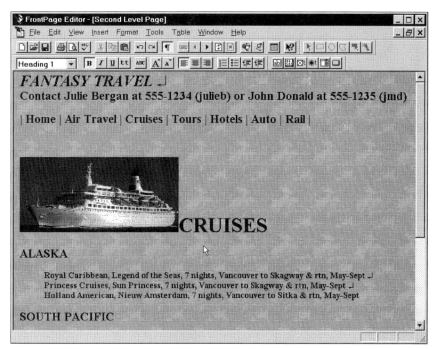

Scanned image used by permission of Princess Cruises.

Page 2 with a scanned image placed on it

FIGURE 4-19

Text and graphics are the foundation of any web, whether you create it or it is created with a template or wizard. The next-most-important element is the hyperlinks that allow you to move around your web, as well as to jump to other webs. See how those are built and used in Chapter 5.

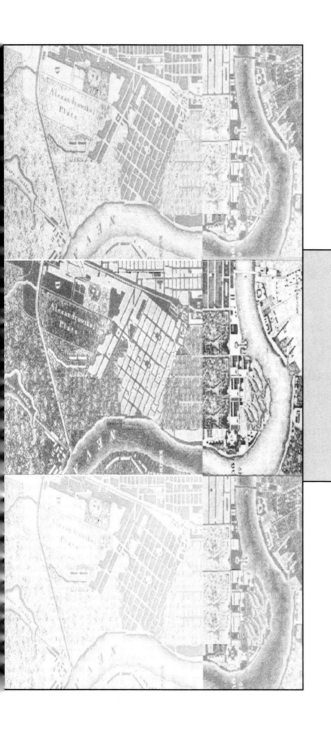

Adding and Managing Hyperlinks and Hotspots

When you open a web page in a browser, you have access to only the single page in the address given to the browser (FrontPage assumes a web page name of index.htm if no other address is given). There is no way to get to another page without giving the browser its address, unless there is a hyperlink on the first page that takes you to the second.

A *hyperlink* or link is an object, either text or graphic, that when you click on it, tells the browser to open another page. The hyperlink, when clicked upon, gives the browser an address called a *uniform resource locator (URL)*. The browser then opens the page at that address. The page can be part of the current web, part of another web at the same site, or any web at any site anywhere on the Internet, anywhere in the world—unless your intranet limits you to its domain.

A hyperlink is an essential part of a web page. It is the element that allows it to be interconnected with other pages producing the "web." Hyperlinks are also why the language behind web pages, HTML, is called *hyper*text markup language. Hyperlinks provide the first and most important level of interactivity in a web page: they give users a choice of where to go when they are done with the current page.

When a hyperlink is viewed in a browser, it is normally a different color than the surrounding text, and it is usually underlined (the person controlling the browser can determine what color a hyperlink is and whether it is underlined). Also, when you move the mouse pointer over a hyperlink, the pointer normally turns into a pointing hand, and either the full or partial URL related to that link is displayed in the status bar at the bottom of the window, as you can see here (with a partial URL of "Project2"):

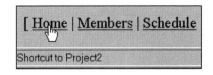

In this chapter you will see how to add hyperlinks to text and graphics, how to assign areas of a graphic—or hotspots—to a hyperlink, and how to manage the hyperlinks in a web page.

Adding Hyperlinks to Text and Graphics

Hyperlinks can be assigned to anything you enter on a web page. Any piece of text—be it a word, a phrase, or a paragraph—or any graphic, from a bullet to a large image, can be assigned a link. While there are many similarities, there are some differences, so let's look separately at assigning hyperlinks to text and to graphics.

Assigning Hyperlinks to Text

Within a web, hyperlinks provide the principal means of getting from one page to another and back again. Begin by assigning hyperlinks for that purpose:

1. If they aren't already loaded, start both the FrontPage Personal Web Server and the FrontPage Explorer. In the FrontPage Explorer, open the Fantasy Travel web that you created in Chapter 4, and then open the three pages, one after the other, in the FrontPage Editor.

2. In the FrontPage Editor display the Home page, and then scroll the page so you can see the Available Travel Options.

3. Drag across the word "CRUISES" in the second line to select that word. You'll make this word a link to the Second Level page displaying a list of cruises.

4. Click on the Create Or Edit Link button in the toolbar. Alternatively, you can choose Link from the Edit menu. In either case the Create Link dialog box will open, as you can see in Figure 5-1.

5. The Second Level page is the one that you want to link to, so double-click on it. The Create Link dialog box will close. When you return to the Home page, you'll see that the word "CRUISES" has changed. If you move the highlight off it, you'll see that it has changed color and is underlined (unless someone changed your FrontPage Editor defaults in the Page Properties dialog box) like this:

1. AIR TRAVEL: Domestic, Canada,

2. CRUISES: Alaska, Panama Canal,

3. TOURS: Domestic, Canada, Europ

6. Right-click on CRUISES and choose Properties to again open the Link dialog box, now called Edit Link. Click on the Current Web tab, and you'll see that the page name second.htm has been assigned to this link. Click on Cancel to close the dialog box.

7. Click on Save in the toolbar to save the Home page.

8. Right-click on CRUISES again and choose Follow Link Forward to see where it will take you. You should end up on the Second Level page. (If you didn't, you somehow did not select the correct page in step 5.)

OTE: *When you choose a page as a link, you are not taken to any particular part of the page. The page is just opened. If you are opening the page for the first time in a session, then you'll be taken to the top of the page. If you have previously opened the page in the current session and scrolled down it, then when you return, you'll be taken to wherever you scrolled. This may or may not be what you want. You can control where you go on a page through bookmarks, which are discussed in "Establishing Bookmarks" later in this chapter.*

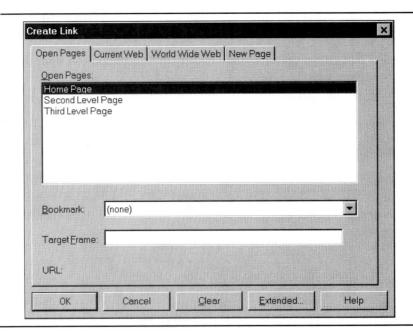

The Create Link dialog box

FIGURE 5-1

Activating a Navbar

Once you are on the second page, you need a way to return to the Home page (ignore for the moment that there is a Back button and a Window menu). To do that, activate the navbar at the top of the page with these steps:

1. Drag across the word "Home" in the navbar, and click on the Create Or Edit Link button in the toolbar. (From now on this will just be called the Link button.)

2. Double-click on Home Page to establish that as the destination of the link.

3. Since you'll copy the navbar to other pages, drag across Cruises in the navbar, and click on the Link button again.

4. Double-click on Second Level Page to establish that as the destination of the Cruises link. Since you have not established pages for the other elements of the navbar, Home and Cruises are the only two you can activate at this time, and your navbar should look like this:

5

FANTASY TRAVEL ⏎
Contact Julie Bergan at 555-1234 (julieb) or John Donald at
| <u>Home</u> | **Air Travel** | <u>Cruises</u> | **Tours** | **Hotels** | **Auto** | **Rail** ‖

Establishing Bookmarks

Since some web pages can be quite long and you may want to direct exactly where on a page a link will take the user, you need to identify a spot on a page where a link will end up. This is done with the use of bookmarks. *Bookmarks* are objects (text or graphics) that have been selected as destinations for a link. Follow these steps to create a bookmark:

IP: *You must identify the bookmark before you establish the link, unless you want to go back and edit the link after it is established.*

1. While still on the Second Level page, drag across the heading "ALASKA" just under the graphic of a cruise ship.

2. Open the Edit menu and choose Bookmark. (There should be a button on the toolbar for this, and hopefully by the time you read this there will be.) The Bookmark dialog box will open, as shown here:

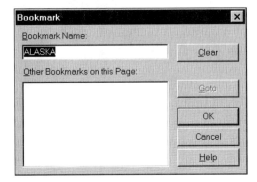

3. Click on OK to make the word "ALASKA" a bookmark. You'll see a dashed line appear under "ALASKA."

4. Drag across the heading "SOUTH PACIFIC," open the Edit menu, choose Bookmark, and click on OK in the Bookmark dialog box. A dashed line will appear under the selected words.

Selecting the bookmarks is only half the procedure; you must also establish the links to the bookmarks. Before going back to the Home page to do that, establish the link to the Third Level page.

Linking to the Third Level Page

The Third Level page is a detailed description of one South Pacific cruise listed on the Second Level page. Therefore, set the line that lists the cruise as the link to the page that describes it, using these steps:

1. With the Second Level page displayed, scroll the page so you can see the list of cruises under the South Pacific heading.

2. Drag across the line that begins "Princess Cruises, Pacific Princess."

3. Click on the Link button in the toolbar to open the Create Link dialog box, and then double-click on Third Level Page. Your Second Level page

with the activated navbar, the two bookmarks, and the link to the third page should look like Figure 5-2.

4. You need to copy the navbar to the Third Level page, so before trying the new link, select the navbar, right-click on it, and choose Copy to copy it to the Clipboard.

5. Click on Save in the toolbar to save the second page.

6. Right-click on the Princess Cruises link you established in step 3 and choose Follow Link Forward. Your Third Level page should open.

7. Select the navbar on the third page, and click on the Paste button in the toolbar. The navbar with the links will replace the original one, as you can see in Figure 5-3.

8. Click on Save in the toolbar to save the third page.

9. Right-click on the word "Home" in the navbar to open the context menu, and choose Follow Link Forward to return to the Home page.

5

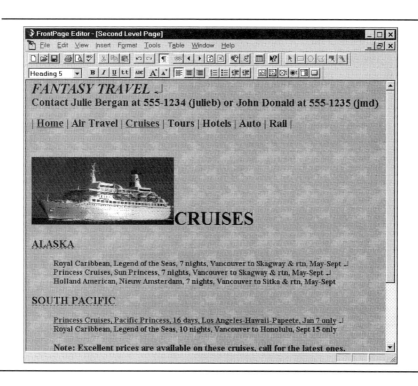

Second Level page with links and bookmarks

▋ **FIGURE 5-2**

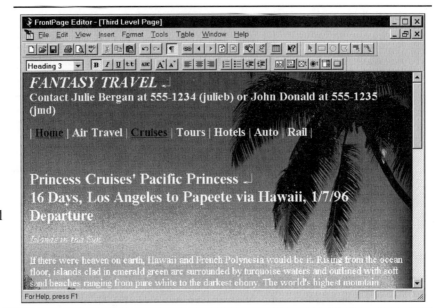

Third Level page with the activated navbar

FIGURE 5-3

You have now followed the links you established from the first to the second page, from the second to the third page, and from the third page back to the first. You can see that they provide a good means of navigating a web. Later in the chapter you'll try them out in a browser, where all you'll need to do is click on them.

Using Bookmarks in Links

On the Home page use the two bookmarks you set to create two detail links within the Cruises travel options:

1. On the Home page, scroll the page so you can see the numbered list of travel options.

2. Drag across the word "Alaska" in the list of cruise destinations, as you can see in the following illustration:

> 1. AIR TRAVEL: Domestic, Canada, Europe, So.
>
> 2. CRUISES: Alaska, Panama Canal, Caribbean,
>
> 3. TOURS: Domestic, Canada, Europe, So. Amer

3. Click on the Link button in the toolbar to open the Create Link dialog box.

4. Click on Second Level Page under Open Pages, and then click on the down arrow on the right of the Bookmark drop-down list box. Your two bookmarks will appear, as shown in Figure 5-4.

5. Click on ALASKA to select that bookmark, and then click on OK to close the dialog box and establish the link.

6. Drag across the words "So. Pacific," click on the Link button, select Second Level Page, open the bookmarks, and click on SOUTH PACIFIC. The URL in the bottom of the Create Link dialog box now includes the bookmark, like this:

> URL: second.htm#SOUTH PACIFIC

7. Click on OK to close the dialog box and to set the link.

5

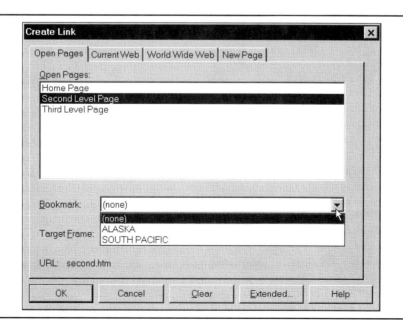

Selecting a
bookmark
to use in a
link

FIGURE 5-4

Setting Links to Other Than Web Sites

All of the links that you have created so far have been to other pages within this single web. Later in this chapter you'll make a link to another web site and web. FrontPage, though, allows you to make a link to other than a web site. The types of sites (shown in the Protocol drop-down list in Figure 5-5) are shown in Table 5-1.

To create a link that can be used to send e-mail:

1. Scroll to the bottom of the Home page in the FrontPage Editor, so you can see the copyright and other information in the footer.

2. Drag across "webmaster@fantasytravel.com," click on the Copy button, and then click on the Link button in the toolbar.

3. Click on the World Wide Web tab, and then click on the down arrow in the Protocol drop-down list box. Here, as you can see in Figure 5-5, are the optional destinations for your links to the Internet.

4. Click on mailto in the Protocol drop-down list box. In the URL text box click to the right of "mailto:" and press CTRL-V to paste the webmaster address in the URL, like this:

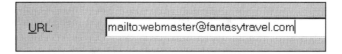

5. Click on OK to close the Create Link dialog box, and then click on Save in the toolbar to save the Home page.

You now have a number of links, so it is time to see if they work.

Testing Your Links in a Browser

The only way to know if your links are really working is to try them on a browser:

1. If you didn't save each of the three pages in the preceding steps, do that now.

Type of Site	How It Is Used
File	To open a file on a local hard disk
Ftp	To download a file on the Internet
Gopher	To perform a Gopher search (based on selections from a series of menus) on the Internet
Http	To open another web (this is the default)
Mailto	To send e-mail
News	To access information on an Internet news server
Telnet	To connect to and remotely use another computer
Wais	To perform a Wais (wide area information service) search (looking for one or more words in text) on the Internet

Types of Internet Sites to Which You Can Establish a Link

TABLE 5-1

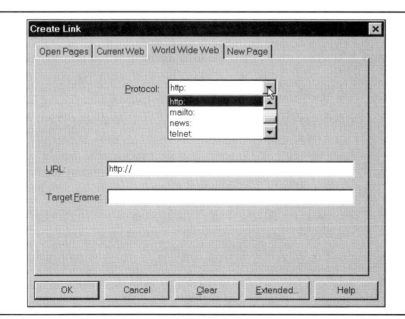

Alternative types of Internet sites available to links

FIGURE 5-5

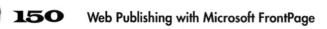

2. Open your web browser and enter the address or URL for your Fantasy Travel web. The address should be in the form *servername/webname/.* You can find this in the FrontPage Page Properties dialog box for any page in a web. For example, here is the URL for the Home page in the Home page Page Properties dialog box:

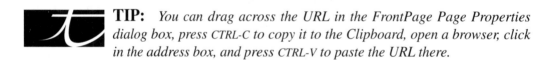**OTE:** *If you include a page filename in the URL when you open a browser, you will open that page, which may not be the home page. You do not need to include the page filename if you want to open a home page named index.htm.*

TIP: *You can drag across the URL in the FrontPage Page Properties dialog box, press CTRL-C to copy it to the Clipboard, open a browser, click in the address box, and press CTRL-V to paste the URL there.*

3. If you have previously opened the Fantasy Travel web in your browser, click on the Refresh button in the browser's toolbar to make sure you are using the latest files.

4. Scroll down the page until you can see the Available Travel Options. Move the mouse pointer until it is over the word "CRUISES." The mouse pointer will turn into a pointing hand, and the URL for the second page will be shown in the status bar at the bottom of the window, as you can see in Figure 5-6.

5. Click once on CRUISES and your second page will be displayed. Your first hyperlink has now opened the Second Level page.

6. Click on Home in the navbar. Your Home page should again be displayed.

7. Scroll down so you can see the Available Travel Options, and then click on So. Pacific. The South Pacific heading will be positioned at the top of the window, as shown in Figure 5-7.

8. Click on the line beginning "Princess Cruises, Pacific Princess." The Third Level page will open.

9. Click on Cruises in the navbar, and you'll be returned to the Second Level page. Notice how the page is positioned where you left it.

10. Scroll up to the navbar and click on Home. When the Home page opens, it will be positioned where you last left it.

11. Scroll to the bottom of the Home page, and click on the webmaster address. Your e-mail system should start and display a new message window with the webmaster address in the To text box, as you can see in Figure 5-8.

12. Close down your e-mail system without trying to send a message (the webmaster@fantasytravel.com is a fictitious address), and then close your browser and return to the FrontPage Editor.

All of your links should have worked, providing an excellent navigation system around your web. If you find that a link did not work, right-click on it, open the Properties dialog box, and correct where the link is pointing.

When a mouse pointer is over a link, its URL is displayed in the status bar

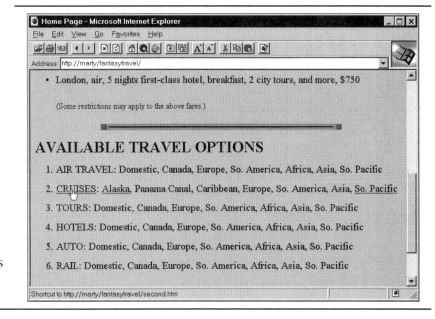

FIGURE 5-6

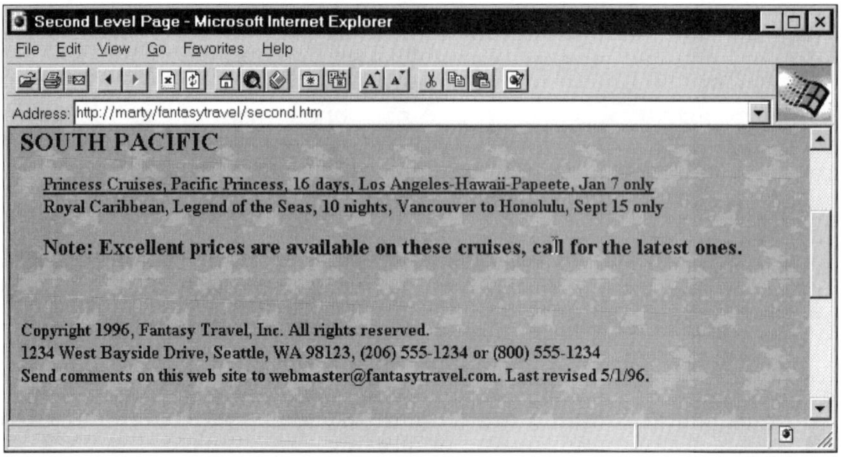

A
bookmark
in a link
will
position the
bookmark
at the top
of the
window

FIGURE 5-7

Assigning Hyperlinks to a Graphic

Although text makes for good links, graphics have even greater possibilities. You
can assign a single link to a graphic, or you can divide a graphic into sections and
make each section a separate link. All of the concepts that you learned about with
text links also apply to graphics. You can have links to the existing web, both with

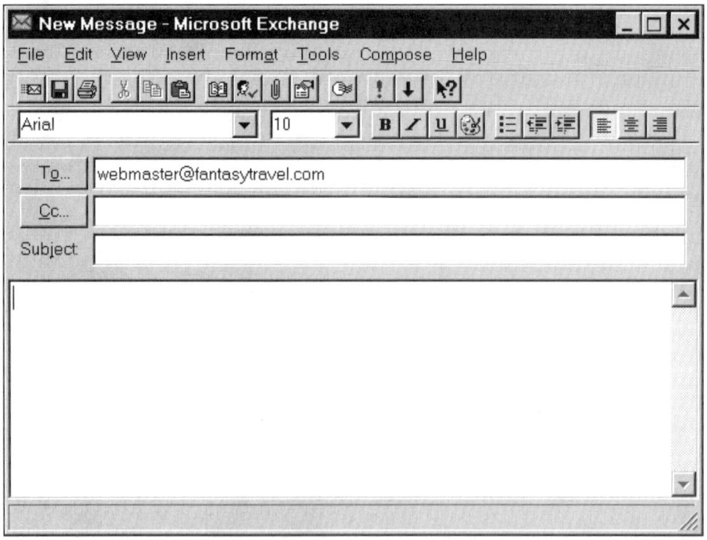

Clicking on
a mailto
link starts
your e-mail
system

FIGURE 5-8

and without bookmarks. You can have external links to web sites as well as to other types of Internet sites. You can make either a single graphic that has been divided or multiple graphics into a navbar. You can test graphic links in your browser.

Making a Graphic a Single Link

Making a graphic a single link is very much like what you did with a piece of text. To do this for a graphic:

1. In the FrontPage Editor, open the Second Level page. Scroll the page down, if necessary, so you can see the picture of the ship.

2. Click on the picture so it is selected with little white boxes in the four corners, like this:

3. Click on the Link button in the toolbar to open the Create Link dialog box, and then double-click on Third Level Page to establish that as the destination of the link.

Now when you move the mouse pointer over the graphic, you'll see "third.htm," the address for the third page, in the status bar.

Linking a Graphic to an External Web

Linking a graphic or text to an external web requires nothing more than specifying the external web's URL in the link:

1. Scroll the Second Level page down so the insertion point is on the blank line just above the footer.

2. Insert a Horizontal Line (you can use the FrontPage Editor-created line from the Insert menu, as is done here, or you can place a graphics line).

3. If a blank line appears above the horizontal line, delete it. If necessary, add a blank line below the horizontal line.

4. On the next line, type **OUTSIDE SOURCES**, format it as a Heading 2, press ENTER, and type **Check these additional sources for cruise information**. Format it as a Heading 4, and press ENTER.

5. Insert two or three small images that can be used for links and center them, as shown in Figure 5-9.

6. Click on one of your images to select it, and then click on the Link button to open the Create Link dialog box.

7. Click on the World Wide Web tab, make sure that http is chosen as the Protocol, and then click in the URL text box to the right of the "http://."

8. Type **www.royalcaribbean.com/** and click on OK. You should see the URL in the status bar when you move the mouse pointer over the graphic.

9. Click on Save to save the second page.

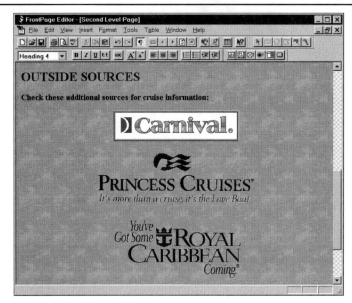

Graphics set up for external links

FIGURE 5-9

"Carnival" and the "reverse-C" are registered service marks of Carnival Cruise Lines. Used with the permission of Carnival Cruise Lines.

"Princess Cruises" and the "Lady with wind-blown hair" are registered service marks of Princess Cruises. Used with the permission of Princess Cruises.

"Royal Caribbean" and the "Crown & Anchor" are registered service marks of Royal Caribbean Cruises Ltd. Used with the permission of Royal Caribbean Cruises Ltd.

Adding Hotspots to Graphics

FrontPage has a feature that allows you to divide a graphic into sections that can be rectangles, circles, or polygons, and assign each of those sections a different link. Each linked, or clickable, section is called a *hotspot*. When FrontPage generates the actual web that is downloaded by the user, it creates an *image map* of the graphic and all of its hotspots. To create a graphic with hotspots:

1. Open the Home page of the Fantasy Travel web in the FrontPage Editor and, if necessary, scroll down the page until you see the Available Travel Options.

2. Drag across the words "AIR TRAVEL," and click on the Link button in the toolbar.

3. Click on the New Page tab. This will create a new page in the current web and link it to the selected object. A suggested page name is generated out of the link object. Accept that page name, type **air.htm** as the URL, accept the option to immediately edit the new page, and, with your dialog box looking like Figure 5-10, click on OK.

4. The New Page dialog box will open, asking which template or wizard you want to use on the new page. Accept the Normal Page template and click on OK. A blank page will open in the FrontPage Editor.

5. Separately, you can copy the header and footer for the page. For now, enter several blank lines to leave room for the header, and then type **Click on the area of the world for which you want air fares.** (including the period) and then press ENTER.

6. From a clipart collection, insert a world map on the page and center it, as shown in Figure 5-11.

7. Select your world map and then use the tools in the upper right of the toolbar to draw the hotspots on the map. For example, select the

Rectangle tool and draw a rectangle around the United States. When you complete the rectangle and release the mouse button, the Create Link dialog box will open. You have all the normal choices for a new link including an existing page, with or without a bookmark, any other site on the Internet, or a new page.

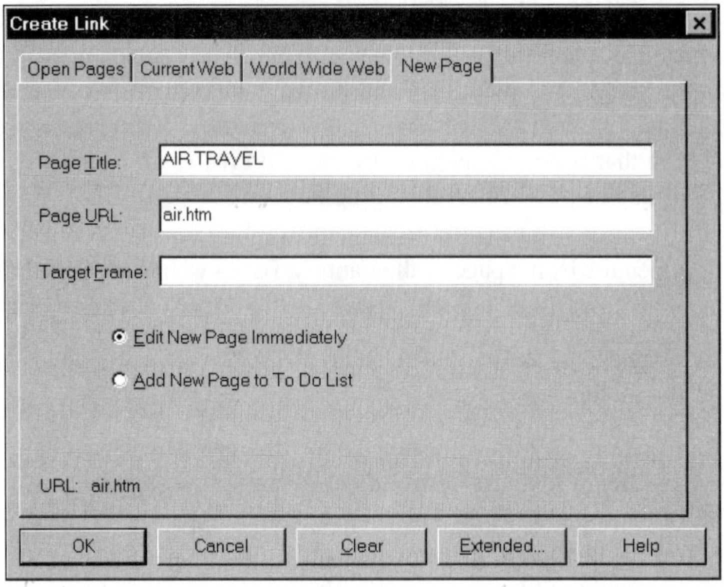

Adding a
new page
while
creating a
link

FIGURE 5-10

A new page
created
with a
world map

FIGURE 5-11

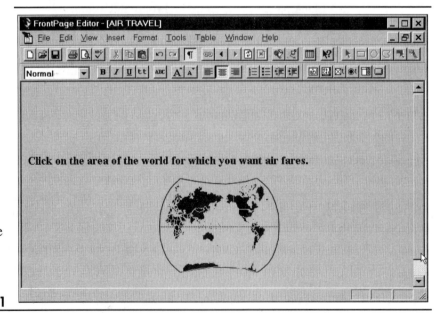

8. When you have completed drawing the shapes you want over the various areas of your map, you'll see all of the shapes on your map. The shapes will not be visible in a browser. When you move the mouse pointer over one of the areas, you'll see the URL in the status bar, as you can see here:

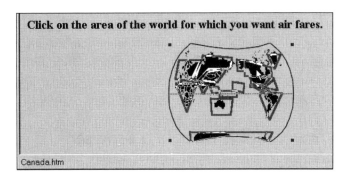

9. Right-click on an area of the map that you have not drawn a hotspot over, choose Properties, and at the bottom of the dialog box in the Default Link URL, enter the link that you want used if someone clicks outside of a hotspot, like this:

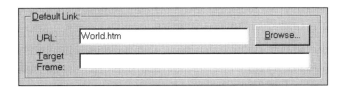

10. To see the hotspots uncluttered by the map, click on the Highlight Hotspots button. The map will disappear, leaving only the shapes you drew, as you can see here:

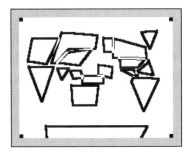

11. Turn off Highlight Hotspots, save your new Air Travel page, return to your Home page, and save it.

OTE: *An image map may be processed either on the client's computer by encoding the URL for each hotspot into the image map, or on the server, by using the FrontPage Server Extensions. This decision applies to an entire web, affecting all of the image maps it contains. While the web is open in the FrontPage Explorer, open the Tools menu, choose Web Settings, click on the Advanced tab, and make sure that Generate Client-Side Image Maps is checked (it's the default) to have the image maps self-contained in the web.*

Testing Your Graphic Links in a Browser

Once again it is prudent to open you browser and see how your links are working:

1. Open your browser with the Fantasy Travel Home page displayed, and click on the Refresh button in the toolbar to make sure you are looking at the most recent copy of your web.

2. Scroll down the Home page until you can see Available Travel Options, and then click on AIR TRAVEL. Your new Air Travel page will open and display the map you placed there.

3. Move the mouse pointer around the map to see the various hotspots you created and their URLs in the status bar. Click on several to see that they work, and then use Back to return to the Home page.

4. Click on CRUISES to open the second page, click on the image of the ship, and your third page should open (click on Refresh if this doesn't work).

5. Click on Cruises in the navbar to return to the second page.

6. Scroll down the page until you can see the two or three graphics you added, one of which you assigned a link to an external web.

7. If you are connected to the Internet and entered the Royal Caribbean URL, click on it, and the Royal Caribbean web will open as you can see in Figure 5-12. You have been transported out of your web and to the Royal Caribbean web in Miami, Florida.

Royal
Caribbean
external
web
opened
from the
Fantasy
Travel web

5

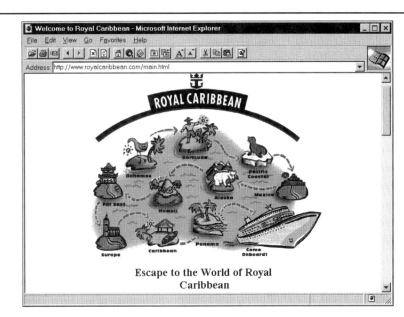

FIGURE 5-12   Royal Caribbean Main.html web page used with the permission of Royal Caribbean Cruises Ltd.

8. Close your browser. If you have any problems, edit the links to see what the trouble is. When all your links are working, close the FrontPage Editor and return to the FrontPage Explorer.

Managing Hyperlinks

The Fantasy Travel web, as it is displayed in your FrontPage Explorer, now looks much different than it did when you started this chapter, because all of your links are now displayed, as you can see in Figure 5-13. As a result, the FrontPage Explorer becomes an excellent tool for managing your links. Besides the obvious visual checking that you can do in FrontPage Explorer, it also has two commands in the Tool menu that help you in link management: Verify Links makes sure that each of the links in fact leads somewhere, and Recalculate Links updates the display of all

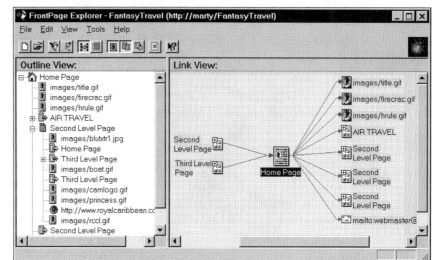

FrontPage
Explorer
showing all
of the links
that have
been added

FIGURE 5-13

links as well as the server databases used by the Include and Search bots. To check out your links:

1. In the FrontPage Explorer, open the Tools menu and click on Verify Links. Each of your internal links is checked and flagged if broken. Your external links also are listed in the Verify Links dialog box, as shown in Figure 5-14. (All the broken links shown in Figure 5-14 result from copying the world map from another web.)

2. Click on Verify and your external links will be checked. (If you are not currently connected to the Internet, this link will also register as broken.)

3. Select a broken link and click on Edit Link. The Edit Link dialog box will open, as shown next, allowing you to replace the current link with a new one. You can also change all pages with this link, or only selected ones.

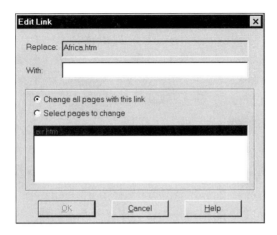

5

4. Close both the Edit Link and Verify Links dialog boxes.

5. Select Recalculate Links from the FrontPage Explorer Tools menu. You are given a warning that the process runs on the web server and will take several minutes. Click on Yes to proceed. Your Web Server task on the task bar will show busy for a few seconds, and then your web will be redisplayed in the FrontPage Explorer.

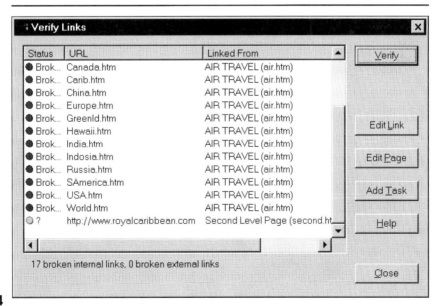

Verify
Links
dialog box
listing the
broken and
external
links

FIGURE 5-14

OTE: *When you have broken a link, the icon for the linked page is broken in the Link View of the FrontPage Explorer, like this:*

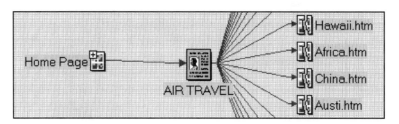

You have seen in this chapter how easy it is to establish links in FrontPage both with text and with graphics, both within a web and externally, and how you can manage those links with some powerful commands in the FrontPage Explorer. Go on now and look at the great tools FrontPage provides to add tables and frames to your webs.

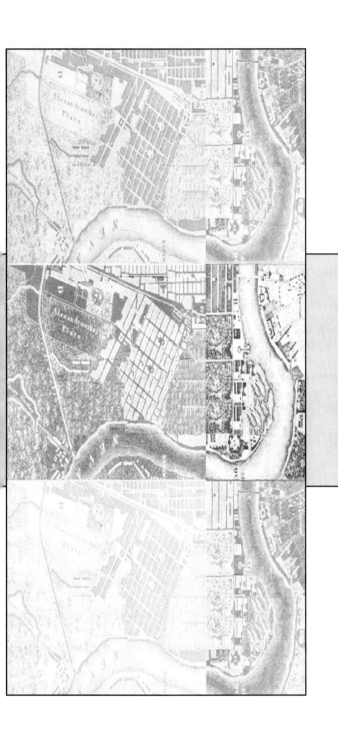

Using Tables and Frames

So far in this book, you have used the full width of a web page for placing all text and graphics. Good layout designs can be accomplished this way, but it does not allow for text or graphics to be placed in independent columns, and the only way to align text within a line (other than at the ends) is to add spaces with the Formatted paragraph style. FrontPage has two features that allow you to break up some or all of a page into sections that can contain text or graphics. These two features are tables and frames.

Designing with Tables

Tables allow you to divide a portion of a page into rows and columns that create *cells* by their intersection. Tables can be used to systematically arrange information in rows and columns, or they can be used to simply lay out text and graphics on a page. In web design, tables are probably the most important tool for creative page layout. Just a few of the ways that you can use tables are as follows:

- Tabular data display, with and without cell borders

- Side-by-side columns of text

- Text on one side, graphics on the other

- Placing borders around text or graphics

- Placing graphics on both sides of text or vice versa

- Wrapping text around a graphic

When you create a table, you can determine the number of rows and columns in the table, the horizontal percentage of a page that will be used by the table, the percentage of the table's width in each column, and whether the table has a caption. After a table has been created, you can add or remove rows and/or columns, you can combine adjacent cells, and you can add to or remove from a cell or groups of cells any formatting available to the table's contents. Within the percentage limits set for the table and column, a cell will automatically expand both horizontally and vertically to contain the information placed in it.

IP: *Although you can create a table based on a percentage of the screen, with columns as a percentage of the table, there are often problems getting the table to display the way you want to. If you use fixed pixel widths based on the minimum 640×480 screen you'll be able to create a more consistent look.*

Displaying Tabular Data in a Table

The classic table, such as you might create in a spreadsheet application, segments text into rows and columns. To build such a table:

1. If they are not already loaded, start both the FrontPage Personal Web Server and the FrontPage Explorer.

2. In the FrontPage Explorer, open the File menu, choose New Web, and click on OK to accept the Normal Web template. Type **Wine** for the Web Name, and click on OK.

3. Double-click on the Normal Page in the right pane to open the FrontPage Editor.

4. Press ENTER to move down the page and leave room at the top.

5. Click on the Insert Table button in the toolbar, or choose Insert Table from the Table menu. The Insert Table dialog box will open, as shown in Figure 6-1.

6. In the dialog box, take a look at the options available when you create a table; they are described in Table 6-1. Then click on OK. A four-cell table appears on your page.

Working with Table Properties

Table properties affect all of the cells in a table and establish how the overall table will look. To see that for yourself:

1. In the new table that was just created, type the number **1** in the upper-left cell, press RIGHT ARROW to move to the cell on the right, and type

   This is a longer statement

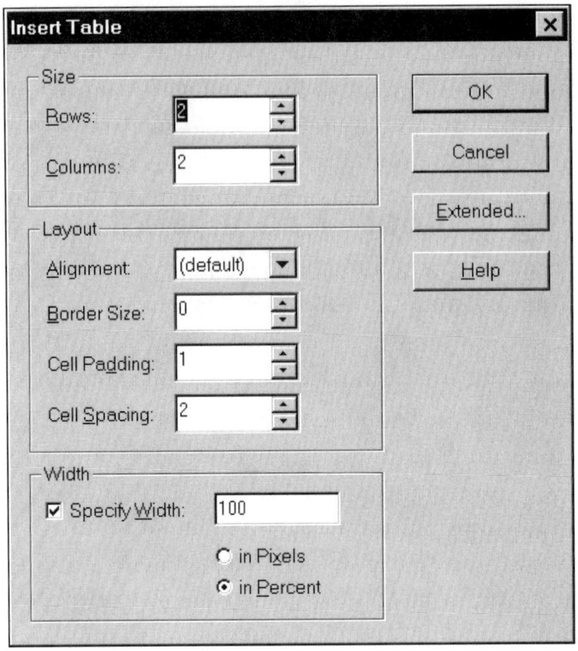

Insert Table
dialog box

FIGURE 6-1

Press RIGHT ARROW again to move to the left cell in the second row, type the number **2**, press RIGHT ARROW once more, and type

This is a statement

Your table should look like the one shown next. The table takes up almost 100 percent of the window's width, and the two cells equally split that width.

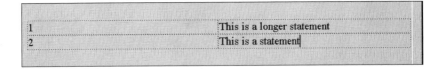

 OTE: *The TAB key, which is often used in other applications to move from cell to cell, does not work that way in FrontPage. You must use the arrow keys instead.*

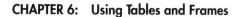

Option	Description
Alignment	This aligns the table on the left, center, or right of the page. Default alignment is the same as left alignment. The paragraph alignment buttons on the Formatting toolbar affect the content of a cell, but not the table itself.
Border Size	This refers to the number of pixels in the border. A 0 pixel border will not appear in a browser, but you'll see a dotted line in the FrontPage Editor when the Paragraph button in the toolbar is enabled. The default is 0.
Cell Padding	This is the number of pixels between the inside edges of a cell and the cell contents on all four sides. The default is 1.
Cell Spacing	This is the number of pixels between adjacent cells. The default is 2.
Width	If Specify Width is selected, you can set the width to be a fixed number of pixels or a percentage of the window size. If you select the percentage method, each cell is given an equal percentage of the table. If you don't select Specify Width, the table width is the sum of the cells, which are individually sized to contain their contents within the size of the window.

Table
Properties

TABLE 6-1

2. Press RIGHT ARROW to move out of the table, and then press ENTER to leave a blank line.

3. Click on the Insert Table button again, click on Specify Width at the bottom of the dialog box to deselect it, and then click on OK. A second, much smaller table appears.

4. Type **1**, press RIGHT ARROW, and type

This is a longer statement

You can see that the new cells automatically size themselves to fit the content, as shown in Figure 6-2.

5. Right-click in the first table to open the context menu shown here. You can see that it has both Table and Cell Properties options. Choose Table Properties, opening that dialog box. It is the same as the dialog box opened with Insert Table and shown in Figure 6-1, except that it does not allow you to specify the number of rows and columns.

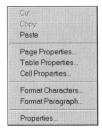

OTE: *If you turn off the Specify Width option in the Table Properties dialog box opened from an existing table, not much happens, either initially or as you enter cell content. You can change and readily see the effect of all the layout options such as Border Size and Cell Padding.*

6. Change Border Size to **5**, Cell Padding to **6**, Cell Spacing to **8**, and click on OK. Your table should look like this:

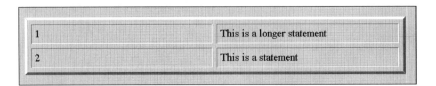

7. Again right-click in the upper table and select Cell Properties. The Cell Properties dialog box will open, as you can see in Figure 6-3. Take a moment and look at the options it contains. They are described in Table 6-2.

Applying Cell Properties

Cell properties apply to just the one or more selected cells in a table, as shown in the following steps.

OTE: *If you change the cell width, you should do so for an entire column, and you should make sure that the sum of the cell widths in a row does not exceed 100 percent, or you will get unpredictable results.*

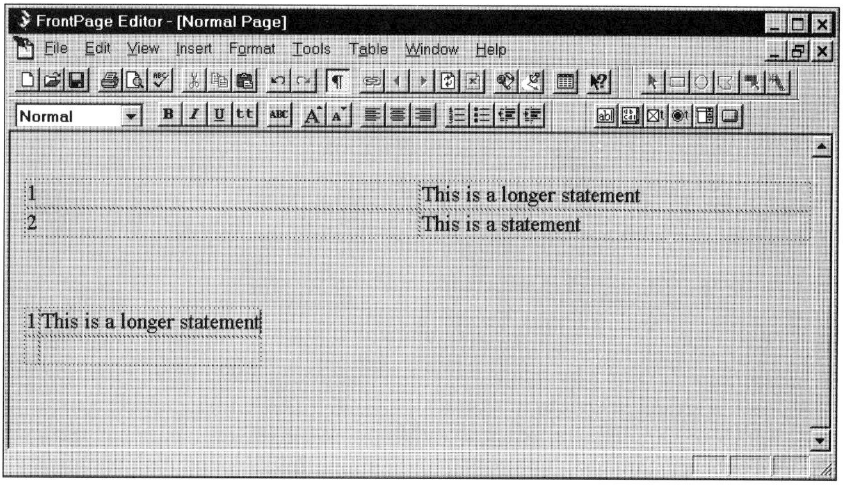

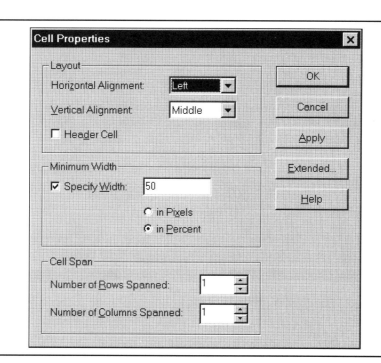

Tables with
and without
a specified
width

FIGURE 6-2

6

Cell
Properties
dialog box

FIGURE 6-3

Option	Description
Horizontal Alignment	This option horizontally aligns the contents of the cell. It can be Left, Center, or Right. Left is the default.
Vertical Alignment	This option vertically aligns the contents of the cell. It can be Top, Middle, or Bottom. Middle is the default.
Header Cell	This option makes the text in the cell bold. (You can also do this with the paragraph or character formatting options.)
Minimum Width	If Specify Width is selected, you can set the width to be a fixed number of pixels or a percentage of the table size. If you don't select Specify Width, the cell width is automatically sized to hold its contents.
Cell Span	This option joins adjacent cells to make a single larger cell.

Cell
Properties
■ **TABLE 6-2**

1. In the Cell Properties dialog box, change Horizontal Alignment to Center, Vertical Alignment to Top, and click on OK. You should see the contents of the cell you selected change accordingly.

 OTE: *Cell padding and spacing may prevent much movement, especially vertically, in a cell when you change the alignment.*

2. Select the left column of cells in the upper table by pointing on the top border of the table and clicking, open the Cell Properties dialog box, uncheck Specify Width, and click on OK. The width of the first column will collapse, as you can see next. (The top-left cell in this illustration had both its vertical and horizontal alignment changed.)

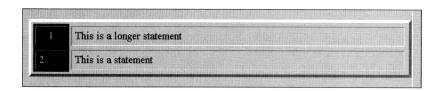

TIP: *To select either a row or a column, move the mouse pointer to the outer edge of the table—the left edge for a row, the top edge for a column—until the mouse pointer changes to a heavy arrow, and click. If you drag the heavy arrow, you can select multiple rows or columns.*

3. Select the bottom row in the second table, right-click in that row, choose Cell Properties, change the Number Of Columns Spanned to **2**, and click on OK. Your bottom table should look like the table shown next. The leftmost cell does span the two upper cells, but you have an extra cell on the right.

6

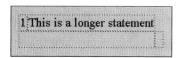

4. Press CTRL-Z or choose Undo from the Edit menu to undo step 3. In a moment you'll see another way to do this that is probably more what you want.

5. Select the top row of the second table, open the Cell Properties dialog box, increase the Number Of Rows Spanned to **2**, and click on OK. The top two cells come down and push the bottom two to the right, like this:

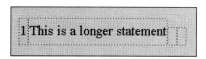

6. Click on the Undo button in the toolbar, select just the top left cell, open the Cell Properties dialog box, click on Specify Width and In Pixels, type **20** for the width, and click on OK. Both cells in the first column increase, as you can see in the following illustration.

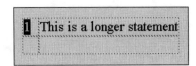

7. Click on Undo, select the bottom right cell, and open the Table menu, which is shown here. Look at the options in this menu, which are described in Table 6-3.

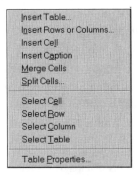

 IP: *To select multiple cells not in a row or column, select the first cell using the Table menu Select Cell option, and then press and hold SHIFT while clicking on the additional cells.*

Employing the Table Menu Options

Tables is the only FrontPage feature to have its own menu, and well it should. The Table menu provides some important options for working with tables. To see for yourself:

1. In the Table menu, choose Insert Table, accept the defaults in the Insert Table dialog box, and click on OK. You should now have a 2×2 table in the cell of your original table, as shown here:

Option	Description
Insert Table	This opens the Insert Table dialog box, where you can select the properties of a table to place at the current insertion point. If the insertion point is in a cell of another table, a second table is placed in that cell.
Insert Rows Or Columns	This opens the Insert Rows Or Columns dialog box, where you can select the number of rows or columns to be inserted above, below, to the left, or to the right of the current selection.
Insert Cell	This inserts a new cell to the left of a selected cell, pushing any cells on the right farther to the right.
Insert Caption	This inserts a blank line, with an insertion point for typing text, immediately above the active table. This line is aligned with and attached to the table. If you select or delete the table, the caption is also selected or deleted. The initial alignment is for the caption to be centered on the table, but it can also be left- or right-aligned on the table.
Merge Cells	This joins two or more selected cells in a row or a column—including an entire row or column—into a single cell that spans the area originally occupied by the cells that were joined.
Split Cells	This opens the Split Cells dialog box, where you can split the selected cell into multiple rows or multiple columns.
Select Cell, Row, Column, or Table	This selects a particular area so that it can be merged, split, or deleted. Use of the Table menu's Select Cell option is the only way to select a cell, so the cell itself, not just its contents, can be copied or cut.
Table Properties	This opens the Table Properties dialog box.

Table Menu
Options

TABLE 6-3

6

2. Click on Undo and on the upper-left cell in the second or smaller of the original two tables. Open the Table menu and choose Insert Rows Or Columns. The Insert Rows Or Columns dialog box will open:

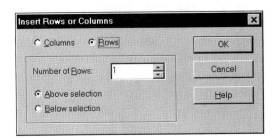

3. Accept the default Rows, 1, and Above Selection options and click on OK. A new row appears at the top of the table.

4. Reopen the Table menu and again select Insert Rows Or Columns. Click on Columns, Left Of Selection, and then on OK. A new column appears on the left so that your table now looks like this:

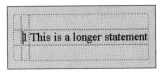

5. Open the Table menu and choose Insert Cell. A new cell appears in the table, pushing the right two cells in the row out to the right.

6. From the Table menu, choose Select Cell, and then press DEL. The new cell disappears.

 OTE: *The only way to delete a cell is to first select it in the Table menu and then press DEL.*

7. Choose Insert Caption from the Table menu. An insertion point appears above and centered on the table. Type

This is a Caption

8. Select the bottom row of the second table. Then, from the Table menu, choose Merge Cells. The bottom row now only contains a single cell, as shown next.

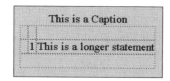

9. Click in the upper-right cell, and then choose Split Cells in the Table menu. The Split Cells dialog box will open, like this:

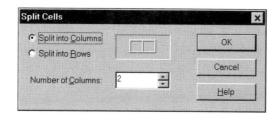

10. Accept the defaults, and click on OK. Your original cell is now split into two.

11. From the Table menu, choose Select Table, and then press DEL. You table disappears. Click on Undo to bring it back.

 IP: *Tables can be selected in the Table menu and by double-clicking in the left margin of the page opposite the table.*

Through the above exercises you can see the incredible flexibility in FrontPage's table capability. And it is all WYSIWYG; you instantly see the table you are building exactly as it will appear in a browser. Next, build a real table and then look at all three of your tables in a browser.

Building a Tabular Table

This web was called "Wine" because you are about to build a table of wines as might be prepared by a winery. To do that:

1. Click below the second, smaller table, press ENTER to leave a blank line, and then click on the Insert Table button.

2. Enter **7** rows, **5** columns, a border size of **2**, a cell padding of **2**, turn off Specify Width, and click on OK. In the resulting table, type the following information:

	Name	Type	Taste	Year
	Sauvignon Blanc	Dry white	Crisp, balanced	1993
*	Fumé Blanc	Dry white	Medium-bodied	1993
**	La Caille de Fumé	Dry white	Medium-bodied	1992
	White Riesling	Medium-sweet white	Light, fruity	1993
**	Merlot	Medium-weight red	Full-bodied	1991
*	Cabernet Sauvignon	Medium-weight red	Full-bodied	1990

 IP: *To get the "é" in Fumé, choose Special Character in the Insert menu, select the character, click on Insert, and then click on Close.*

3. When you are done typing, your table should look like the one shown in Figure 6-4. Look at your table and ask yourself "how can the table be improved?"

4. Right-click on the table and choose Table properties. Change the alignment to Center, decrease the border size to **1**, increase the cell padding to **4**, and click on OK.

5. Select the top row, right-click on a cell in the first row, open the Cell Properties dialog box, click on Header cell, and click on OK.

6. From the Table menu, choose Insert Caption. Click on the Bold button and on the Increase Text Size button, both in the Formatting toolbar, and then type

   Fair Mountain Wines Currently Available

   When you are done, your table should look like the one in Figure 6-5. You may have further ideas about how to improve the table. Try them out. You can always click on Undo if you don't like a change.

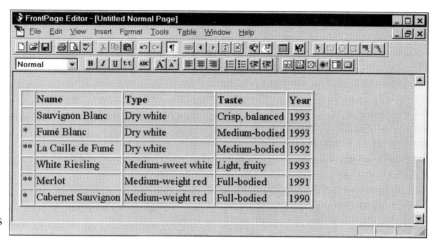

Wine table
before
improvements

▮ FIGURE 6-4

7. Click on Save to save the tables you have built. Close your Wine web in both the FrontPage Editor and FrontPage Explorer.

8. Open Microsoft Internet Explorer 2.0 or later, and enter your server name and **wine**. Your three tables should look like Figure 6-6. Close the Internet Explorer when you are done.

9. Open Netscape Navigator 2.0 or later and enter your server name and **wine**. The table will look like Figure 6-7. Close the Navigator when you are done.

10. If you have some other browser, like Spry Mosaic, open it and view your tables page. The tables in Spry Mosaic will look like Figure 6-8. Close your other browser when you are done.

As you can see, there is a considerable difference in how various browsers display tables—if they even can. You need to decide how these differences affect you. In the Internet arena, Netscape and Microsoft have the lion's share, with Netscape's share twice that of Microsoft.

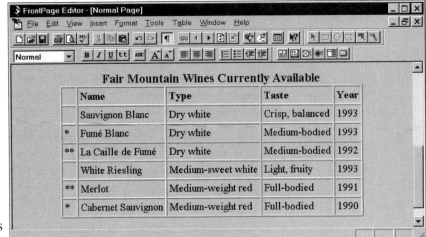

Wine table
after
improvements

FIGURE 6-5

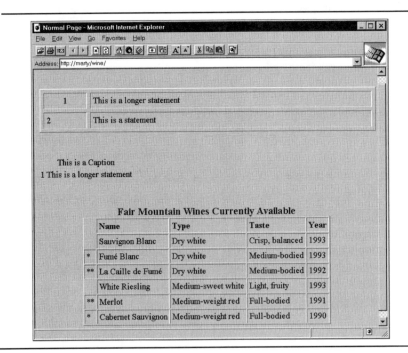

Tables in
Microsoft
Internet
Explorer

FIGURE 6-6

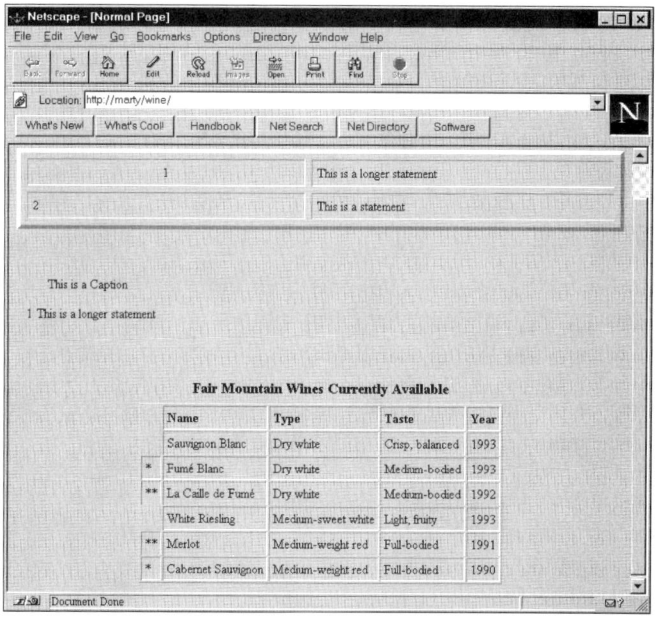

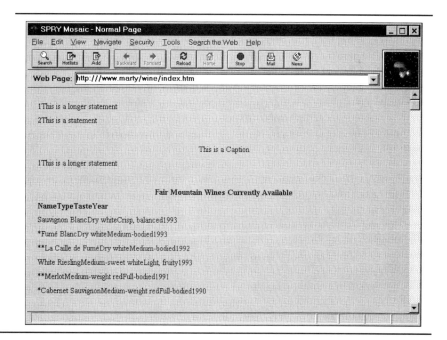

Tables in
Netscape
Navigator

FIGURE 6-7

Tables in
Spry
Mosaic

FIGURE 6-8

Using a Table to Enhance a Layout

While tabular tables are the classical way that you think of tables, in web page design, tables are extensively used to lay out a page. Seldom are you aware that there is a table behind the layout. To use the third page of your Fantasy Travel web and look at some layout ideas:

1. In the FrontPage Editor, open as a file the third page of your Fantasy Travel web. You don't have to open the web itself, just the page. If you installed FrontPage in the default directories, the page will be at C:\FrontPage Webs\Content\FantasyTravel\third.htm.

2. So that you don't affect the original page, resave the page as a file in a different directory and name it **New3.htm**.

3. To prepare the page for tables, open the Page Properties dialog box (right-click on the page and select Page Properties), turn off both the Background Image and Use Custom Text Color options, and then click on OK.

4. Click at the top left of the page, click on Insert Table, change Rows to **1**, and click on OK.

5. Cut and paste the words "Fantasy Travel" into the left cell and the contact information into the right cell. Then drag across the words "Fantasy Travel" and change the font to Size 6 (24 pt), Bold, and Italic.

6. Move the insertion point down to the navbar and insert another table of a single row, seven columns, and a border of **1**. Cut and paste the seven navbar entries into the table, and then delete the remaining vertical lines and blank line.

7. Select the row, change the font to Size 4 (14 pt) and Bold, and then change the cell horizontal alignment to Center. When you are done, your title and navbar should look like this:

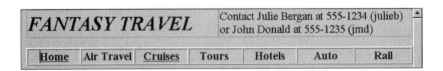

8. Move the insertion point down to the blank line below the navbar and insert a single-cell table (1 row and 1 column), with a border of **3** and a cell padding of **5**. Cut and paste the two-line title of the cruise into the new table, delete the original line the title was on, and reformat the text in the table to Size 5 (18pt) and Bold.

9. Move the insertion point down to the line containing "Islands in the Sun" and insert a fourth table with one row, two columns, and all the other options at their defaults. Cut and paste the "Islands in the Sun" and its following paragraph into the right cell. The font size is 4 (14pt) and the title line is Bold Italic. Press SHIFT-ENTER after the title line, and delete the resulting blank line.

10. Size a graphic outside of FrontPage in, for example, Adobe Photoshop, so it fits in about one-third of a page (the graphic used here was about 250×350 pixels). Then place it in the left cell. Adjust the Cell Properties so the vertical alignment is Top and the specified width is 33 percent. When you are done, this part of your page should look like Figure 6-9.

11. Save your new third page, and close both the FrontPage Editor and FrontPage Explorer.

12. Look at the new third page in different browsers. You'll notice that some of the text may wrap differently, for example, you may find that "Fantasy Travel" is on two lines and that the contacts wrap at a different point, as shown in Figure 6-10. Also look at this at different screen resolutions. By using percentages everywhere except for the graphic, and with the graphic sized to about one-third of the width of the minimum 640×480 screen, this page should work well in all browsers that handle tables.

You may have some other ideas of how to apply tables to this page. Try them. Play with your ideas until you have the look you want—that is how good designs are created. FrontPage's table capability gives you an extremely powerful tool to create what you want.

Laying Out with Frames

While both frames and tables divide up a page into sections, they do so very differently with very different results. *Tables* are typically a smaller section of a page

Table used
to separate
text and
graphics

FIGURE 6-9

Fantasy
Travel page
3 with
tables in a
browser

FIGURE 6-10

that has been divided, while *frames* are actually several pages that have each been allocated a section of the viewing window. In FrontPage, frames can only be built by use of the Frames Wizard in the FrontPage Editor. The Frames Wizard establishes a structure of blank pages and the HTML code to view them in frames within a single window. Each frame is a full page when you view it in the FrontPage Editor. You do not get a WYSIWYG view of the finished frame, nor is your editing limited to the portion of the page normally viewable in the frame, although frames are scrollable. The only way to view the final result is to open the web in Netscape's Navigator 2.0 or later.

OTE: *At this writing, only Netscape's Navigator 2.0 and later will display frames. Microsoft's Internet Explorer 3.0, due out in the second half of 1996, will also have frame capability.*

Explore FrontPage's frames capability by rebuilding the Fantasy Travel home page with frames:

1. In the FrontPage Explorer, create a new web, name it **Frames**, select the Normal Web template, and double-click on Normal Page to open the FrontPage Editor.

2. In the FrontPage Editor click on New Page to open its dialog box, and double-click on Frames Wizard.

3. The Frames Wizard opens and asks you to choose between using a template and creating a custom grid. Accept the default of using a template, and click on Next.

4. The Frames Wizard—Pick Template Layout appears asking you to choose a layout. Look at each of the choices. They offer most of the ways a page can be laid out. When you are ready, select Navigation Bars With Internal Table Of Contents, as shown in Figure 6-11, and then click on Next.

5. You are asked for the alternate page URL to use if your frame page is viewed with a browser that doesn't support frames. This is important, because currently only the Netscape Navigator supports frames. For this exercise, click on Browse, select the default index.htm (your original blank page you started this web with), click on OK, and then click on Next.

Frames Wizard - Pick Template Layout

Select a frame set layout from the list of templates below.

| top |
| contents | main |
| bottom |

Layout:

Banner with nested Table of Contents
Main document plus footnotes
Navigation bars with internal Table of Contents
Top-down three-level hierarchy
Nested three-level hierarchy
Simple Table of Contents

Description

Creates static navigation bars at the top and bottom, with an interior Table of Contents for the main frame.

< Back   Next >   Cancel

Choosing
the frame
template

FIGURE 6-11

6. Accept the default title and URL, and click on Finish. The original blank home page appears, giving you no indication that the Frames Wizard did anything. You'll see in a minute that it did.

7. The blank page that you are looking at will be what is seen if a user's browser cannot display frames. Therefore you want this page to display the original Fantasy Travel home page. To copy this here, open the Insert menu, choose File, and select the Fantasy Travel index.htm page (if you used the default directories when installing FrontPage, the path to this file is C:\FrontPage Webs\Content\FantasyTravel\index.htm).

8. The Fantasy Travel home page will appear with broken-link symbols for all the graphics on the page. Under normal circumstances you would want to fix these (the easiest way is to replace the art), but here replace the top graphic with the words **FANTASY TRAVEL** formatted with Heading 1 and the largest type size (Size 7). Then delete the other two graphics. Save this page.

9. Open the FrontPage Explorer, scroll down the Outline view until you see "New Frameset," and then click on that to open it in the Link view, as you can see in Figure 6-12. The New Frameset refers to the four frames in the

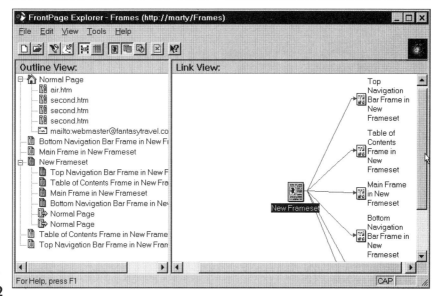

The New
Frameset
with its
four frames

FIGURE 6-12

frame design that was chosen, plus it references the Normal Page. (Ignore, for this exercise, the four broken links from the Normal Page.)

10. Double-click on New Frameset in the Link view. The FrontPage Editor does not open; rather, the Frames Wizard - Edit Frameset Grid dialog box opens. In this and subsequent dialog boxes, you get a chance to edit all of the characteristics that were automatically applied when the frameset was created.

    In this first dialog box you can change the grid you want to use in the frameset. (Each cell in the grid will become a frame.) You can change the overall structure, select a particular cell (by holding down SHIFT while clicking on it) and split it, select two cells and merge them, or drag the borders to change the size of any of the cells, as shown in Figure 6-13.

11. Keep the original grid layout and click on Next. The Edit Frame Attributes dialog box, where you can change the names, URLs, and appearance of each frame, will open. Accept the original settings and click on Next.

12. The third dialog box, Choose Alternate Content, allows you to change the URL that is chosen if the user cannot display frames. Click on Next

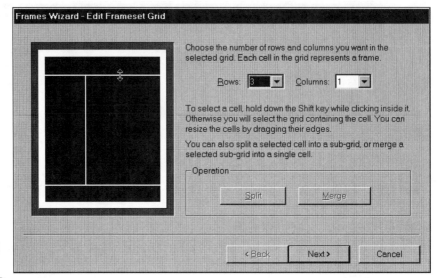

Frames
Wizard -
Edit
Frameset
Grid dialog
box

FIGURE 6-13

without making a change. Finally, you can change the name and URL of the frameset. Click on Finish without changes.

13. Click on the Top Navigation Bar Frame in the Outline view, and then double-click on it in the Link view. The page representing the Top Navigation Bar Frame will open in the FrontPage Editor. On the page are some comments about how the page and its resulting frame are expected to be used. The most important of these comments is that the *target frame* for this page is the contents frame on the left of the middle section. You can change this target frame in the Page Properties dialog box.

14. The purple (using default colors) comments in the initial Top Navigation Bar Frame page will not be seen in a browser, but the top text in black needs to be replaced. Select it now and press DEL. Then open the Normal Page with the original Fantasy Travel home page material in it. Copy the top four lines, down through the contact information, to the new frame page. Add a blank line to separate the title from the comments, and if necessary, delete any blank lines at the top of the page. Your Top Navigation Bar Frame page should now look like Figure 6-14. Save it when it does.

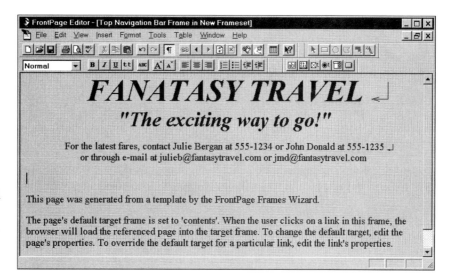

Completed
top
navigation
bar frame
page

FIGURE 6-14

15. Return to the FrontPage Explorer, and open the Table Of Contents Frame in the FrontPage Editor. Note that the target frame for this page is the Main frame. Delete the top three lines on this page, and copy and paste the Available Travel Options from the Normal Page to the Table Of Contents Frame page.

16. In the Table Of Contents Frame page, delete the word "Available" and then edit the remainder of the material so that it fits into a narrow column on the left, as shown in Figure 6-15 (very little reformatting is necessary, because the text will wrap to fit the frame width). Save this page when you are done.

17. In the FrontPage Explorer, open the Main Frame in the FrontPage Editor, and replace the top three lines with the Current Specials information on the Normal page. This does not need any editing, so simply save it.

18. As you did with the previous frames, open the Bottom Navigation Bar Frame in the FrontPage Editor, and copy the material at the bottom of Normal Page to it. (If the text loses its format, reformat it as Heading 5.) Save this new page. Close the FrontPage Editor, and see what you have.

19. Open the Netscape Navigator (2.0 or later) and bring up *servername*/**frames/frameset.htm**. After only minor adjustment of the scroll bars, your set of frames should look like those shown in Figure 6-15 (this figure was taken at a screen resolution of 1024×768; at lower resolutions, you'll see less of each of the frames).

20. Considering that you used the frame's default sizing, the result is pretty good. You might want to make the top frame larger and the contents frame narrower. In the Netscape Navigator you can drag the vertical frame borders to see how it will look, and then go back to the FrontPage Explorer, open the New Frameset Frames Wizard - Edit Frameset Grid as you did earlier, and drag the grid where you want it.

21. Close your browser, make any final adjustments to your frameset, save it, and close FrontPage.

The
Fantasy
Travel
home page
using
frames

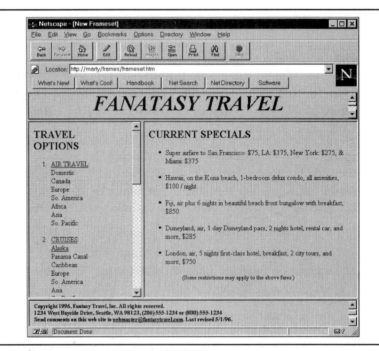

FIGURE 6-15

Frames provide some powerful layout capabilities, especially the ability of a frame to scroll and the target-frame concept. Based on the default target frames, anything that you open by clicking on a link in the top frame will appear in the contents frame, and contents frame links will appear in the main frame instead of on a separate page. This means that instead of appearing on separate pages as they did in the original Fantasy Travel web, the second and third pages, if they were properly linked, would appear in the main frame on the home page. You would not have to worry about the common title and the common footer on each page.

Tables and frames provide real depth to your ability to create sophisticated, state-of-the-art web pages in FrontPage. And you can do it very easily and, at least with tables, with true WYSIWYG ability to see the final results.

6

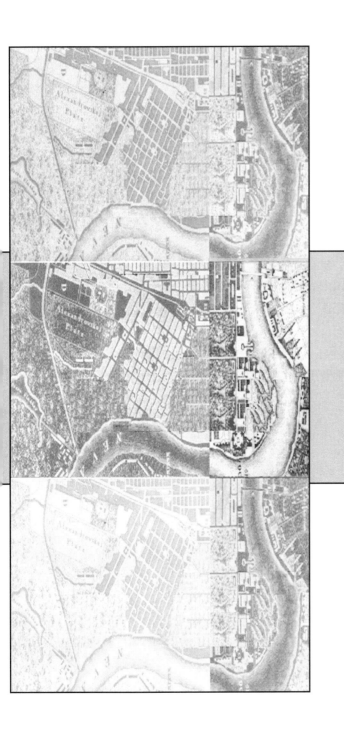

Working with Forms and WebBots

In Chapters 4 through 6, the focus has been on how to present text and graphic information to users of your web. In this chapter, the tables will be turned—you'll learn how to get information back from users. *Forms* are the obvious mechanism for collecting user input and are the major focus of this chapter. *WebBots,* the secondary focus, also provide means for user input and are instrumental in the use of forms. Both forms and WebBots have classically (meaning "last year," in terms of the Web) required either programming or the use of canned programs on a web server. FrontPage has replaced this with its Server Extensions and WebBots, which save you from any programming or from using canned programs with their arcane HTML calls. FrontPage then goes further by giving you powerful tools to perform these functions in a WYSIWYG environment. See for yourself, starting with using forms.

Using Forms

Forms in a web are very similar to those on paper, as you saw in Chapter 2. You are given boxes to fill in, options to select, and choices to make. The advantages of computer forms over paper forms are that computer forms can be easily modified, you don't have to decipher someone's handwriting, and the data starts out in computer form, so it does not have to be retyped into a computer. As with paper forms, though, the design of a form is very important if you want the user to fill it out willingly and properly. The three cardinal rules of forms are

- Keep it simple

- Keep it short

- Make it very clear what the user is supposed to do

FrontPage provides a comprehensive Form Page Wizard to lead you through the development of a form. In addition, FrontPage has a complete set of tools both in the toolbar and in the Insert menu to allow you to create any form you

can dream up. You'll work with both of these in this chapter, beginning with the Form Page Wizard.

Creating Forms with the Form Page Wizard

To create a form, you need to figure out what questions to ask and what fields are necessary for the user to answer them. Go through that process with the idea of creating a questionnaire for prospective project team members. First use the Form Page Wizard to generate the form, then examine and modify the results.

Generating the Form

Like the other wizards you have seen, the Form Page Wizard asks you a series of questions, which it then uses to build a form. To work with the Form Page Wizard:

1. If necessary, start the FrontPage Personal Web Server and then the FrontPage Explorer.

2. In the FrontPage Explorer create a new web based on the Normal Web template and name it **Forms**. When the Normal Page appears, double-click on it to open the FrontPage Editor.

3. In the FrontPage Editor choose New from the File menu, select Form Page Wizard, and click on OK. The Form Page Wizard's introductory dialog box will appear telling you about web forms, what the wizard will do, and what you can do with the result. Click on Next after reading this.

4. You are asked for the Page URL or filename and Page Title. Type **memform.htm** for the URL and **Project Team Questionnaire** for the Page Title. Click on Next when you are done.

5. The Form Page Wizard dialog box that opens will eventually show the questions that you are asking on your form. Currently it is blank. Click on Add to select the first question.

6. In the next dialog box (shown in Figure 7-1) there is a list of types of questions at the top. Click on Contact Information. As you can see in Figure 7-1, a description of the fields that will be placed on the form appears in the middle of the dialog box, and the actual question is displayed at the bottom, where you can change it as you want. Accept the default and click on Next.

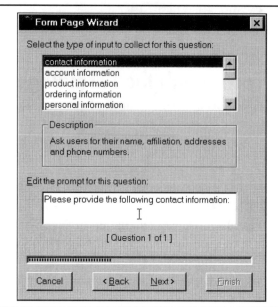

Choosing
the type of
questions
to be on the
form

FIGURE 7-1

7. You are then asked to select the specific fields that you want on the form for your first question (see Figure 7-2). All of these are related to an individual contact. For the Name entry you can use one, two, or three fields. Click on First, Last, which is the two-field choice. Also click on Postal Address and Home Phone, and then click on Next, leaving the suggested name for the group of variables (Contact) as is.

8. You are returned to the list of questions, which now shows the contact information question you just selected. Use steps 5 through 7 to include questions dealing with account information and personal information, and keep the suggested defaults, except that you don't want to repeat the Name field.

OTE: *After you are done using the Form Page Wizard, you can add to, change, and delete what the wizard has produced.*

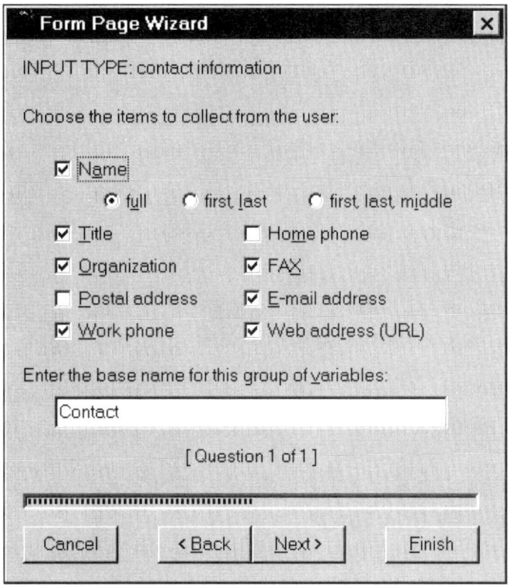

> **Form Page Wizard** ☒
>
> INPUT TYPE: contact information
>
> Choose the items to collect from the user:
>
> ☑ Name
>   ◉ full   ○ first, last   ○ first, last, middle
> ☑ Title   ☐ Home phone
> ☑ Organization   ☑ FAX
> ☐ Postal address   ☑ E-mail address
> ☑ Work phone   ☑ Web address (URL)
>
> Enter the base name for this group of variables:
>
> | Contact |
>
> [Question 1 of 1]
>
> Cancel   < Back   Next >   Finish

Selecting the specific fields to use for gathering contact information

FIGURE 7-2

9. Click on Add, select the One Of Several Options question, change the prompt to

Choose the city you want to be located in:

click on Next, and enter **New York**, **Dallas**, and **San Francisco** as three separate labels on three lines in the upper list box. Then click on radio buttons, enter the word **Location** as the variable name, and click on Next.

10. Click on Add, select the Any Of Several Options question, change the prompt to

Select two areas you want to be associated with:

click on Next, and enter

Initial design
Detail plan
Project management
Plan implementation
Evaluation

on five separate lines. Enter **Preferred areas** as the name for the group, and click on Next.

11. Click on Add, select the Date question, change the prompt to

    Enter the date you are available:

    click on Next, leave the default top date format, enter **Availability** for the variable name, and click on Next.

12. Click on Add, select the Paragraph question, change the prompt to

    Why do you want to be on this project?

    click on Next, enter **Why** as the variable name, and click on Next. When you are done, your list of questions will look like the one in Figure 7-3.

13. Look at your list of questions. Do you want to change any of them or reposition them in the list? While you can change the finished product, it is easier to change it now, before the form is generated. Click on No. 6, the availability date. Click twice on Move Up to move the date ahead of the city question. Click on any question you want to edit and click on Modify. When you are done editing and are returned to the list of questions, click on Next to continue with the form creation.

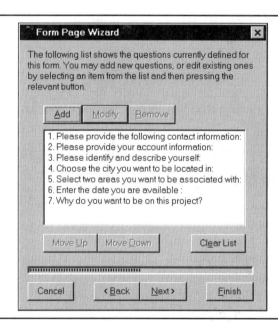

Final list of selected questions

FIGURE 7-3

14. You can then choose the type of list that you want to use. Leave the default normal paragraph without a table of contents, and click on Next.

15. You are asked how you want to save the results of the questionnaire. Choose text file, enter the filename of **memans**, click on Next, and then click on Finish to generate the form page, which appears as shown in Figure 7-4.

IP: *If you want to transfer the results of a web form to a database or spreadsheet, it is best to use a text file to collect the information. You can choose a comma-, tab-, or space-delimited file (tab probably being the best), which is fairly easy to import into most products.*

Reviewing and Editing a Form

As with most documents that you create, you'll want to go through your form in detail and make any necessary changes. In the real world, you would need to replace the introductory paragraph with an explanation of the form. This should tell users how the form will be used and why they should fill it out. In this case you might use

7

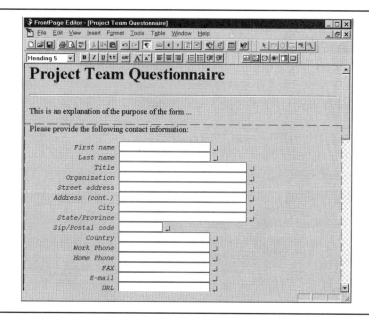

The form as it is generated by the wizard

FIGURE 7-4

something like "This form will be used to qualify prospective members of the Project Team. If you are interested in being a member, please fill out this form."

You can customize many areas of the form. The things that you can do are discussed in the following sections.

CHANGING THE FIELD'S LABEL OR TEXT   Change the label or text on the left of each field by simply typing over or adding to the existing text. This will change the field alignment. For example, add **& middle** to the first label, and you'll get the alignment change shown here:

Please provide the following contact information:

```
    First & middle name  [                    ]
            Last name    [              ]
                Title    [                    ]
```

CHANGING THE FIELD'S ALIGNMENT   Change the alignment by deleting the spaces on the left. But, as in the case of adding "& middle" in the preceding example, there aren't always enough spaces. In that case you need to choose among leaving a field unaligned, removing the left indent that affects the entire paragraph, and/or adding or removing spaces on all the other fields. In the case of "& middle," the left indent had to be removed and space added to all the other fields.

CAUTION: *If you change the paragraph style on the form fields from Formatted to any other style, you'll lose all the leading spaces that produce the original field alignment. This can easily happen by backspacing up to the first paragraph. If this happens to you, click on Undo to quickly recover.*

CHANGING THE FIELD'S PLACEMENT AND SIZE   Change the field placement, for example, by moving the last name up to the same line as the first name, as shown next. (It is probably easier for a user to work through an aligned list, though.)

Please provide the following contact information:

```
    First & middle name  [              ]   Last name  [            ]
                  Title  [              ]
           Organization  [              ]
```

Change the size of a field by dragging the field's selection box, as you can see here:

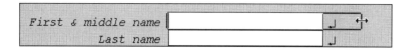

DELETING A FIELD   Delete a field by selecting the label and the field and pressing DEL. You can also delete an entire section by selecting the question, labels, and fields, and pressing DEL.

CHANGING A FIELD'S PROPERTIES   Right-clicking on a field (not its label) and selecting Properties opens the field's properties dialog box, shown next:

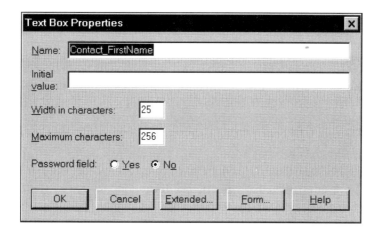

7

Here you can

- Change the field's name

- Establish an initial value, such as a state abbreviation, if most people filling out a form are from one state

- Set the width of the text box, which can also be changed by dragging the end of a field

- Set the maximum number of characters that can be entered into the field

- Determine if the field contains a password so its contents can be encrypted

Form
Properties
dialog box

FIGURE 7-5

CHANGING THE FORM'S PROPERTIES A *form* is a group of fields enclosed within a dashed border on a page. From within the properties dialog box of any field in the form, click on the Form button to open the Form Properties dialog box shown in Figure 7-5 above. This allows you to set

- The form handler that will return the contents of a form to you. You have a choice of a custom CGI script that you create, the Discussion or Registration bots for those particular types of web forms, and the Save Results bot, which is the default (and what you should use most of the time).

- The target frame in which you want the form to appear.

- The hidden fields that you want to appear in the data collected from the form, but not on the form itself. Through the Add, Modify, and Remove buttons, you can add a field name and a value that appear in the data. For example, if you use the same form on several web pages, you could add a field named "Source" that identifies where this set of data originated.

- The settings for the form handler. By clicking on the Settings button, you open the Settings For Saving Results Of Form dialog box, shown in Figure 7-6. Here you can change the name and format of the results file, include (or exclude) the field names, add additional fields and data, and establish the URL for a confirmation page to be sent on the receipt of a form. In the Advanced tab you can set up a second file to save the results with its format and the selection of fields to be included.

In the lower part of the form in Figure 7-4 there are different types of fields, as you can see in Figure 7-7. Each of these fields has slight variations in its properties dialog box. Open each of these in turn and look at their differences. Note the following features:

- The group of radio buttons is a single field, and the value is the button selected.

- Each of the check boxes is its own field, and the value is "on" if a box is selected.

- In the scrolling text box, you can select the number of lines as well as the width. The total content, though, can be far greater than you might think by looking at the width and number of lines (5 lines of 35 characters, or 175 characters), since each line can contain up to 256 characters.

7

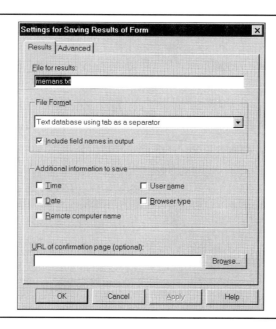

Settings
For Saving
Results
Of Form
dialog box

FIGURE 7-6

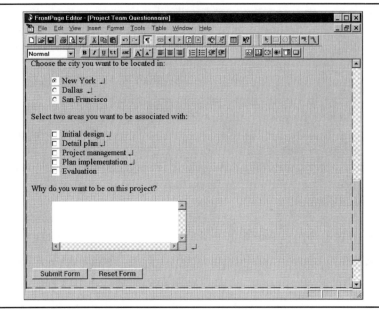

Different
types of
fields in the
lower part
of the form

FIGURE 7-7

- You can change the label on the push buttons, but the only functions that can be performed are submitting a form and resetting it (erasing any entries made and not submitting it).

Given the considerable customization that can be done to a wizard-created form, if your form looks anything like a form the wizard can build, it will probably save you time to use the wizard. The wizard also makes the necessary settings for the Save Results bot that you otherwise would have to remember to do.

Building Forms from Scratch

As good as the Form Page Wizard is, there will always be the need for forms that are different enough from the standards that it is worthwhile building them from scratch. Now that you're familiar with wizard-created forms, take on the building

of a form from scratch and see the differences in the following exercise using the Forms toolbar. (Here you will build a request for literature, which could be built with a wizard, but the design calls for it to be laid out quite differently from what the wizard would do.)

1. With the Project Team Questionnaire still open in the FrontPage Editor, click on the New page button to open a blank page.

2. Open the Page Properties dialog box from the File menu, and type **Literature Request** for the title. Click on OK to close the dialog box.

3. At the top of the New page type **LITERATURE REQUEST**, center it, and format it as Heading 1.

4. Insert a horizontal line under the title using the Horizontal Line option in the Insert menu, and then press ENTER to be positioned at the left of the line under the horizontal line.

5. Select the One-Line Text Box tool from the Forms toolbar, type **First** for the name, change the width to **25**, leave the other defaults as shown next, and click OK. A text box will appear within the dashed line representing a form.

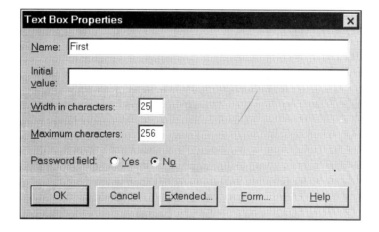

6. Move the insertion point to the left of the new text box, select the Formatted paragraph style, type **First Name:**, and leave a space before the text box.

7. Move the insertion point to the right of the text box, leave two spaces, type **Last Name:**, leave a space, and insert a second one-line text box named **Last** with a width of **25**. Press SHIFT-ENTER to start a new line within the form.

8. Type **Company:**, leave four spaces, insert a one-line text box named **Company**, change the width to **65** characters, click on OK, and press SHIFT-ENTER.

9. Type **Address:**, leave four spaces, insert a one-line text box named **Address1** with a width of **25**, and click on OK.

10. Leave two spaces, type **Address 2:**, leave a space, insert a one-line text box named **Address2** with a width of **25**, click on OK, and press SHIFT-ENTER.

11. Type **City:**, leave seven spaces, insert a one-line text box named **City** with a width of **25**, leave two spaces, type **State:**, leave a space, insert a one-line text box named **State** with an initial value of **WA**, change the width to **9** characters, leave two spaces, type **Zip:**, leave a space, insert a one-line text box named **Zip** with a width of **12** characters, and press SHIFT-ENTER.

12. Type **Phone:**, leave six spaces, insert a one-line text box named **Phone** with a width of **25**, leave two spaces, type **E-mail:**, leave four spaces, insert a one-line text box named **Email** with a width of **25**, and press SHIFT-ENTER.

 13. Click on the Check Box button in the Forms toolbar, give it a name of **Literature**, accept the defaults shown next, and click on OK. Without intervening, type

    Click here if you wish literature.

    (include the period), and then leave three spaces.

Check Box Properties				✕
Name:	Literature			
Value:	ON			
Initial State:	○ Checked	⊙ Not checked		
OK	Cancel	Extended...	Form...	Help

14. Type **Which products?**, leave a space, click on the Drop-Down Menu button in the Forms toolbar, type **Lit_Products** for the name, and click on Add to open the Add Choice dialog box. Type **Portable model**, and click on Selected as the initial state, as shown here:

15. Click on OK and then click on Add twice more to add the choices of **Desktop model** and **Floor model**. In both cases leave the initial state as not selected. In the Drop-Down Menu Properties dialog box, click on Yes to allow multiple selections, so that your dialog box looks like Figure 7-8.

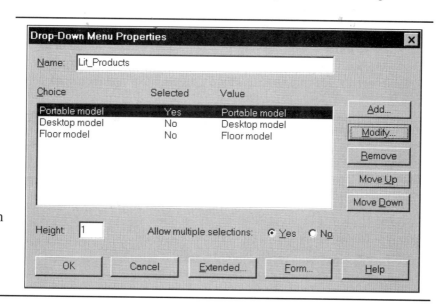

Drop-Down
Menu
Properties
dialog box

FIGURE 7-8

7

16. Click on OK. Select both the "Which products?" label and the drop-down menu box, and press CTRL-C to copy them to the Clipboard. You'll use this twice again. Move the insertion point to the end of the line and press SHIFT-ENTER.

17. Insert a check box named **Use**, accept the defaults, and click on OK. Immediately type

Click here if you use our products.

leave two spaces, and press CTRL-V to paste in your "Which products?" label and drop-down menu. Right-click on the drop-down menu, choose Properties, change the name to **Use_Products**, and click on OK. Move the insertion point to the end of the line and press SHIFT-ENTER.

18. Insert a check box named **Plan**, accept the defaults, and click on OK. Immediately type

Click here if planning our products.

leave a space and press CTRL-V to paste in your "Which products?" label and drop-down menu. Right-click on the drop-down menu, choose Properties, change the name to **Plan_Products**, and click on OK. Move the insertion point to the end of the line and press SHIFT-ENTER.

19. On a new line, type

What is your company size?

leave three spaces, and click on the Radio Button button in the Forms toolbar. In the Radio Button Properties dialog box, enter a group name of **Size**, a value of **Less than 50**, as shown next, and then click on OK.

Radio Button Properties	☒
Group Name:	Size
Value:	Less than 50
Initial State:	○ Selected ⦿ Not selected
OK Cancel Extended... Form... Help	

20. Immediately type

> **Less than 50,**

(include the comma), leave two spaces, insert a radio button with a group name of **Size** and a value of **50 to 500**, immediately type

> **50 to 500,**

leave two spaces, insert a third radio button with a group name of **Size** and value of **Over 500**, type **Over 500**, and press SHIFT-ENTER.

21. Type

> **Please give us any comments you wish:**

click on the Scrolling Text Box button in the Forms toolbar, type a name of **Comments** in the Scrolling Text Box Properties dialog box, enter a width of **34**, click on OK, and press SHIFT-ENTER twice.

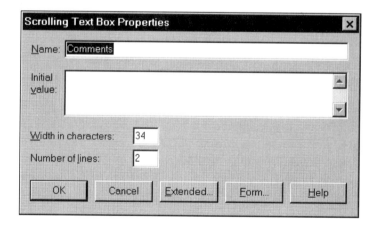

22. Click on the Push Button button in the Forms toolbar. In the Push Button Properties dialog box, type a name of **Submit**, and a value/label of **Submit Form**. Make sure the Button Type is Submit, as shown next, and click on OK.

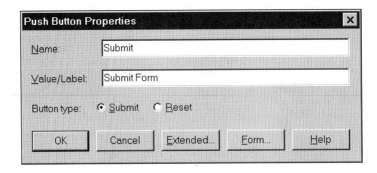

23. Leave four spaces, insert a second push button named **Reset** and a value/label of **Reset Form**, select a button type of Reset, click on OK, save your form, and you're done! The result should look like Figure 7-9.

24. Well, almost done. You still need a handler to process the input from the form. Click on any field in the form, choose Properties, and when the Properties dialog box opens, click on Form. In the Form Properties dialog box, select Save Results Bot for the Form Handler, and click on Settings.

25. In the Settings For Saving Results Of Form dialog box, type **Literate.txt** for the filename, select Text Database Using Tab As A Separator for the file format, turn off Include Field Names, select Date and User Name for Additional Information, and click on OK three times to get back to your form. Now you are done, so save your form once more.

OTE: *Much of the spacing and wording in this form was done interactively—in other words, by use of the "try it and see what it looks like" approach. The beauty of a WYSIWYG form editor is that you can immediately see what the form you're building looks like and change it if needed.*

Part of the purpose of this "from scratch" example is to see what the Form Page Wizard does for you. You must admit it's a lot. The wizard saves you the hassle of naming, spacing, and layout, let alone the setup of the Save Results bot. There aren't many situations where "from scratch" will pay off.

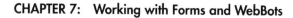

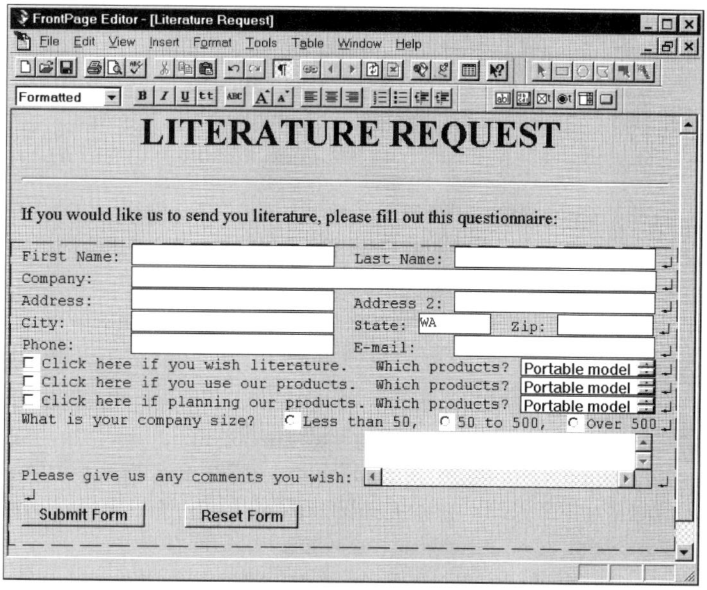

Completed
form built
from scratch

FIGURE 7-9

Handling Form Input

The next step is to look at your forms in a browser. The web called Forms should still be active on your screen and should have three pages: a blank Normal Page, a Project Team Questionnaire page built with the Form Page Wizard, and a Literature Request form built from scratch. To use the web, you'll need to put some links on the Normal Page to the two forms. To do that, and then try out the forms in a browser:

1. From the FrontPage Editor, open the Window menu and choose Normal Page. At the top of the page type **FORMS EXAMPLES**, format it as Heading 1, and press ENTER.

2. On the next line, type **Form Page Wizard**, format it as Heading 4, select the three words you just typed, and click on Create Or Edit Link. In the Create Link dialog box Open Pages tab, select Project Team Questionnaire, and click on OK. Move the insertion point to the end of the line and press ENTER twice.

3. Type **Custom Form**, select the words, and click on Create Or Edit Link. In the Create Link dialog box Open Pages tab, select Literature Request, and click on OK. Your Normal Page should now look like Figure 7-10. Save this page, put a "Home" link back to the Normal Page at the bottom of each form, save each of them, and close the FrontPage Editor.

4. Open your favorite browser and display the Forms web. Select the Project Team Questionnaire and then fill it out and submit it. Almost immediately you'll see another benefit of FrontPage—an automatic confirmation form is created for you and is used here to confirm your input, as you can see in Figure 7-11. Click on Return To The Form at the bottom of the confirmation page.

5. Use the Home link to get back to the Normal Page, and then select the Literature Request form. Fill it out and click on Submit Form. Again you'll see the automatic confirmation report. Click on Return To The Form and then close your browser.

OTE: *The "beautiful" symmetry of the form in the FrontPage Editor has not carried over to the browser, as shown in Figure 7-12. If you look at the form in different browsers, you'll notice different spacing. The user can also change the spacing by selecting different fonts in the browser.*

Normal Page with links to the forms

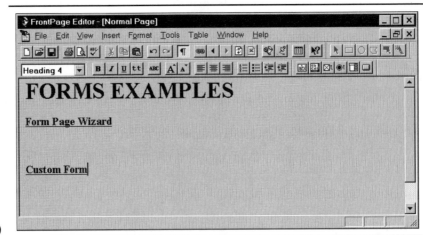

FIGURE 7-10

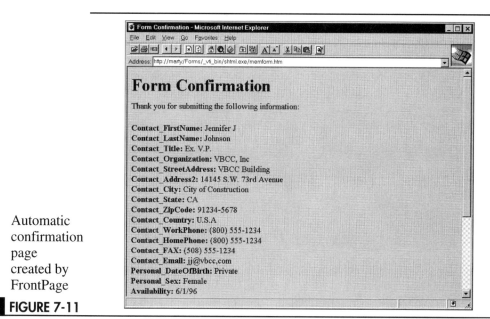

Automatic
confirmation
page
created by
FrontPage

FIGURE 7-11

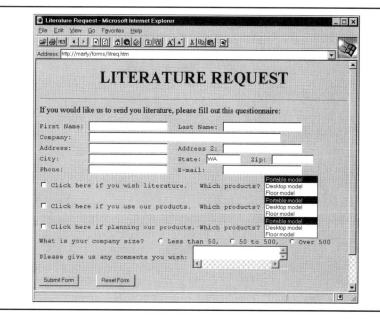

Literature
Request
form
loses its
symmetry
in a browser

FIGURE 7-12

7

6. Open the file that was created by the Save Results bot from the Project Team Questionnaire. If you used the default directories when you installed FrontPage, this should be located at **C:\FrontPage Webs\Forms\Memans.txt**. Use the Windows 95 Explorer or My Computer to locate it, and then double-click on it to open it in the Notepad. What you see should look like this:

7. You can also open the files saved from either form in a database program or in a spreadsheet. Figure 7-13 shows the Literature Request data in Microsoft Access and the Project Team Questionnaire in Microsoft Excel.

8. Close Notepad and any applications other than FrontPage that you have open. In the FrontPage Explorer close your Forms web.

As you can see, FrontPage not only provides significant power for creating a form, but it also does a lot to get the data collected on the form back to you. Also, in the data collection area, a form created with the Form Page Wizard does not have an advantage over a properly set up custom form.

Using WebBots

As you have read in earlier chapters, a WebBot or "bot" is a way you can add automation to your web, often to provide interactivity with the user. Some WebBots are buried in other features, such as the Save Results bot you just used, while others are stand-alone tools that you can use directly. The stand-alone bots, shown in the following illustration of the Insert Bot dialog box, are the subject of the remainder of this chapter (they are also listed in Chapter 2's Table 2-7). Open a new Normal

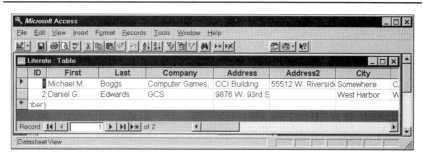

The Literature Request data in Microsoft Access and the Project Questionnaire data in Microsoft Excel

FIGURE 7-13

Web named **Bots**, open its Normal Page in the FrontPage Editor, and then try some of the stand-alone bots in the following sections.

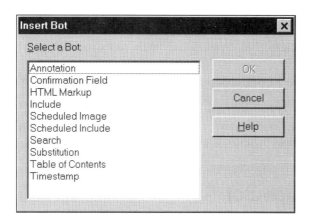

Annotation Bot

The Annotation bot allows you to insert notes that you want to be visible while the web is in the FrontPage Editor, but invisible or hidden while the web is being viewed in a browser. To see how that works:

1. On a blank page in the FrontPage Editor, type

This is normal text

and press ENTER.

2. From the Insert Menu choose Bot. The Insert Bot dialog box opens.

3. Double-click on Annotation. The Annotation Bot Properties dialog box opens. Here you can type any text you want to see in the FrontPage Editor, but not in a browser.

4. Type

This is annotation text that should not be visible in a browser.

(include the period), and then click on OK. The annotation text will appear in the FrontPage Editor as shown next. If you move the mouse pointer over it, you'll see the WebBot icon (shown here in the margin).

> This is normal text
>
> This is annotation text that should not be visible in a browser.

5. Save your web page, open it in a browser, and all you'll see is the normal first line.

6. Minimize your browser, close the open page in the FrontPage Editor, and return to the FrontPage Explorer, where you should close the Bots web.

Confirmation Bot

The Confirmation bot allows you to build a confirmation page that echoes the contents of a web form that has been submitted. Such a page would replace the automatic confirmation form you saw earlier in this chapter. To build a confirmation page for your Literature Request form:

1. In the FrontPage Explorer open the Forms web you created earlier, and then open the Literature Request form in the FrontPage Editor.

2. In the FrontPage Editor create a new Normal Page. On the new page you'll create a brief confirmation letter. Begin by putting a heading on the page like **Great Products Company**, formatting it as Heading 1 and centering it.

3. On the left margin type **To:** and press SHIFT-ENTER.

4. From the Insert menu choose Bot and double-click on Confirmation Field. In the Confirmation Field Bot Properties dialog box type **First**, as shown next, and then click on OK.

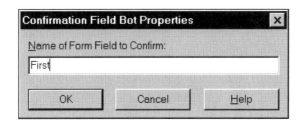

5. Leave a space, again open the Confirmation Field Bot Properties dialog box, type **Last**, click on OK, and press SHIFT-ENTER for a new line.

OTE: *There is no easy way to get a list of field names—you need to either remember them or write them down as you are creating a form, or open the properties dialog box for each field. A suggestion has been made to Microsoft that a "Browse" feature be added to the Confirmation Field Bot Properties dialog box.*

6. Repeat step 4 to enter confirmation fields for **Company**, **Address**, and **Address2** all on separate lines ending with SHIFT-ENTER.

7. Again repeat step 4 to enter confirmation fields for **City**, **State**, and **Zip** all on one line with a comma and a space between "City" and "State," and a space between "State" and "Zip."

8. Type the body and ending of the letter, something similar to that shown in Figure 7-14. Follow this with a link that says **Return to the Form** and points to the Literature Request form. When you are done, save the confirmation letter with a page title of **Literature Request Confirmation** and a URL of **Litreqcf.htm**.

9. Open the Literature Request form, right-click in any field, choose Properties, click on Form, and then on Settings. At the bottom of the Settings For Saving Results Of Form dialog box it asks for the URL of the confirmation page. Click on Browse, double-click on Literature Request Confirmation, and then click on OK three times. Save the Literature Request form and close the FrontPage Editor.

10. In your browser open the Forms web, click on Custom Form, fill out the form, click on Submit Form, and you'll see a confirmation letter similar to the one in Figure 7-15.

11. Close your browser and your Forms web.

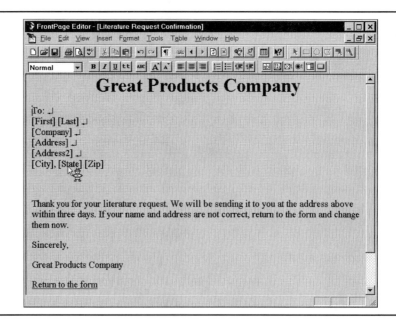

Literature
Request
confirmation
letter

FIGURE 7-14

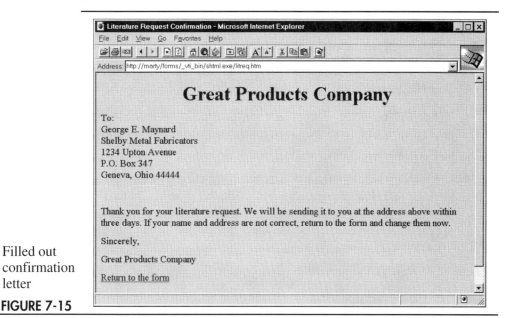

Filled out
confirmation
letter

FIGURE 7-15

For more on confirmation forms, see the "Confirmation Form Template" section of Chapter 3.

HTML Markup Bot

The HTML Markup bot allows you to include an HTML command that is not otherwise supported, directly on a web page. This bot will be discussed in Chapter 9.

Include and Scheduled Include Bots

The Include bot allows you to include one web page on another. For example, if you wanted an identical header on every page, as you did in the Fantasy Travel web, you could put the header on a web page and then include that page on all others in the web. The Scheduled Include bot allows you to include one page on another for a given period. When that time expires, the included page is no longer included. To try this:

1. In the FrontPage Explorer open the Bots web, and double-click on the Normal Page to open the FrontPage Editor.

2. Click on the New button to create a new page. At the top of the page type

This is a page heading, it should be on all pages

Save this page with the page title **Included Header** and the Page URL of **Inchead.htm**.

3. Return to the Normal Page, place the insertion point at the top of the page, choose Bot from the Insert menu, and double-click on Include to open the Include Bot Properties dialog box.

4. Click on Browse to get a list of pages in the current web, double-click on the Included Header page, and then click on OK to return to the web page. You should see the heading appear on this page and the WebBot icon appear when you move the mouse pointer over it, as you can see here:

> This is a page heading, it should be on all pages
>
> This is normal text
>
> This is annotation text that should not be visible in a browser.

The real beauty of using the Include bot is that not only are you saved from retyping or copying the heading onto each page, but also that changes you make need only be typed once. The Scheduled Include bot works similarly to the Include, except that it has a start and stop date and time, as will be demonstrated next with the Scheduled Image bot.

Scheduled Image Bot

The Scheduled Image bot allows you to display an image on a page for a fixed period. When the time expires, the image disappears. To see how this works:

1. On the Normal Page of the Bots web in the FrontPage Editor move the insertion point below the annotation line.

2. Open the Insert menu, choose Bot, and double-click on Scheduled Image. The Scheduled Image Bot Properties dialog box will open:

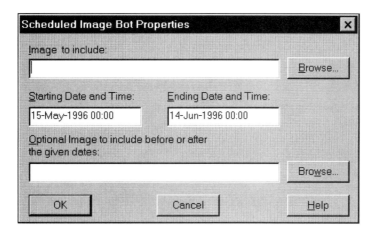

3. Click on Browse next to the Image To Include text box, and then double-click on the Undercon.gif file (this is the Under Construction icon). Set the ending time for a couple of minutes past the current time and click on OK. You should see the image appear in the FrontPage Editor.

4. Save your web page, and open your browser and the Bots web. If necessary, click on the Refresh button in the Standard toolbar and you should see your Under Construction icon, like this:

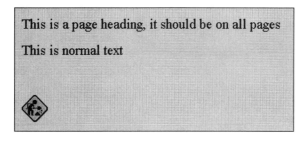

5. After the time has expired, go back to the FrontPage Editor displaying the Bots Normal Page and click on Refresh. The Under Construction icon will be replaced with the message "[Expired Scheduled Image]." If you save this page again, return to your browser, and refresh it, the icon will also disappear from there.

6. Minimize your browser.

Search Bot

The Search bot creates a form in which users can enter any text that they want to search for in the current web. After users enter such text and click on the Search button, the Search bot carries out the search and returns the locations where the text was found. To look at how this is done:

1. At the bottom of the Normal Page of the Bots web open the Insert menu, choose Bot, and double-click on Search. The Search Bot Properties dialog box will open, as shown in Figure 7-16.

2. Accept the defaults in this dialog box and click on OK. The search form will appear on the Normal Page.

3. Save the web page, open your browser, refresh the page, and the search form will appear here.

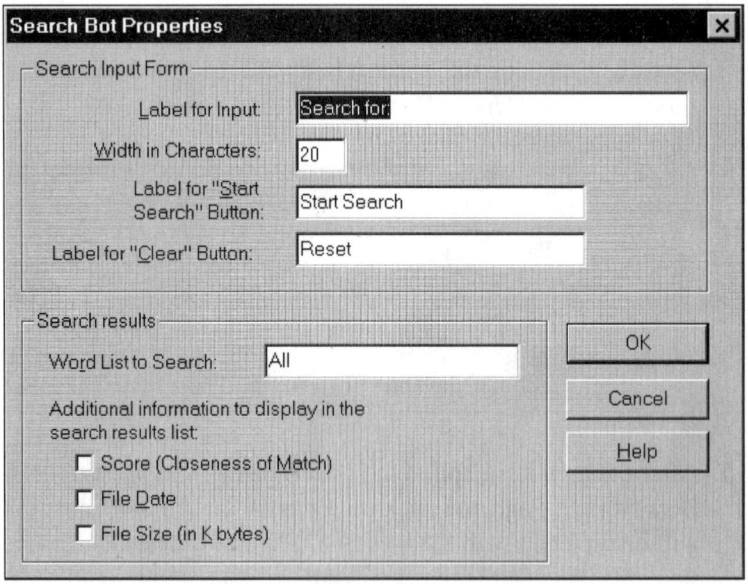

Search Bot
Properties
dialog box

FIGURE 7-16

Search Bot Properties ✕

Search Input Form

Label for Input: `Search for:`

Width in Characters: `20`

Label for "Start Search" Button: `Start Search`

Label for "Clear" Button: `Reset`

Search results

Word List to Search: `All`

Additional information to display in the search results list:

☐ Score (Closeness of Match)
☐ File Date
☐ File Size (in K bytes)

OK

Cancel

Help

4. In the Search For text box type **normal** and click on Start Search. In a moment, you will get the results, which should look like this:

> **Search for:** normal
>
> Start Search   Reset
>
> **Number of documents found: 1. Click on a document to view it, or submit another search.**
>
> **Search Results**
> **Document Title**
> Normal Page

5. Minimize your browser and return to the FrontPage Editor.

IP: *If you want a page* not *to be found by the Search bot (like style pages and included pages), place the pages in the _private directory of the current web; that directory is not searched. By use of FrontPage's default directory structure and the Forms web you created earlier in the chapter, the full path to the _private directory for that web is* C:\FrontPage Webs\Content\Forms_private.

Substitution Bot

The Substitution bot replaces a value on a web page with a configuration variable when the page is viewed by the user. A *configuration variable* contains specific information about either the current page or the current web. There are four predefined configuration variables, as shown in Table 7-1, and you can define additional ones in the Web Settings dialog box opened from the Tools menu in the FrontPage Explorer. You can see how this works with the following instructions:

1. Open the FrontPage Explorer while it is still displaying the Bots web, and then from the Edit menu click on Properties. The web's Properties dialog box will open.

2. Click on the General tab of the web's Properties dialog box so you can see and potentially change the Page URL field. Click on the Summary tab to see but not change the Created By and Modified By fields, and to both see and change the Comments field.

Variable	Description
Author	The name that is in the Created By field of the FrontPage Explorer's Properties dialog box.
Description	The contents of the Comments field of the FrontPage Explorer's Properties dialog box.
ModifiedBy	The name of the person who most recently changed the page, contained in the Modified By field of the FrontPage Explorer's Properties dialog box.
Page-URL	The filename in the Page URL field of the FrontPage Explorer's Properties dialog box.

Configuration Variables

TABLE 7-1

3. In the Comments field type

This is a great web!

click on OK to close the Properties dialog box, and then double-click on the Normal Page to reopen the FrontPage Editor.

4. At the bottom of the Normal Page type

This page was last modified by

leave a space, choose Bot from the Insert menu, and double-click on Substitution. The Substitution Bot Properties dialog box will open.

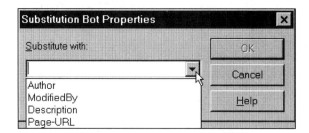

5. Click on the down arrow to see the list of variables shown next. Click on ModifiedBy and then on OK. You'll see the name of the person who last modified the page appear on the Normal Page in the FrontPage Editor.

6. Leave a space and then type

who left these comments:

leave a space, and from the Substitution Bot Properties dialog box choose Description. The comments you left should appear, as you can see here:

This page was last modified by Marty who left these comments: This is a great web!

Table of Contents Bot

The Table of Contents bot creates and maintains a table of contents for a web, with links to all the pages in the web. Whenever the web's contents are changed and resaved, the table of contents is updated. The Table of Contents bot builds the structure of the Table of Contents based on the links that are on each page. For example, if the home page has three pages directly linked to it and the second page has two other pages linked to it, the following structure would be built:

Home Page

      First Page
      Second Page

            Linked Page One
            Linked Page Two

      Third Page

If there are pages in the web that are not linked to other pages, they are listed at the end of the table of contents.

Chapter 3 has a discussion and several examples of the Table of Contents bot as used in web and page wizards and templates. See the "Using the Corporate Presence Wizard" and the "Table of Contents Template" sections in Chapter 3 as well as Figures 3-21, 3-27, and 3-28.

OTE: *When you add the Table of Contents bot to a page, you do not see the full table of contents. It is only when you open the page in a browser that the full table is displayed. See Figures 3-27 and 3-28.*

When you select the Table of Contents bot from the Insert menu, the Table Of Contents Bot Properties dialog box will open, as shown here:

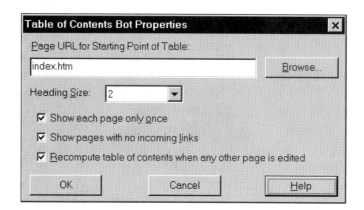

The options in this dialog box are as follows:

- **Page URL for Starting Point of the Table** should be the home page of the web, unless you want a subsidiary table of contents for a section of a web.

- **Heading Size** is the size of the top entry in the table. Each subsidiary entry is one size smaller.

- **Show each page only once** prevents a page that has links from several pages from being listed under each page.

- **Show page with no incoming links** allows unlinked pages to be listed.

- **Recompute table of contents when any other page is edited** forces the table to be rebuilt if any page in the web is changed. Since this can take a significant amount of time, you may not want to do this. A table of contents is also rebuilt every time the page it is on is saved, which should normally be adequate.

 IP: *Using the Table of Contents bot can be a good way to initially establish a link from the home page to all the other pages in the web.*

A good example of using the Table of Contents bot requires a web with a number of pages and several levels. Since such an example was described in Chapter 3 in the "Table of Contents Template" section, an example will not be repeated here.

Timestamp Bot

The Timestamp bot automatically puts the date, and optionally the time, that a page was last modified on the page. To try it:

1. At the bottom of the Normal Page of the Bots web in the FrontPage Editor type

   This page was last modified on

   leave a space, and then using the Bot option in the Insert menu, double-click on Timestamp. The Timestamp Bot Properties dialog box will open like this:

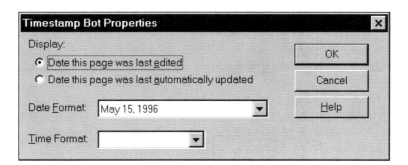

OTE: *In the Timestamp Bot Properties dialog box, "Date this page was last edited" refers to the last time the page was saved. "Date this page was last automatically updated" refers to either the last date the page was saved or the last date an included page was saved, whichever is the most recent.*

2. Accept the defaults and click on OK. The date appears, as you can see next:

> This page was last modified on May 15, 1996

3. Save the Normal Page and close the FrontPage Editor, FrontPage Explorer, and your browser.

Forms and WebBots represent a high level of sophistication that gives you significant power to build the web you want. Much of the "gee wiz" that you saw in the wizards and templates in Chapter 3 came from these tools.

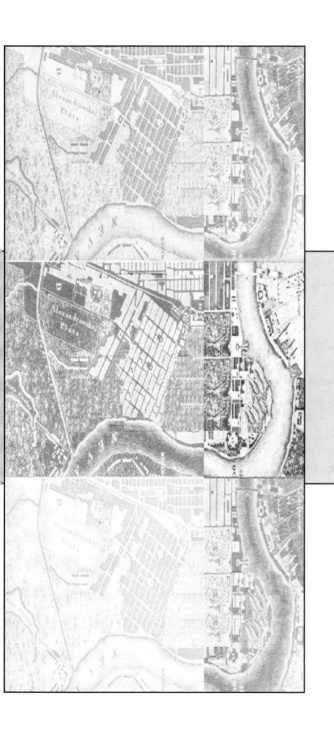

Importing and Integrating Office and Other Files

You are probably going to want to augment your FrontPage web with files imported from other applications—if for no other reason than because the files already exist in the other format. This is especially true with multimedia files, since FrontPage does not have multimedia capability. FrontPage has several ways of working with information created outside of it, including importing information onto an existing page, importing information onto a new page, and attaching or linking to a non-FrontPage file from a web. Let's look at this first from the standpoint of Microsoft Office and other productivity application files and then in terms of multimedia files.

In the next several sections of this chapter, as you are working with Microsoft Office products, you will need to have downloaded and installed several programs that Microsoft provides for free on its web site. These products allow you to create HTML web files which you can use directly on the Web and import into FrontPage. The products that are needed here are Internet Assistant for Microsoft Word, Internet Assistant for Microsoft Excel, Internet Assistant for Microsoft PowerPoint, and the PowerPoint Animation Player. If you connect to *http://www.microsoft.com/internet/* you'll find links to all of the separate pages where these can be downloaded. For each product you'll find instructions for downloading and installing them. After you have downloaded the files, you'll see readme files that have been included and that give you additional pointers. To help you further, Microsoft has posted an online tutorial on using Internet Assistant at *http://www.microsoft.com/smallbiz/ leverage/nbackgrnd.htm.*

Importing Microsoft Office and Other Productivity Files

FrontPage is part of Microsoft's Office family, and thus is tightly integrated, if not bundled, with the other Office products. If you use the Office products Word, Excel, PowerPoint, and Access, you can see a definite similarity in the menus, toolbars, and behavior of FrontPage. Of equal or even greater importance, though, is how easy it is to bring files created in the Office products into FrontPage. Here you'll

look at several Office products and see how you can bring information they create into FrontPage. If you use other productivity applications, such as those from Corel WordPerfect or Lotus, you should be able to follow along with only slight differences.

Using Text from Microsoft Word and Other Word Processors

FrontPage can bring into a web externally created text, especially Microsoft Word text, in a number of ways. Among these are

- Pasting text from the Clipboard onto an existing page in the FrontPage Editor.

- Inserting a file on an existing page from within the FrontPage Editor. The file can be in the HyperText Markup Language (HTML) of the World Wide Web, in the industry standard Rich Text Format (RTF) for heavily formatted word processing files, or in plain text (TXT) format.

- Opening a file onto a new page from within the FrontPage Editor. The file can be in HTML, RTF, or TXT format.

- Importing a file onto a new page(s) in either HTML format or its native format, if that format has been associated with its native editor in the FrontPage Explorer (Microsoft Word's .DOC format has been).

To see how these methods differ, you'll need a text document from Microsoft Word or another word processing application to use as an example.

Creating a Text Document

The document that you want to create should include different character and paragraph formats. It should also be saved in several file formats. To do that:

1. Open a new document in Microsoft Word or your word processor.

2. Type a document with several fonts, several type sizes, several character styles (bold, italic, and underline), several paragraph styles (centered, right-aligned, and a numbered list), and a table, such as the document shown in Figure 8-1.

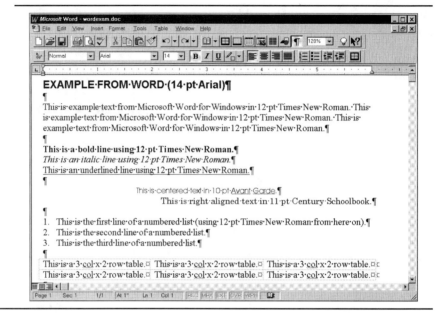

Example
document
in
Microsoft
Word

FIGURE 8-1

3. Select all of the text you entered (CTRL-A in Word), and copy it to the Windows Clipboard by pressing CTRL-C in most applications.

4. Save the document in its native format. If that format is not Microsoft Word for Windows version 6 or 7 and you can save the document in Word format, do so.

5. Save the document in the RTF format, then the HTML format, and finally in the plain TXT format (be sure to save the file in the order shown, or you may lose formatting that would otherwise be there).

OTE: *If you have not installed Microsoft's Internet Assistant for Microsoft Word you won't be able to save in the HTML format.*

6. Close Microsoft Word or your word processor.

Pasting Text from the Clipboard

Probably the easiest way to bring in a small amount of text from almost any Windows application is through the use of the Windows Clipboard. To see how it works with FrontPage:

1. Start the FrontPage Personal Web Server and then the FrontPage Explorer.

2. Create a new web by using the Normal Web template, name it **Import**, and double-click on its Normal Page to open the FrontPage Editor.

3. In the FrontPage Editor, click on the page to place the insertion point, and then press CTRL-V to paste the contents of the Clipboard there. Your result should look like Figure 8-2.

4. Press CTRL-A to select all of the text, and press DEL to get rid of it.

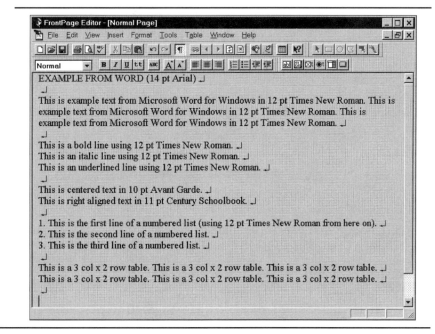

Text
brought
in on the
Clipboard
loses its
formatting

FIGURE 8-2

As you can see, all the formatting gets lost when you bring text into FrontPage from the Windows Clipboard.

Inserting a File onto an Existing Page

You can insert a file onto an existing page by using three different formats: HTML, RTF, and TXT. You'll look at each of these next.

BRINGING IN TXT FILES The Text (.TXT) option of inserting a file has several alternatives. To try these alternatives:

1. On the blank FrontPage Editor page, open the Insert menu and choose File. The Insert dialog box will open.

2. Click on the down arrow in the Files Of Type drop-down list box. Here you can see the three ways you can bring files into FrontPage:

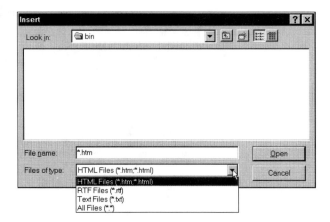

3. Click on Text Files, select the directory and file where you saved the TXT file, and click on Open.

4. In the Convert Text dialog box, click on Formatted paragraphs, and then click on OK. The text comes in using the FrontPage Formatted paragraph style, but all of the formatting from Microsoft Word is gone, as you can see in Figure 8-3.

   If you were to use the One Formatted Paragraph option, you would have no paragraph breaks, only new-line (SHIFT-ENTER) breaks throughout. With the Formatted paragraphs option, you get paragraph

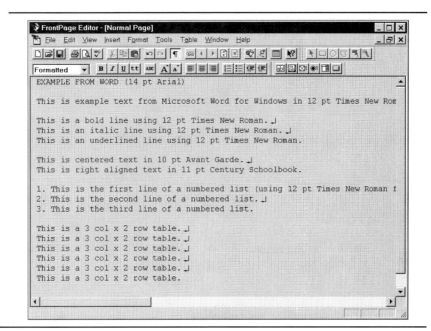

A text file inserted in .TXT format with Formatted paragraphs

FIGURE 8-3

breaks wherever you had a blank line or two paragraph breaks in the original text.

5. Click on Undo, open the Insert menu, choose File, select Text Files, and double-click on your TXT file. Select Normal Paragraphs With Line Breaks and click on OK. The text comes in using FrontPage's Normal style, but again has no other formatting.

   If you were to use the Normal paragraphs option, the only paragraphs breaks you would get are where you had blank paragraphs in the original (or two paragraph marks together).

6. Click on Undo.

The text format does not give you much more than using the Clipboard does, unless you want to bring in some plain text in FrontPage's Formatted paragraph style.

INSERTING AN HTML FILE   An HMTL file (with a file extension on a PC of .HTM) is the normal format of all text files on the Web, including FrontPage text files. For that reason it is the default when you insert a new file. As was mentioned at the beginning of the chapter, some applications, specifically Microsoft Word, Excel,

PowerPoint, Schedule+, and Access for Windows 95 have free add-ins that you can download from *http://www.microsoft.com/internet* that will allow you to create HTML files directly. The HTML files come into FrontPage nicely, as you can see:

1. With a blank page in FrontPage Editor, open the Insert menu, choose File, and accept the default file type of HTML.

2. Double-click on the Microsoft Word example that you saved with the HTML format. The file will appear on the open page, as shown in Figure 8-4.

3. At the right end of the heading that begins "EXAMPLE FROM WORD," type **–INSERTED HTML** to distinguish this page from others that you will create.

4. Open the File menu and choose Save As. Type **Inserted Word HTML File** for the page title, type **Wrdhtml.htm** as the page URL, and click on OK.

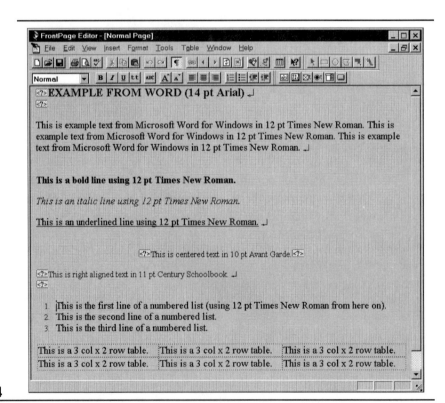

A text file inserted in HTML format

FIGURE 8-4

The HTML format retains much of the formatting present in the original document. There are two exceptions—the specific font and the right alignment. The right alignment was lost when word saved the file to HTML and is therefore a problem that originates with Word's Internet Assistant. (Hopefully, this will be fixed before you encounter this problem.) The fonts are actually present on the page, but the FrontPage Editor does not recognize them and places a question mark icon at either end of the affected text. If you right-click on the question mark icon and choose Properties, you'll see the HTML code for the font change, shown next. (Chapter 9 will discuss HTML in depth.)

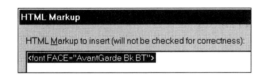

There is one other small difference between the original and this HTML version—the 11-point right-aligned line is 10 points. That is because there is no standard HTML size of 11 points; the closest standard sizes are 10 or 12 points.

INSERTING AN RTF FILE   The RTF file format was created to communicate the majority of text formatting. Many applications, not just word processing programs, have the ability to export files in RTF. To see how well FrontPage handles these files:

1. From the FrontPage Editor, click on the New button in the Standard toolbar to open a new page using the Normal template.

2. Open the Insert File dialog box, choose RTF as the file type, and double-click on the RTF version of your Microsoft Word file. The file will appear on the new page, as you can see in Figure 8-5.

3. At the right end of the heading at the top, type **–INSERTED RTF**, select Save As from the File menu, type **Inserted Word RTF File** for the page title, type **Wrdrtf.htm** for the page URL, and click on OK.

The results of the RTF import are not that good. Not only are the fonts and right alignment missing, but all the type sizing also is gone and the "centered" text isn't centered. In addition, a 1-point border has been added to the table, which you may or may not want.

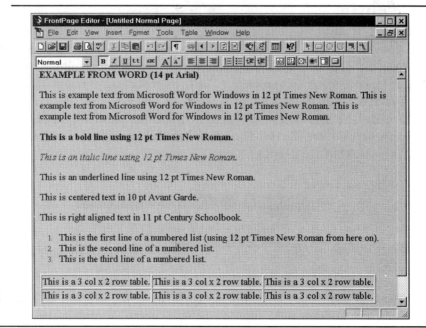

A file
inserted in
RTF format

FIGURE 8-5

Opening a File onto a New Page

The second way you can bring text files into a FrontPage web is through the
FrontPage Editor's File menu Open File command. This yields the Open dialog box,
from which you can again select the HTML, RTF, and TXT file types, as shown in
Figure 8-6. To explore this method:

1. From the FrontPage Editor open the File menu, choose Open File, select
   the Text Files type, and double-click on the TXT version of your Word file.

2. As you saw when you inserted a text file, the Convert Text dialog box
   opens asking you the format to convert the text to. Click on Normal
   Paragraphs With Line Breaks, and click on OK. The page that opens is
   exactly like the one you saw when you inserted a text file in this format,
   as shown in Figure 8-7.

3. In the Heading, type **–OPENED TEXT**, select Save As from the File
   menu, type **Opened Word Text File** for the page title, type **Wrdtxto.htm**
   for the page URL, and click on OK.

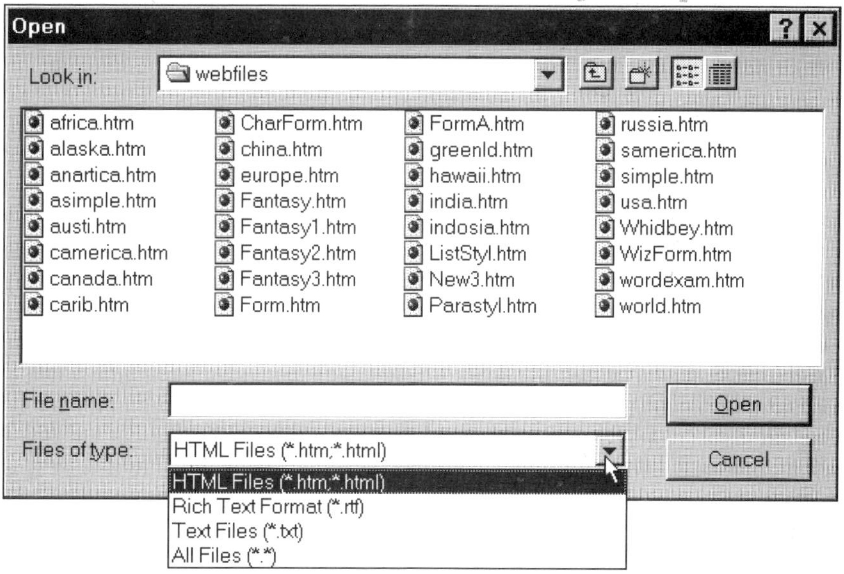

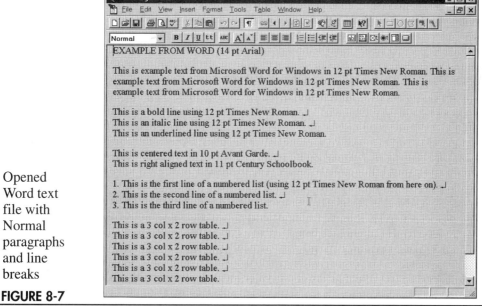

Open dialog box with the allowed formats

FIGURE 8-6

Opened Word text file with Normal paragraphs and line breaks

FIGURE 8-7

4. From the File menu choose Open File, select the HTML Files type, and double-click on the HTML version of your Word file. The file will come in on a new page, just as it did earlier (as shown in Figure 8-4).

5. Type **–OPENED HTML** in the heading, select Save As from the File menu, type **Opened Word HTML File** for the page title, type **Wrdhtmlo.htm** for the page URL, and click on OK.

 OTE: *The original filename is suggested here; since it is an HTML file, it can be used.*

6. Choose Open File from the File menu, select the RTF Files type, and double-click on the RTF version of your Word file. The file will come in on a new page, just as it did earlier (as shown in Figure 8-5).

7. Type **–OPENED RTF** in the heading, select Save As from the File menu, type **Opened Word RTF file** for the page title, type **Wrdrtfo.htm** for the page URL, and click on OK.

You can see that the Open File command produces the same results as Insert File, except that it creates a new page each time a file is brought in.

Importing a File onto a New Page

The third method for bringing text files into FrontPage is to use the FrontPage Explorer's Import command in the File menu. Try that next:

1. Open the FrontPage Explorer, and then from its File menu choose Import. The Import File To Web dialog box will open.

2. Click on Add and the Add File To Import List will open. Click on the down arrow in its Files Of Type drop-down list box. Notice that you do not have all the choices here that you had in the FrontPage Editor Insert and Open methods, as you can see in Figure 8-8.

3. Choose Web Pages as the file type, select the directory and filename of the HTML version of your Word file, and then click on Open. The file is added to the Import File To Web dialog box.

File types
available
when
importing
a file

FIGURE 8-8

4. Click on Add again, select All Files as the type, and then double-click on the .DOC version, the native Word for Windows format of your Word file.

OTE: *Opening or inserting a .DOC file in the FrontPage Editor does not work, so it was not tried in the preceding examples.*

5. With your Import File To Web dialog box looking like the one shown next, click on Import Now. After the files disappear, click on Close.

8

6. Back in the FrontPage Explorer you will see two new pages, one is the .DOC file (wordexam.doc) and the other is a file with your heading or first line of text as its page label, like this:

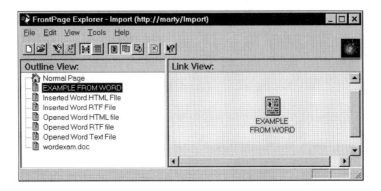

IMPORTING HTML FILES The FrontPage Explorer gives you two ways to import text files—in HTML format and in the native format of the original document. Take a quick look at the HTML file now:

1. Select the HTML file, the one that is not the .DOC file (in this example, the "EXAMPLE FROM WORD" file), and double-click on it in Link view to open the file in the FrontPage Editor. Again you'll see the same HTML page you have seen twice before and in Figure 8-4.

2. Type **–IMPORTED HTML** in the heading, select Save As from the File menu, type **Imported Word HTML file** for the page title, type **Wrdhtmli.htm** for the page URL, and click on OK.

3. Return to the FrontPage Explorer and notice that in renaming your imported page, you actually created an additional page. To correct this, delete the original imported HTML file (not the .DOC file), and click on Yes to confirm the deletion.

IMPORTING FILES IN THEIR NATIVE FORMAT The ability to import a file in its native format is very important, but it, of course, has limitations. You'll see how this works with the Microsoft Word file next. Later, in the "Bringing Files from Other

Productivity Applications" section, you'll see how this works with other applications.

1. Click on the .DOC file in Outline view, and double-click on the same file in Link view. The Microsoft Word application will load, and the file will be displayed and ready to edit as you saw in Figure 8-1.

   Instead of opening the FrontPage Editor, the .DOC extension has been associated with Microsoft Word, and that application is opened to edit the file. While you may have such an association in your Windows Registry, the association that opens Word here is maintained in FrontPage.

2. Close Microsoft Word, open the FrontPage Explorer's Tools menu, and click on Configure Editors. The Configure Editors dialog box will open, as shown here. This dialog box associates a file extension with the application that the FrontPage Explorer will open to edit the file.

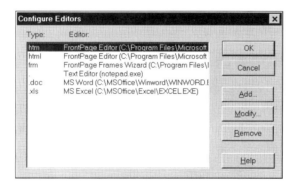

3. Click on Add. The Add Editor Association dialog box will open. Type **.ppt** as the file type, press TAB, type **PowerPoint** for the editor name, press TAB again, and then click on Browse and locate the PowerPoint application (with the default installation it should be C:\MSOffice\Powerpnt\Powerpnt.exe, as you can see in the following illustration). Click on OK. If you don't have PowerPoint, pick some other application that you do have and put it on instead.

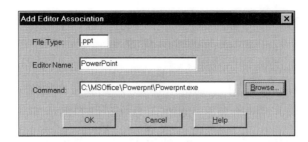

4. Your new application will appear in the Configure Editors dialog box. Click on OK to close it.

AUTION: *There is one catch to using a file in its native format in a web—you are assuming that users have the application on their computer so they can view the file. This is made easier for Microsoft Office products, because Microsoft offers free viewers on its web site (http://www.microsoft.com/ internet) that can be used with Microsoft Internet Explorer.*

Bringing Files from Other Productivity Applications

Using HTML, RTF, or potentially the native format if you think the user can open it, you can bring applications into FrontPage. Recently a number of applications have made add-ins available that convert their files to HTML or otherwise allow publishing them on the Internet. Microsoft has made add-ins, called Internet Assistants, available for Word, Excel, PowerPoint, Access, and Schedule+ applications that are part of Office 95. In addition, Microsoft has the PowerPoint Animation Player and Publisher available, which provides the means to create and deliver a PowerPoint animated presentation, complete with sound, on the Web. While the PowerPoint Player and Publisher come together as one product, they are two separate programs. One, the Animation Player, is an add-on for your browser. The other, the Animation Publisher, is an add-on for PowerPoint. As mentioned earlier, all of the Microsoft add-ins are available for free if you download them from *http://www.microsoft.com/internet*. Now you'll see how this works with Microsoft Excel and PowerPoint files.

Using Microsoft Excel Files

In Microsoft Excel, like most spreadsheet applications, you can create both tabular information and charts or graphs, as shown in Figure 8-9. When you bring this into FrontPage, you must either use the native format—which handles both types of data—and hope the user has the product or the viewer, or you must handle the two data types separately. Try this with Microsoft's Internet Assistant for Excel (if you don't have Excel, see if your application has the same capability).

1. In Microsoft Excel or your spreadsheet application create the tabular and chart example shown in Figure 8-9. Save this both in its native format and in TXT format (if your spreadsheet can also directly save the file in HTML or RTF, do so; Excel can't).

2. In Excel with the Internet Assistant installed, open the Tools menu, choose Add-Ins, click on Internet Assistant Wizard if it isn't already checked, and click on OK.

8

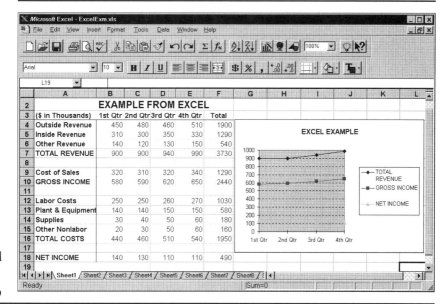

Excel example with both tabular and chart data

FIGURE 8-9

3. Select a range on the spreadsheet that you want to bring into FrontPage, and then from the Tools menu choose Internet Assistant Wizard. The first step of the wizard will open as shown here:

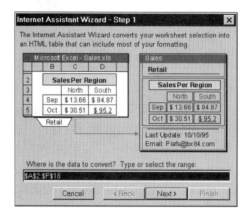

4. Click on Next. You can choose to create an independent HTML file with a header, body table, and a footer, or just to insert the table in an existing HTML file. Choose the independent HTML file and click on Next.

5. Enter the title, header, and footer; decide if you want lines separating them; and then click on Next. Choose to convert the formatting, and again click on Next. Enter the path and filename to use, and click on Finish.

> **NOTE:** *The best way to bring in the chart from Excel is to select and copy it to the Windows Clipboard and then paste it onto an existing page in FrontPage. FrontPage will generate a name for it (like wrdhtml.jpg) and place it in the Images directory when you save the page onto which you pasted the chart.*

6. In the FrontPage Explorer, open the Import File dialog box, click on Add File, select the Excel HTML file, click on Open, click on Add File again, choose All Files as the file type, and double-click on the Excel file in its native format. Click on Import now to complete the process, and then close the Import File dialog box.

7. Open the HTML file in the FrontPage Editor, and you'll see the table with a lot of unknown HTML commands as shown in Figure 8-10. Since your

browser supports these commands, though, you'll be able get the benefit of them. You'll see this in the "Looking at Imported Files in a Browser" section later in this chapter.

8. Close the FrontPage Editor. Click on the native Excel file, and then double-click on it in Link view. Excel will open and display the file as Word did. Close Excel.

Bringing in PowerPoint Files

PowerPoint with both the Internet Assistant and the PowerPoint Animation Publisher installed gives you three choices for getting the files on the Internet: in native format, in HTML, and in PowerPoint Animation. To look at each of these:

1. Load PowerPoint and then either create a new presentation, use an existing presentation, or use the AutoContent Wizard to create a quick example presentation, as I have done for this example.

Excel
HTML
example in
the
FrontPage
Editor

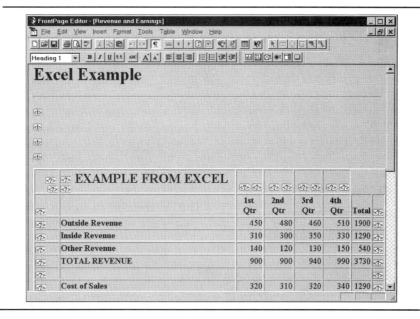

FIGURE 8-10

2. Save the presentation in its native format, and then open the File menu again and choose Export As HTML. The HTML Export Options dialog box will open as shown here.

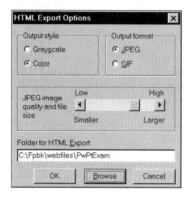

Accept the defaults of Color and JPEG, and browse for the correct path and filename. Finally, click on OK. You'll see several message boxes telling you that the presentation is being created and then one that says that the presentation was successfully saved as HTML. Click on OK again to close the final message box.

OTE: *The Export As HTML command creates a number of files that are placed in their own directory complete with a home page (Index.htm) and a number of graphics. In other words, a complete web is created by this command.*

3. Using the Windows Explorer, open the directory in which you saved the PowerPoint HTML example and observe the complete web that has been created. Close the Windows Explorer and return to PowerPoint

4. If you have installed the Animation Publisher/Player, open the File menu once more, choose Export For The Internet, select As PowerPoint Animation, enter the appropriate path and filename, and click on Save. Close PowerPoint.

5. In the FrontPage Explorer, open the Import File To Web dialog box from the File menu, click on Add File, select the path to the animation file (not

the new directory that was created), choose All Files for the file type, select the .HTM, .PPT, and .PPZ files for the PowerPoint example, click on Open, click on Import Now, and then click on Close. This brings in both the native PowerPoint file and the animation file.

OTE: *The PowerPoint example that was created with the Internet Assistant and placed in a separate directory is a separate web and cannot be easily imported into FrontPage. This occurs because the PowerPoint Internet Assistant (as is true with the Word Internet Assistant) uses relative references to its graphics files, causing all the links to the graphics files to be broken. If you want to import the PowerPoint web, you can replace all the graphics, or you can copy the graphics files from the Images subdirectory to the web's root directory (Import, in this example). For the instructions here, you won't import the web, but you will look at it in the "Looking at Imported Files in a Browser" section shortly.*

6. Click on the PowerPoint .HTM file, and then open it in the FrontPage Editor. What you get is not very exciting, as you can see in Figure 8-11. But if you right-click on the first link and choose Follow Link Forward, you'll get a full-screen view of your presentation. Click on it to go to the next slide, or right-click on it and select End Show to immediately do so. In the right browser this will work beautifully.

8

OTE: *The .PPZ file that you imported into the web, and that is linked to the .HTM file, is the means for producing the animated presentation, which can include sound.*

7. Close the FrontPage Editor. Next, click and then double-click on the .PPT file to see it opened in the PowerPoint application like the other native files you've seen. Close PowerPoint when you are ready.

All of the Microsoft Office applications, including Access and Schedule+, have an impressive ability to create HTML and other files that are usable in a web and importable with FrontPage. This is a great way to quickly generate web content.

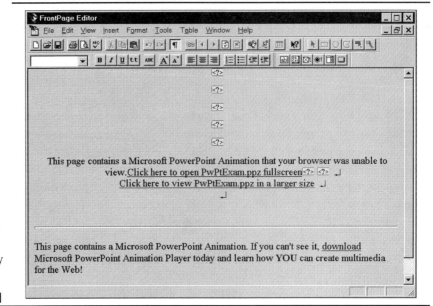

PowerPoint
Animation
introductory
page

FIGURE 8-11

Using Legacy Files on an Intranet

An intranet provides an excellent opportunity to make good use of, or even improve, *legacy* (previously created) files. Manuals and sets of procedures are particularly good examples of this. Instead of maintaining around the office 20 (or 50, or 500!) sets of company manuals that rarely get used except to settle an argument, maintain one set on your intranet. Here people can use a search capability to quickly find what they are looking for, whenever they want and wherever they are.

Manuals and sets of procedures almost surely exist as word processing files that can be easily transferred to FrontPage. Once you do that, you can add the Table of Contents bot to quickly index the files, the Search bot to search all of the text, and the Include bot to place headers and footers on each page with navbars, time stamps, and contacts.

Company reports and company periodicals are more good candidates for your intranet—not only future editions, but also previous issues, so they can be searched and read, and are in one place where everyone can easily access them.

The easy addition of FrontPage's search capability makes getting at information on an intranet so easy, that that could be the primary reason for putting it there. In

the same vein, the Table of Contents and Include bots can add significantly improved usability to existing documents. In other words, putting your legacy documents on your intranet with FrontPage not only gives them a new way to be distributed and read, but features like the Search bot, the Table of Contents bot, and the Include bot make them substantially more usable, and therefore, probably more used.

Looking at Imported Files in a Browser

The real test of a web is how it looks in a browser. See for yourself in this next set of steps:

1. Open the very first "Normal Page" you created for this web in the FrontPage Editor. This should be your home page with a filename of Index.htm. If you do not find it, use any other page to open the FrontPage Editor and create a new page. In either case title the page **Import Home Page**, formatted with Heading 1 and centered, and insert a Table of Contents bot.

OTE: *This is a great demonstration of how the Table of Contents bot can automatically create links to all the .HTM pages. Unfortunately, it will not create links to the .DOC, .XLS, and .PPT files.*

8

2. Accept the defaults for the bot; this gives you a link to all of the .HTM files (although they won't appear until you open the web in a browser). Create links to the .DOC, .XLS, or .PPT files by typing **Link to Word .DOC file** (or Excel .XLS, or PowerPoint .PPT), clicking on the Link button, and selecting the link in the current web using the Browse button.

3. Save the Home Page with the **Import Home Page** title and the **index.htm** page URL. Close the FrontPage Editor. You should see all of the links in the FrontPage Explorer, like this:

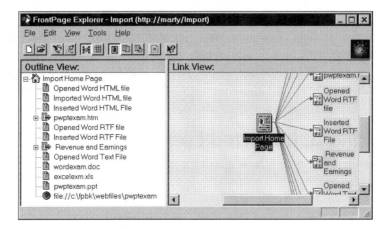

4. Open your browser, which has a web name of Import. The Import Home Page will appear, as you can see in Figure 8-12.

5. Click on each of the links to view the imported (or opened, or inserted) files, using the browser's Back button to return to the Home Page. You will not find many surprises.

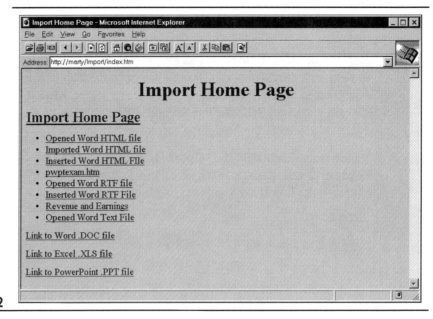

Import Home Page with the links to imported pages

FIGURE 8-12

6. If you have a second browser, open the same web in it, and go through each of the links. Note the differences.

In Microsoft Internet Explorer 2.0 the Word HTML files display the different fonts and all the other formatting except the right alignment, as shown in Figure 8-13. In Netscape Navigator 2.01 the different fonts are gone, as is the underlining; also there is considerable difference in spacing and what is considered to be a "12-point" font, as you can see in Figure 8-14.

The Excel HTML file in both the Internet Explorer and the Navigator comes out reasonably well, as shown in Figures 8-15 and 8-16. The Navigator once again does not display the sans serif font and uses a smaller type size. In both cases, the table title needs to be edited in FrontPage to span several columns and not cause the second column to be so wide.

The PowerPoint Animation should work in Netscape Navigator 2.0 and later if the Animation Player has been properly installed, but it will not work in Microsoft Internet Explorer 2.0 (it will work in Internet Explorer 3.0). The three native files opened in Internet Explorer will all

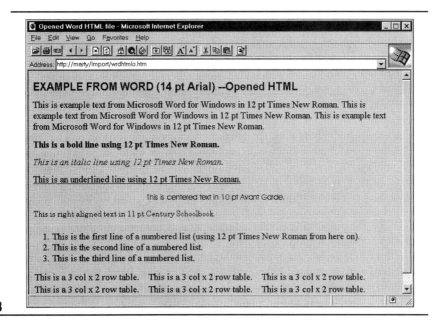

Word
HTML
file in the
Internet
Explorer

FIGURE 8-13

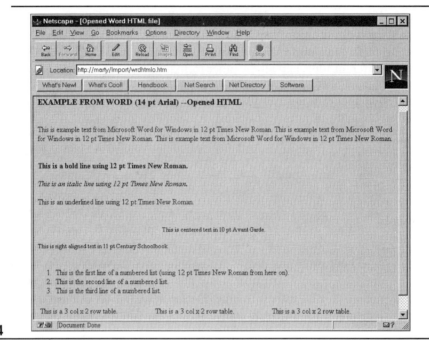

Word
HTML
file in the
Netscape
Navigator

FIGURE 8-14

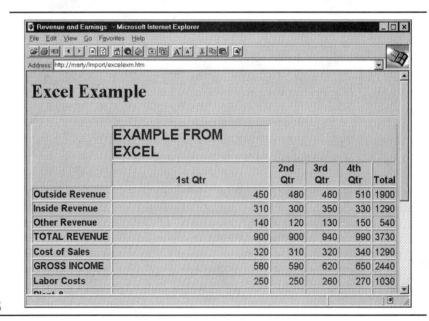

Excel
HTML
file in the
Internet
Explorer

FIGURE 8-15

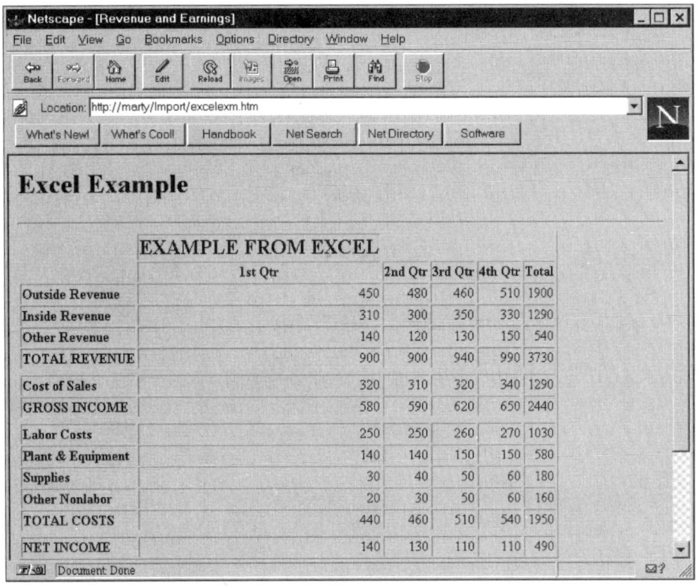

Excel
HTML
file in the
Netscape
Navigator

FIGURE 8-16

load their applications and display the file with only a virus warning to interrupt the process. In Netscape Navigator, both the Word and Excel files require that you identify the application needed to view the file (unless this has already been done). This might be either the creating application or a viewer. For PowerPoint, the Player that you installed for the Animation file includes a viewer, so the file opens directly in the Netscape Navigator.

7. In both browsers open the separate PowerPoint web as a file by identifying the path and then the Index.htm file. In both cases the web looks the same, like the image in Figure 8-17. By clicking on the arrows, you can move through the presentation.

8. Close the one or two browsers you have open.

Importing Multimedia Files

Multimedia is becoming a more significant part of the World Wide Web. In webs you'll see links to .WAV and .AFFI audio files or to .AVI and QuickTime (.MOV) video files. These files are first downloaded and then automatically or manually

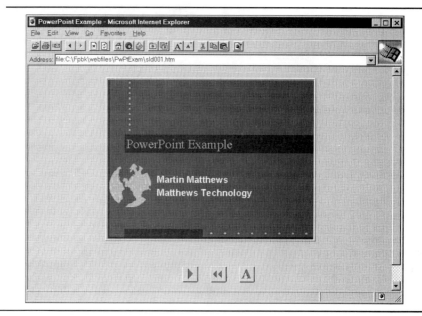

PowerPoint
web
opened in
the Internet
Explorer

FIGURE 8-17

played. There are also products like RealAudio (http://www.realaudio.com) and StreamWorks (http://www.xingtech.com) for both distributing and playing audio and/or video pieces as they are received (instead of waiting for them to be fully transferred).

FrontPage currently does not specifically support the incorporation of any multimedia files. What you can do is import the files into your FrontPage web using the All Files file type and then link to them in your web like you did with the .DOC and .XLS files earlier in this chapter. Assuming that your users have the necessary player, they can play back the files by clicking on them in your web. This works well with .WAV and .AVI files if your users have Windows 95, because Windows 95 includes players for these files. Also, the Microsoft Internet Explorer will automatically start the player when these files are clicked (Netscape Navigator 2.0 requires that you identify the player the first time you click on these files).

IP: *Remember that sound and especially video files can get quite large and take significant time to download even at 28.8 Kbps.*

You can also insert HTML code to play both .AVI and .WAV files automatically when a web page is opened by the user. You'll see how to do this in Chapter 9.

Importing files into a FrontPage web, be they text, tables, presentations, or even multimedia, provides a great deal of ready-made content. When these files are artfully used, they can quickly give a web a lot of depth. As you are building a web site, remember the many existing files that are available. Their use in a web will further leverage their original investment.

8

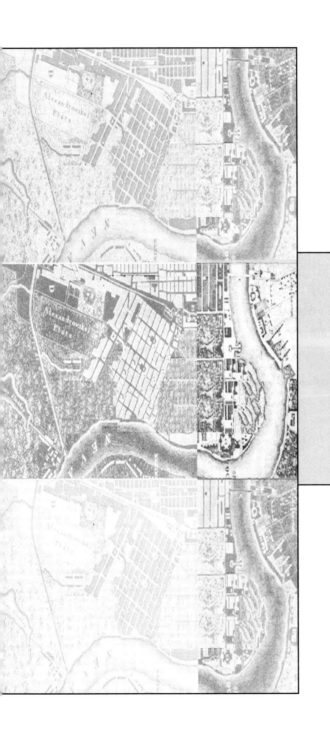

Working with HTML

Throughout the previous chapters you have read that by using FrontPage you don't have to learn HTML (HyperText Markup Language), the programming language of the Web. You *can* build great web pages without ever learning HTML or even reading this chapter. But this chapter is for those who either want to go further—to put the last bit of flourish on their web page—or who just want to understand the HTML behind their FrontPage-created web. Since, with access to FrontPage, you probably will not have to create many webs from scratch in HTML, this chapter will not provide exhaustive coverage of that topic, nor will it cover every nuance of every HTML tag. Both areas are fully covered by sites on the Web, as listed at the end of this chapter. What this chapter will cover is how to understand the HTML that is generated by a FrontPage web and how to add specific capabilities to a FrontPage web with HTML.

OTE: *HTML is an evolving language that's a little out of control. With Netscape and Microsoft adding their own (incompatible) tags, the standards committee is playing catch-up. BGCOLOR (the attribute that controls background color), for example, will respond differently with named colors depending on your browser. Adding to this problem is that both Netscape and Microsoft are rushing ahead with new browsers with many more features. While I have tried to identify what tags work on which products, it is a bit like describing a melting snowball: as soon as you get done describing it, it has changed. The best answer is to use the browsers that you want to write for and test your web on those browsers to make sure it behaves the way you want it to.*

Introducing HTML

HTML is a series of tags that identify the elements in a web. *Tags* or *markup tags* consist of a tag name enclosed in angle brackets and normally come in pairs. Tags are placed at the beginning and end of an element, with the ending tag name preceded by a slash. For example,

```
<TITLE>This is a title</TITLE>
```

uses the Title tag to identify a piece of text that will be placed in the title bar of the browser window. Tags are not case-sensitive, so they can be all uppercase, all lowercase, or a mixture. While tags are often placed around text to control its formatting and placement on a page, they can also be used to identify a hypertext link; to identify a graphic, sound, or video to be loaded; or to identify a particular area of a web.

In addition to a tag name, a tag may contain one or more *attributes* that modify what the tag does. For example, if you want to center a paragraph on the page, you would use this tag:

```
<P ALIGN=CENTER>This will be a centered paragraph</P>
```

The `ALIGN=CENTER` is an *attribute* for the Paragraph tag.

 IP: *Just because an HTML tag exists doesn't mean that you have to use it. As in most other endeavors, the KISS principle applies to the use of HTML.*

Using Basic Tags

All webs should contain a basic set of tags. These tags identify the document as being an HTML document and identify the major parts of the document. The Body tag is also used to identify the page defaults, such as the background color or image, and the text color. The basic tags, some of which are shown in Listing 9-1, are described in Table 9-1.

OTE: *In the listings in this chapter, tags are shown in all capital letters and bold, while attributes are just all capital letters. Also, continuation lines are indented from their parents. These conventions are used solely for readability. Tags and attributes can be any mixture of cases, and there is no need to indent.*

Listing 9-1
Basic set of
HTML tags

```
<!DOCTYPE HTML PUBLIC "-//IETF//DTD HTML X.X//EN">
<HTML>
<HEAD>
  <TITLE>This is a title</TITLE>
  <META NAME="GENERATOR" CONTENT="FrontPage 1.1">
</HEAD>
<BODY BGCOLOR=BLUE TEXT=WHITE>
  This is text that is the body of
  this web document
</BODY>
</HTML>
```

 OTE: *In the tables of tags and attributes in this chapter, tags are shown with their angle brackets, and attributes are indented from the left.*

Tag or Attribute	Description
`<!DOCTYPE ... >`	This tag identifies the document as adhering to the given HTML version. This tag is optional, but becoming common.
`<HTML> </HTML>`	This tag identifies the intervening text as being coded in HTML.
`<HEAD> </HEAD>`	This tag contains the title and identifying information.
`<TITLE> </TITLE>`	This tag identifies the title that is placed in the browser's title bar.
`<META ... >`	This tag assigns content to an element that may be used by a server or browser and cannot otherwise be assigned in HTML; "FrontPage 1.1" is assigned to "GENERATOR" in Listing 9-1.
`<BODY> </BODY>`	This tag specifies the part of the page that is shown to the user and defines overall page properties.
BACKGROUND	This attribute identifies the background image that will be tiled if necessary to fill the window.

Basic Set
of HTML
Tags

TABLE 9-1

Tag or Attribute	Description
BGCOLOR	This attribute identifies the background color that will be used as either a color name or a hexadecimal number representing a color value.
BGPROPERTIES	This attribute specifies that the background will not scroll with the window if BGPROPERTIES=FIXED.
LEFTMARGIN	This attribute sets the left margin for the entire page and overrides any default margin (a margin of 0 will be exactly on the left edge).
LINK	This attribute identifies the color of links that have not been used as either a color name or a hexadecimal number representing a color value.
TEXT	This attribute identifies the color of text on the page as either a color name or a hexadecimal number representing a color value.
TOPMARGIN	This attribute sets the top margin for the page and overrides any default margin (a margin of 0 will be exactly on the top edge).
VLINK	This attribute identifies the color of links that have been used as either a color name or a hexadecimal number representing a color value.

Basic Set of HTML Tags (*continued*)

TABLE 9-1

N **OTE:** *Color* names *that can be used with BGCOLOR, LINK, TEXT, and VLINK as well as other tags with the Microsoft Internet Explorer 2.0 are Black, White, Green, Maroon, Olive, Navy, Purple, Gray, Red, Yellow, Blue, Teal, Lime, Aqua, Fuchsia, and Silver. Netscape Navigator supports 140 named colors including the 16 Microsoft uses. The color value is a combination of three pairs of hexadecimal numbers, one pair (256 possibilities) each for Red, Green, and Blue. Over 16 million color values can therefore be generated, compared with the 16 or 140 color names. There are several sources for color charts from which to determine the color values. One of the best is the RGB Hex Triplet Color Chart by Doug Jacobson on his home page at* http://www.phoenix.net/~jacobson/rgb.html.

Setting Paragraph Styles

Paragraph styles include basic paragraph definition and alignment; headings; the line break; bulleted, numbered, and definition lists; preformatted (called "formatted" in FrontPage) paragraphs; comments; and horizontal lines or rules. Unless the preformatted style is used, normal line endings, extra spaces over one, and tabs are ignored in HTML. Lines simply wrap to fit the space allotted for them, unless you use the Paragraph tag. Listing 9-2 shows examples of paragraph styles. This listing is combined with the tags in Listing 9-1 to produce the web page shown in Figure 9-1. Paragraph styles are described in Table 9-2.

IP: *It is not necessary to have a </P> if it would be immediately followed by a <P>. All browsers will assume the last paragraph has ended if a new one is started. (Netscape Navigator actually puts in another paragraph when it sees a </P>.)*

OTE: *You can nest lists within lists and get automatic indenting.*

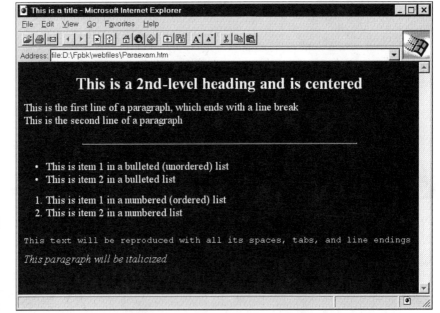

The web page resulting from placing Listing 9-2 between the Body tags of Listing 9-1

FIGURE 9-1

Listing 9-2
Examples of
using
paragraph
style tags

```
<H2 ALIGN=CENTER>This is a 2nd-level heading and is centered</H2>
<P>
  This is the first line of a paragraph, which ends with a line break<BR>
  This is the second line of a paragraph
</P>
<HR SIZE=3 WIDTH=70%>
<UL>
  <LI>This is item 1 in a bulleted (unordered) list
  <LI>This is item 2 in a bulleted list
</UL>
<OL>
  <LI>This is item 1 in a numbered (ordered) list
  <LI>This is item 2 in a numbered list
</OL>
<!-- This is a comment, it is ignored by a browser and not displayed -->
<PRE>This text will be reproduced with all its spaces, tabs, and line
  endings</PRE>
<ADDRESS>This paragraph will be italicized</ADDRESS>
```

9

Tag	Description
`<P>` `</P>`	Identifies the start and end of a paragraph and its alignment with `ALIGN=` and `LEFT`, `CENTER`, or `RIGHT`
`<Hn>` `</Hn>`	Identifies a heading in one of seven heading styles ($n = 1$ to 7) and its alignment with `ALIGN=` and `LEFT`, `CENTER`, or `RIGHT`
` `	Forces a line break similar to pressing SHIFT-ENTER in FrontPage
`<HR>`	Creates a horizontal rule or line where you can specify the alignment, color, shade, size (height), and width across the page
`<OL>` `</OL>`	Contains an ordered (numbered) list
`<UL>` `</UL>`	Contains an unordered (bulleted) list
`<LI>`	Identifies an item in either a numbered or bulleted list
`<DL>` `</DL>`	Contains a definition list

Paragraph
Style
HTML Tags

TABLE 9-2

Tag	Description
`<DT>`	Identifies a term to be defined, displayed on the left of a window
`<DD>`	Identifies the definition of the term that immediately precedes it, indented from the left
`<ADDRESS>` `</ADDRESS>`	Identifies a paragraph of italicized text
`<BLOCKQUOTE>` `</BLOCKQUOTE>`	Identifies a paragraph that is indented on both the left and right, as you might do with a quotation
`<CENTER>` `</CENTER>`	Center all text and images contained within it
`<!-- -->` or `<COMMENT>` `</COMMENT>`	Identifies a comment that the browser will ignore and not display; `<COMMENT>` `</COMMENT>` is *not* used in Netscape Navigator
`<DIV>` `</DIV>`	Identifies a division of a page for which the alignment is set with `ALIGN=` and `LEFT`, `CENTER`, or `RIGHT`
`<PRE>` `</PRE>`	Identifies preformatted text in which all spaces, tabs, and line endings are preserved (called "formatted" in FrontPage)

Paragraph
Style
HTML Tags
(*continued*)

■ **TABLE 9-2**

Applying Character Styles

Character styles determine how one or more characters will look or behave. There are two forms of character styles. *Logical* character styles are defined by the browser and may be displayed in any way that the browser has established. *Physical* character styles have a strict definition that will be the same in all browsers. Examples of character style tags are shown in Listing 9-3, while Figure 9-2 shows how the Netscape Navigator 2.01 and the Microsoft Internet Explorer 2.0 display them—note the differences. Table 9-3 describes most character styles.

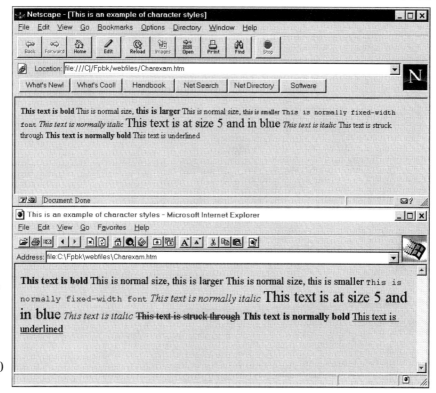

Character
style tags
displayed
in Netscape
Navigator
2.01 and
Microsoft
Internet
Explorer 2.0

FIGURE 9-2

 OTE: *Figure 9-2 demonstrates that browsers ignore line endings unless they are marked with either <P>, <BR>, or other paragraph styles.*

Listing 9-3
Examples of
using
character
style tags

```
<B>This text is bold</B>
This is normal size, <BIG>this is larger</BIG>
This is normal size, <SMALL>this is smaller</SMALL>
<CODE>This is normally fixed-width font</CODE>
<EM>This text is normally italic</EM>
<FONT SIZE=5 COLOR=BLUE>This text is at size 5 and in blue</FONT>
<I>This text is italic</I>
<S>This text is struck through</S>
<STRONG>This text is normally bold</STRONG>
<U>This text is underlined</U>
```

Tag	Description
`<B> </B>`	Applies the Bold physical character style to the enclosed characters
`<BASEFONT>`	Establishes the font size, and/or color, and/or typeface for a web (color and typeface are not used in Netscape Navigator 2.0)
`<BIG> </BIG>`	Makes the enclosed characters one size larger; not used in Internet Explorer 2.0
`<BLINK> </BLINK>`	Applies the Blink physical character style to the enclosed characters; not used in Microsoft Internet Explorer 2.0
`<CITE> </CITE>`	Applies the Citation logical character style to the enclosed characters, normally italic
`<CODE> </CODE>`	Applies the Code logical character style to the enclosed characters, normally a fixed-width font
`<DFN> </DFN>`	Applies the Definition logical character style, normally italic, to the enclosed characters
`<EM> </EM>`	Applies the Emphasis logical character style to the enclosed characters, normally italic
`<FONT> </FONT>`	Applies the font size, and/or color, and/or typeface specified to the enclosed characters (color and typeface are not supported by Netscape Navigator 2.0); if `<BASEFONT>` is used, `<FONT>` size can be relative to the base font size
`<I> </I>`	Applies the Italic physical character style to the enclosed characters
`<KBD> </KBD>`	Applies the Keyboard logical character style to the enclosed characters; normally a fixed-width font

Character
Style
HTML Tags

TABLE 9-3

Tag	Description
`<S> </S>` or `<STRIKE> </STRIKE>`	Applies the Strikethrough physical character style to the enclosed characters; `<S> </S>` is not used in Netscape Navigator 2.0
`<SAMP> </SAMP>`	Applies the Sample logical character style to the enclosed characters; normally a fixed-width font
`<SMALL> </SMALL>`	Makes the enclosed characters one size smaller; not used in Internet Explorer 2.0
`<STRONG> </STRONG>`	Applies the Strong logical character style to the enclosed characters; normally bold
`<SUB> </SUB>`	Applies the Subscript physical character style to the enclosed characters
`<SUP> </SUP>`	Applies the Superscript physical character style to the enclosed characters
`<TT> </TT>`	Applies the Typewriter Text physical character style to the enclosed characters; a fixed-width font
`<U> </U>`	Applies the Underline physical character style to the enclosed characters; not used in Netscape Navigator 2.0

Character Style HTML Tags (*continued*)

TABLE 9-3

Displaying Characters

HTML defines that the less-than, greater-than, and ampersand characters have special meanings and therefore cannot be used as normal text. To use these characters normally, replace them as follows:

Less-than (<)	< or <
Greater-than (>)	> or >
Ampersand (&)	& or &

All other characters that you can type on your keyboard will be displayed as they are typed. In addition, HTML has defined a number of other characters that can be displayed based on entering an *escape sequence* where you want the character displayed. The escape sequence can take either a numeric or a textual format, as was shown with the three characters earlier. In either case the escape sequence begins with an ampersand (&) and ends with a semicolon (;). In the numeric format the ampersand is followed by a number sign (#) and a number that represents the character. All characters, be they on the keyboard or otherwise, can be represented with a numeric escape sequence. The textual format has been defined only for some characters and excludes most characters on the keyboard. Additional examples of the two formats are shown in Table 9-4.

 OTE: *Unlike the rest of HTML, escape sequences are case-sensitive—for example, you cannot use* < *for the less-than symbol.*

For complete lists of the escape sequences, see the Microsoft Internet Explorer 3.0 Specification Character Set at *http://www.microsoft.com/intdev/author/html30/char_set.htm.*

Working with Images and Image Maps

Images are added to a web by using the Image (<IMG>) tag, which specifies the path and filename of the image as well as a number of attributes such as size,

Character	Name	Numeric Sequence	Text Sequence
…	Ellipses	`&#133;`	
•	Bullet	`&#149;`	
™	Trademark	`&#153`	
©	Copyright	`&#169`	`&Copy;`
Æ	AE ligature	`&#198;`	`&Aelig;`
ä	a umlaut	`&#228;`	`&auml;`
é	e acute accent	`&#233;`	`&eacute;`
õ	o tilde	`&#245;`	`&otilde;`

Samples of Character Escape Sequences

TABLE 9-4

positioning, margins, and border. One of the attributes, `ISMAP`, identifies the image as having an image map attached to it. The image map is a separate .MAP file used by the server to relate areas of the image to URLs. To use `ISMAP`, the Image tag must be included in an Anchor tag (see the next section, "Adding Hyperlinks and Bookmarks"). A couple of examples are given in Listing 9-4 and shown in Figure 9-3. Many of the Image attributes are described in Table-9-5.

 OTE: *The   in Listing 9-4 is a nonbreaking space and is used with the Paragraph tags to create a blank line (paragraph) that HTML will not get rid of.*

Listing 9-4
Examples of using the Image tag

```
<P><IMG SRC="parthenon.jpg" ALT="Parthenon on the acropolis"
  ALIGN="bottom" BORDER="2" HSPACE="3" WIDTH="200" HEIGHT="134">
  This is a picture of the Parthenon ...</P>
<P> </P>
<P ALIGN="center"><IMG SRC="undercon.gif" ALT="Under Construction"
  ALIGN="top" WIDTH="40" HEIGHT="38">This image is centered...</p>
```

Attribute	Description
ALIGN	Positions text at the TOP, MIDDLE, or BOTTOM of the image, or positions the image on the LEFT or RIGHT of the text
ALT	Identifies alternative text that is displayed if the image cannot be
BORDER	Specifies that a border of so many pixels be drawn around the image
HEIGHT	Specifies the height, in pixels, of the image
HSPACE	Specifies the blank space on the left and right of the image
ISMAP	Indicates that the image has an image map
SRC	Identifies the path and filename or URL of the image
USEMAP	Identifies the name of the image map that is to be used
VSPACE	Specifies the blank space on the top and bottom of the image
WIDTH	Specifies the width, in pixels, of the image

Image Tag Attributes
TABLE 9-5

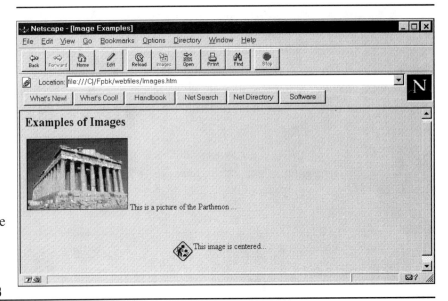

Examples
of using the
Image tag
in Listing
9-4

FIGURE 9-3

OTE: *Netscape Navigator will automatically scale the other dimension based on the current aspect ratio of the image if just one of the dimensions (HEIGHT or WIDTH) is given.*

IP: *Specifying the HEIGHT and the WIDTH speeds up loading, because a quick placeholder will be drawn for the image, allowing the text to continue to be loaded while the image is drawn. Without these dimensions, the loading of the text must wait for the image to be drawn and thereby determine where the remaining text will go.*

Adding Hyperlinks and Bookmarks

Hyperlinks provide the ability to click on an object and transfer what is displayed by the browser (the *focus*) to an address associated with the object. HTML implements hyperlinks with the Anchor tag (<A> </A>), which specifies that the text or graphic that it contains is a hyperlink or a bookmark or both. If the tag is a *hyperlink* and the contents are selected, then the focus is moved to either another location in the current page or web, or to another web. If the tag is a *bookmark,* then another Anchor tag may reference it and potentially transfer the focus to it.

An image used as just described assumes that the entire image is the hyperlink. An image may also be broken into sections, where each section is a link or a *hotspot*. To break an image into multiple links requires an *image map* that is implemented with the Map tag. The Map tag contains Area tags that define the shape of a specific area of the image and the link that it is pointing to.

Listing 9-5 provides some examples of the Anchor, Map, and Area tags, which are shown in Figure 9-4. Table 9-6 describes these tags and their attributes.

Listing 9-5
Examples of hyperlinks and bookmarks

```
<P>This is a link to the <A HREF="index.htm">Home Page.</A></P>
<P><A NAME="This ">This </A>is a bookmark.</P>
<P>This <A HREF="#This ">link </A>takes you to the bookmark.</P>
<P><MAP NAME="ComputerMap">
   <AREA SHAPE="POLYGON" COORDS="163, 121, 197,
      145, 91, 183, 55, 157" HREF="#Keyboard">
   <AREA SHAPE="POLYGON" COORDS="6, 90, 147, 87,
      148, 115, 46, 145, 2, 124" HREF="#Processor">
   <AREA SHAPE="RECT" COORDS="30, 6, 124, 70" HREF="#Screen"></MAP>
  <A HREF="computer.map">
   <IMG ALIGN="bottom" SRC="computer.gif" WIDTH="200" ISMAP
   USEMAP="#ComputerMap" HEIGHT="186"></A></P>
```

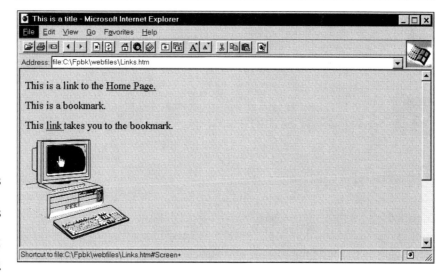

Hyperlinks and bookmarks defined in Listing 9-5

FIGURE 9-4

Tag or Attribute	Description
<A> </A>	Specifies the definition of a hyperlink
HREF	Identifies the destination bookmark, web, or URL
NAME	Identifies the bookmark at this location
TARGET	Identifies a specific frame in the link destination
TITLE	Identifies a name for a link that is displayed when the mouse passes over the link; otherwise the link address is displayed
<MAP> </MAP>	Specifies the definition of an image map
NAME	Identifies the name of the image map
<AREA> </AREA>	Specifies the definition of one image area
SHAPE	Identifies the type of shape being defined to be CIRC, CIRCLE, POLY, POLYGON, RECT, or RECTANGLE
COORDS	Identifies the coordinates of the shape being defined using X and Y positions in terms of image pixels for each point
HREF	Identifies the bookmark or URL to which the focus is transferred
NOHREF	Indicates that a given area causes no action to take place

Anchor Tag
Attributes

TABLE 9-6

 OTE: *The SHAPE attribute of the Area tag may be left out, and a rectangular shape will be assumed.*

Defining Forms

A form in HTML is defined by the input fields that it contains. Each input field is defined by its type, name, and potentially a default value. There are a number of field types around which you can wrap text and formatting to get virtually any form you want to define. One example is shown in Listing 9-6 and displayed in Figure 9-5. Table 9-7 describes the tags and attributes related to forms.

This is a form - Microsoft Internet Explorer

File   Edit   View   Go   Favorites   Help

Address: file:C:\Fpbk\webfiles\H1.htm

This is a form

```
          Name: [                              ]
       Address: [                              ]
                                                    ┌─────────────┐
                                                    │Floor model  │
Send Data? Yes  ○   No  ○    For what product? │Desk model   │
                                                    └─────────────┘
Check if a member  ☐

   [  Send It  ]      [  Forget It  ]
```

Form
created
with
Listing 9-6

■ FIGURE 9-5

OTE: *The Microsoft Internet Explorer does not correctly display the <SELECT NAME="Product" MULTIPLE SIZE="1">, as shown in Figure 9-5. The SIZE="1" says that only one of the multiple entries should be displayed. Netscape Navigator will correctly display this.*

9

Listing 9-6
Example of a
form

```
<H1>This is a form</H1>
<FORM ACTION="-vermeer-self-" METHOD="post">
<PRE>
  Name: <INPUT TYPE=TEXT SIZE=50 MAXLENGTH=256 NAME="Name"><BR>
  Address: <INPUT TYPE=TEXT SIZE=50 MAXLENGTH=256
    NAME="Address"><BR><BR>
  Send Data? Yes <INPUT TYPE=RADIO NAME="Send" Value="Yes">
    No <INPUT TYPE=RADIO NAME="Send" Value="No">
  For what product? <SELECT NAME="Product" MULTIPLE SIZE="1">
    <OPTION VALUE="Floor" SELECTED>Floor model
    <OPTION VALUE="Desk">Desk model</SELECT><BR>
  Check if a member <INPUT TYPE=CHECKBOX NAME="Member" Value="TRUE">
    <BR><BR>
    <INPUT TYPE=SUBMIT VALUE="Send It"> <INPUT TYPE=RESET
      VALUE="Forget It">
</PRE></FORM>
```

Tag or Attribute	Description
`<FORM> </FORM>`	Specifies the definition of a form
`<INPUT>`	Identifies one input field
`TYPE`	Specifies the field type to be `CHECKBOX`, `HIDDEN`, `IMAGE`, `PASSWORD`, `RADIO`, `RESET`, `SUBMIT`, `TEXT`, or `TEXTAREA`
`NAME`	Specifies the name of the field
`VALUE`	Specifies the default value of the field
`ALIGN`	If `TYPE=IMAGE`, positions text at `TOP`, `BOTTOM`, or `CENTER` of image
`CHECKED`	If `TYPE=CHECKBOX` or `RADIO`, determines if by default they are selected (`TRUE`) or not (`FALSE`)
`MAXLENGTH`	Specifies the maximum number of characters that can be entered in a text field
`SIZE`	Specifies the width of a text field in characters, or the width and height in characters and lines of a text area
`SRC`	Specifies the URL of an image if `TYPE=IMAGE`
`<SELECT> </SELECT>`	Specifies the definition of a drop-down list box
`NAME`	Specifies the name of a list box
`MULTIPLE`	Specifies that multiple items can be selected in a list box
`SIZE`	Specifies the height of the list box
`<OPTION>`	Identifies one option in a list box
`SELECTED`	Specifies that this option is the default
`VALUE`	Specifies the value if the option is selected

Form Tags and Attributes

TABLE 9-7

Creating Tables

HTML provides a very rich set of tags to define a table, its cells, borders, and other properties. As rich as the original HTML table specification was, there are many extensions to it by both Microsoft and Netscape. Since these extensions are not consistent between the two companies, they need to be used with caution. Listing 9-7 provides an example of the HTML for creating the simple table shown in Figure 9-6. Table 9-8 shows the principal table tags and their attributes.

Listing 9-7
Table
example

```
<H2>A New Table</H2>
<TABLE BORDER=2 CELLPADDING=3 CELLSPACING=4 WIDTH=100%>
  <CAPTION ALIGN=CENTER>THIS IS THE TABLE CAPTION</CAPTION>
  <TR><TH ALIGN=LEFT WIDTH=25%>Cell 1, a header</TH>
    <TD COLSPAN=2 WIDTH=25%>Cell 2, This cell spans two columns</TD>
    <TD WIDTH=10%>Cell 3</TD>
    <TD WIDTH=10%>Cell 4</TD></TR>
  <TR><TD WIDTH=25%>Cell 5, 25%</TD>
    <TD WIDTH=25%>Cell 6, 25%</TD>
    <TD WIDTH=25%>Cell 7, 25%</TD>
    <TD WIDTH=10%>10%</TD></TR>
  <TR><TD ROWSPAN=2 WIDTH=25%>Cells 9/13, These cells were merged</TD>
    <TD WIDTH=25%>Cell 10</TD>
    <TD WIDTH=25%>Cell 11</TD>
    <TD WIDTH=10%>Cell 12</TD></TR>
  <TR><TD WIDTH=25%>Cell 14</TD>
    <TD WIDTH=25%>Cell 15</TD>
    <TD WIDTH=10%>Cell 16</TD></TR>
</TABLE>
```

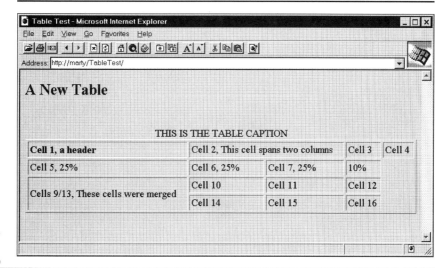

Table
created
with
Listing 9-7

FIGURE 9-6

 OTE: *A table without the BORDER attribute will not have a border, but will take up the same space as if it had a border of 1. Therefore, specifying a border of zero (0) will take up less space.*

Tag or Attribute	Description
`<TABLE> </TABLE>`	Specifies definition of a table
`ALIGN`	Specifies that the table will be aligned on the `LEFT` or `RIGHT` of the page, allowing text to flow around it
`BACKGROUND`	Specifies that a URL containing an image be used as a background; not used in Netscape Navigator 2.0
`BGCOLOR`	Specifies a background color for an entire table; not used in Netscape Navigator 2.0
`BORDER`	Specifies the size, in pixels, of a border to be drawn around all cells in a table
`BORDERCOLOR`	Specifies a border color if a border is present; not used in Netscape Navigator 2.0
`BORDERCOLORLIGHT`	Specifies the lighter of 3-D border colors if a border is present; not used in Netscape Navigator 2.0
`BORDERCOLORDARK`	Specifies the darker of 3-D border colors if a border is present; not used in Netscape Navigator 2.0
`CELLSPACING`	Specifies the amount of space, in pixels, between cells; a default of 2 is used when not specified
`CELLPADDING`	Specifies the amount of space, in pixels, between the cell wall and its contents on all sides; a default of 1 is used when not specified

Table Tags
and
Attributes

■ **TABLE 9-8**

Tag or Attribute	Description
HEIGHT	Specifies the height of a table as either a certain number of pixels or a percentage of the window
VALIGN	Specifies that the text in the table can be aligned with the TOP or BOTTOM of the cells; if not specified, text is center-aligned—not used in Netscape Navigator 2.0
WIDTH	Specifies the width of a table as either a certain number of pixels or a percentage of the window
<TR> </TR>	Identifies the cells in a single row of a table
ALIGN	Specifies that the text in the cells of this row is aligned on the LEFT, CENTER, or RIGHT of each cell. BGCOLOR, BORDERCOLOR, BORDERCOLORLIGHT, BORDERCOLORDARK, and VALIGN are the same as described for <TABLE>
<TD> </TD>	Identifies a single data cell in a table
ALIGN	Specifies that the text in this cell is aligned on the LEFT, CENTER, or RIGHT of the cell. BACKGROUND, BGCOLOR, BORDERCOLOR, BORDERCOLORLIGHT, BORDERCOLORDARK, HEIGHT, WIDTH, and VALIGN are the same as described for <TABLE>
COLSPAN	Specifies the number of columns a cell should span

Table Tags and Attributes (*continued*)

■ **TABLE 9-8**

Tag or Attribute	Description
ROWSPAN	Specifies the number of rows a cell should span
NOWRAP	Specifies that the text in the table cannot be wrapped to fit a smaller cell, forcing the cell to enlarge
<TH> </TH>	Identifies a single header cell in a table (uses the same attributes as <TD>)
<CAPTION> </CAPTION>	Identifies the caption for a table
ALIGN	Specifies that the caption is aligned to the LEFT, CENTER, or RIGHT of the table
VALIGN	Specifies that the caption should appear at the TOP or BOTTOM of the table; not used in Netscape Navigator 2.0

Table Tags and Attributes (*continued*)

TABLE 9-8

Incorporating Frames

HTML frames allow the definition of individual panes or *frames* within a browser window. Each frame contains a separate page that can be scrolled independently of the other frames. HTML defines frames in terms of *frame pages,* which contain Frameset tags, which in turn contain Frame tags. In a frame page, the *Frameset tag* replaces the Body tag and provides the overall structure of the frames to be created in a browser window. Similarly, the *Frame tag* is used to define the structure of a single frame. Figure 9-7 shows a simple frame page that was created with the tags displayed in Listing 9-8. (The banner, contents, and main pages are separately defined to contain the information you see.) The tags and attributes related to frames are described in Table 9-9.

 OTE: *Frames are not supported in Microsoft Internet Explorer 2.0, but are in 3.0.*

 OTE: *No tags that would be within a Body tag can precede the first Frameset tag, although Frameset tags can be contained within another Frameset tag.*

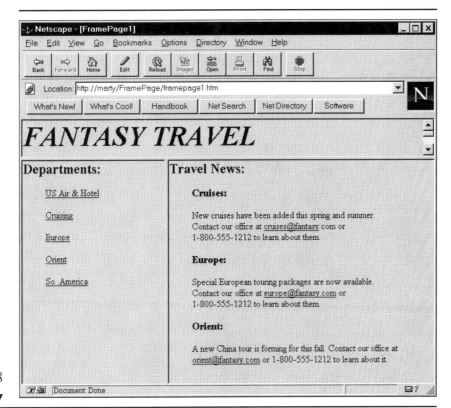

A frame page produced with Listing 9-8

FIGURE 9-7

9

Listing 9-8

A frame page with Frameset and Frame tags

```
<HTML>
<HEAD>
<TITLE>FramePage1</TITLE>
</HEAD>
<FRAMESET ROWS="15%,85%">
  <FRAME SRC="frbanner.htm" NAME="banner" MARGINWIDTH="1"
    MARGINHEIGHT="1">
  <FRAMESET COLS="35%,65%">
    <FRAME SRC="frconten.htm" NAME="contents" MARGINWIDTH="1"
      MARGINHEIGHT="1">
    <FRAME SRC="frmain.htm" NAME="main" MARGINWIDTH="1"
      MARGINHEIGHT="1">
  </FRAMESET>
<NOFRAMES>
<BODY>
<P> </P>
```

```
<P>This web page uses frames, but your browser doesn't
   support them.</P>
</BODY>
</NOFRAMES>
</FRAMESET>
</HTML>
```

Tag or Attribute	Description
`<FRAMESET> </FRAMESET>`	Specifies the definition of a set of frames
COLS	Identifies the number of vertical frames (columns) in the frameset and their absolute or relative size (see comments on this attribute)
ROWS	Identifies the number of horizontal frames (rows) in the frameset and their absolute or relative size (see comments on this attribute)
FRAMEBORDER	Turns on (FRAMEBORDER="Yes") or off (="No") the border around a frame; not used in Netscape Navigator 2.0
FRAMESPACING	Identifies extra space, in pixels, inserted between frames; not used in Netscape Navigator 2.0
`<FRAME> </FRAME>`	Specifies the definition of a single frame
FRAMEBORDER	Turns on (FRAMEBORDER="Yes") or off (="No") the border around a frame
FRAMESPACING	Identifies extra space, in pixels, inserted between frames

Frame Tags
and
Attributes

TABLE 9-9

Tag or Attribute	Description
MARGINWIDTH	Identifies the size, in pixels, of the left and right margin in a frame
MARGINHEIGHT	Identifies the size, in pixels, of the top and bottom margins in a frame
NAME	Identifies the name of the frame so it can be referred to by TARGET attributes
NORESIZE	Prevents the frame from being resized by the user
SCROLLING	Turns the appearance of scroll bars on or off with SCROLLING="Yes"/"No"/"Auto"; Auto is the default
SRC	Identifies the URL of the web page that will occupy the frame
<NOFRAMES> </NOFRAMES>	Specifies HTML that will be displayed by browsers that cannot display frames, but ignored by browsers with frame capability

Frame Tags and Attributes (*continued*)

■ **TABLE 9-9**

OTE: *If FRAMEBORDER and FRAMESPACING are specified in the Frameset tag, they will automatically apply to all the Frame tags contained within it and only need to be specified for the Frame where a change is desired.*

OTE: *The Target attribute, which you have seen with other tags, is used to load pages into specific frames.*

Within the ROWS and COLS attributes are a list of values separated by commas, one for each horizontal frame ("row") or vertical frame ("column") in the frameset. These values can be

The absolute width of a column or height of a row, in pixels. For example,

```
COLS="200, 100, 300"
```

sets up three columns that, from left to right, are 200, 100, and 300 pixels wide, respectively.

A percentage of the window's width for a column or the window's height for a row. For example,

```
ROWS="15%, 85%"
```

sets up two rows, one taking 15 percent of the window and the other, 85 percent.

A relative value to the other rows or columns. For example,

```
COLS="*, 2*"
```

sets up two columns, the right one getting twice as much space as the left one (this is the same as using "33%, 67%").

Any combination of absolute, percentage, and relative. For example,

```
ROWS="100, 65%, *"
```

sets up three rows: the top is 100 pixels high, the middle is 65 percent of the window, and the bottom gets the remaining space.

 AUTION: *Using absolute pixel values with the ROWS and COLS attributes can cause some weird-looking frames, due to the many differences in screen sizes and resolutions.*

Using Multimedia

Multimedia is the inclusion of audio, video, and animation pieces in a web. As you read in Chapter 8, you can simply offer a user a multimedia file to be downloaded by clicking on its link, and then, depending on the availability of players, the file can be automatically or manually played. If you want to make multimedia an automatic part of a web (called "inline" audio or video)—for example, to automatically play an audio piece when a web opens—you must use some of the newest extensions to HTML. These include the <BGSOUND> tag for playing inline audio and the DYNSRC attribute for the Image tag to play inline audio-video. Also <MARQUEE>, which is a scrolling bar of text across the window, is included here as a form of animation. These HTML extensions are *only* supported by Microsoft Internet Explorer 2.0 and to a lesser extent NSCA Mosaic. Listing 9-9 provides some examples of using multimedia, and Table 9-10 describes the related tags.

Listing 9-9
Examples of the HTML to use multimedia

```
<BGSOUND SRC="all.wav" LOOP=2>
<IMG SRC="parthenon.jpg" DYNSRC="goodtime.avi" CONTROLS START=MOUSEOVER>
<MARQUEE BEHAVIOR=SLIDE, DIRECTION=RIGHT>The marquee will scroll this
  text</MARQUEE>
```

Tag or Attribute	Description
<BGSOUND>	Specifies a sound to be played automatically as a page is loaded
SRC	Identifies the URL of the .WAV, .AU, or .MID file that will be played as soon as it is downloaded
LOOP	Identifies the number of times the sound will play; if LOOP=-1 or INFINITE, the sound will play until the page is closed
<IMG>	Specifies a video or animation clip is to be played
DYNSRC	Identifies the URL of the inline video .AVI file to be played

Multimedia Tags and Attributes

TABLE 9-10

9

Tag or Attribute	Description
START	Identifies when the file should start playing (START=FILEOPEN or MOUSEOVER); FILEOPEN is the default, and MOUSEOVER means the file will start playing when the mouse is moved over the alternative image
CONTROLS	Specifies that the video player control panel should be displayed
LOOP	Identifies the number of times the sound will play; if LOOP=-1 or INFINITE, the sound will play until the page is closed
LOOPDELAY	Identifies how long to wait, in milliseconds, between repetitions in a loop
SRC	Identifies the image to display if the browser cannot play the video
<MARQUEE> </MARQUEE>	Specifies the definition of a scrolling bar of text across the browser window
ALIGN	Identifies the alignment of the text in the marquee to be at its TOP, MIDDLE, or BOTTOM
BEHAVIOR	Identifies how the text should behave; BEHAVIOR=SCROLL means the text will continuously scroll from one side to the other; =SLIDE means it will move from one side to the other and stop; =ALTERNATE means the text will continuously bounce from one side to the other; SCROLL is the default
BGCOLOR	Identifies the background color

Multimedia Tags and Attributes (*continued*)

TABLE 9-10

Tag or Attribute	Description
DIRECTION	Identifies the direction that the text will scroll (=LEFT or =RIGHT); LEFT is the default
HEIGHT	Identifies the height of the marquee in either pixels or percentage of the window
HSPACE	Identifies the right and left margins of the marquee in pixels
LOOP	Identifies the number of times that the text will loop; if LOOP=-1 or INFINITE, the sound will play until the page is closed
SCROLLAMOUNT	Identifies the number of pixels between successive loops of text
SCROLLDELAY	Identifies the number of milliseconds between successive loops
VSPACE	Identifies the top and bottom margins of the marquee
WIDTH	Identifies the width of the marquee, either in pixels or as a percentage of the window

Multimedia Tags and Attributes (*continued*)

TABLE 9-10

OTE: *The Image tag attributes in Table 9-10 are in addition to all the regular Image tag attributes listed in Table 9-5, which can all be used with video and animation clips.*

Understanding FrontPage-Generated HTML

Many of the example listings in the "Introducing HTML" section have been created with FrontPage and only slightly modified to fit the needs of the section. Look at three more examples in increasing complexity and get a feeling for the HTML generated by FrontPage. First, though, explore the ways of looking at FrontPage's HTML.

How to Look at FrontPage HTML

You have at least three ways to look at the HTML generated by FrontPage. Two of these are in the FrontPage Editor. The third is in your browser. If you have more than one browser, you can look at the HTML in each. Use the following steps to see the differences among the views:

1. Load both the FrontPage Personal Web Server and the FrontPage Explorer if they are not already loaded. Create a new web with the Normal template, name it **Simple HTML**, and open it in the FrontPage Editor.

2. Enter a heading, a couple of short paragraphs with some formatting, and place an image with text after it, as shown in Figure 9-8. Save the page.

3. Open the View menu and choose HTML. The View HTML window will open, as you can see next. Notice that there are two option buttons in the lower left of the window: Original and Generated. Generated should be selected.

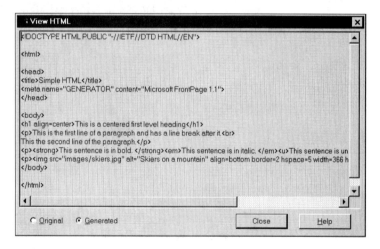

4. Click on Original and you should see no differences, if you have made no changes since saving the page in step 2.

5. Close the window, make some small change to your web page like centering the image, and *without saving* the page, reopen the View HTML window. In Generated view you should see the change you just made, like this:

```
This the second line of the paragraph.</p>
<p><strong>This sentence is in bold. </strong><em>This sentence is in italic. </em><u>This sentence is und
<p align=center><img src="images/skiers.jpg" alt="Skiers on a mountain" align=bottom border=2 hspace=5
</body>
```

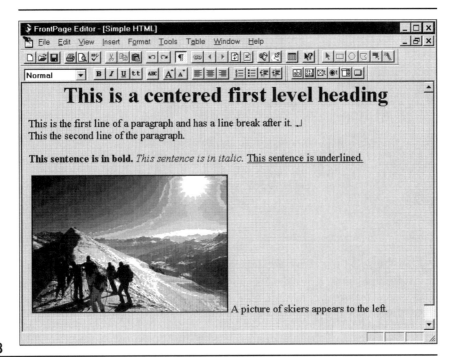

A simple
web page

FIGURE 9-8

6. Click on Original and you should see the HTML the way it was *prior* to your change, as shown in the illustration following step 3. Go back and forth between Original and Generated, and the change will be very obvious, because only the changes will move on the screen.

OTE: *The Original and Generated views are important, because they allow you to see the effect on the HTML of the changes you make in FrontPage.*

7. Close the HTML window, save your changes, and reopen the HTML window. Now you won't see any differences between Original and Generated.

8. Close the HTML window and open the Simple HTML web in Microsoft Internet Explorer if you have it. Open the View menu and choose Source. The Windows Notepad will open and display the HTML behind the Simple HTML web page, as you can see in the following:

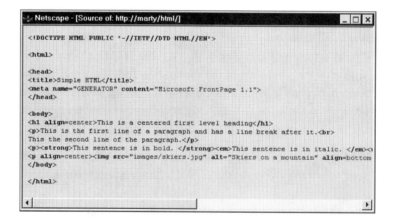

9. Close Notepad and the Internet Explorer, and open Netscape Navigator if you have it. Open the View menu and choose Document Source. A Netscape window will open as shown next. Onscreen you can see that tags are one color, attributes another, and text a third.

10. Close the Netscape window and the Navigator, and reopen the FrontPage Editor window.

   In the three or four views in which you have just seen the Simple HTML example, there are no major differences, although you will see some as the examples become more complex. In this example it just depends on your preference and what you want to do with what you are looking at. If you just want to look, Netscape offers the

advantage of having different colors for the different HTML components, which neither FrontPage nor Microsoft Internet Explorer offers. If you want to directly change the HTML, opening Microsoft Internet Explorer's Notepad editor allows you to do that. In all three views you can select and copy the HTML to the Windows Clipboard, copy it to another editor, and then easily move the HTML from both FrontPage and the Navigator to, for example, Notepad.

In the next several sections of this chapter, try all three methods (if you have both browsers), and by the end of the chapter you'll be able to decide which you like best.

Looking at a Simple HTML Example

Take a closer look at the tags and attributes that were created by FrontPage in the Simple HTML example. Listing 9-10 shows the HTML for this example. It was copied to the Clipboard and then pasted in the manuscript for this book. The tags and attributes were put in capital letters, the tags were made bold, and tags contained in other tags or lines that were a continuation of the previous line were indented. Otherwise this listing has not changed from that generated by FrontPage.

Listing 9-10
A simple HTML example

```
<!DOCTYPE HTML PUBLIC "-//IETF//DTD HTML//EN">
<HTML>
<HEAD>
  <TITLE>Simple HTML</TITLE>
  <META NAME="GENERATOR" CONTENT="Microsoft FrontPage 1.1">
</HEAD>
<BODY>
  <H1 ALIGN=CENTER>This is a centered first level heading</H1>
  <P>This is the first line of a paragraph and has a line break after
    it.<BR>
    This the second line of the paragraph.</P>
  <P><STRONG>This sentence is in bold. </STRONG>
    <EM>This sentence is in italic. </EM>
    <U>This sentence is underlined.</U></P>
  <P ALIGN=CENTER><IMG SRC="images/skiers.jpg" ALT="Skiers on a
    mountain" ALIGN=BOTTOM BORDER=2 HSPACE=5 WIDTH=366 HEIGHT=248>
    A picture of skiers appears to the left.</P>
</BODY>
</HTML>
```

9

There are no surprises in Listing 9-10. All of the tags and attributes were discussed in the "Introducing HTML" section earlier in the chapter. There are, however, several interesting items to note. Among these are

- In the Doctype statement, FrontPage doesn't say what version of HTML it is using, even though that is a major part of the reason to have the statement.

- FrontPage uses the new `ALIGN=CENTER` attributes of Heading and Paragraph tags instead of embedding the tags in a Center tag.

- The Strong and Emphasis tags are used in place of the Bold and Italic tags.

- The `HEIGHT` and `WIDTH` attributes are added to the Image tag to establish the area to be occupied by the image and allow the following text to be displayed while the image is loaded.

Looking at Fantasy Travel HTML

For a second example, close your Simple HTML example and open the Fantasy Travel Home Page you created in Chapters 4 and 5. The beginning of the web page is shown in Figure 9-9, and the HTML that creates it is provided in Listing 9-11 (to

Fantasy
Travel
Home Page

FIGURE 9-9

reduce the bulk and repetition, the middle three items in the bulleted list and the middle four items in the numbered list were removed, as were two lines of text and a Break tag in the contact section and a line of text and a Break tag at the bottom).

Listing 9-11
Fantasy
Travel Home
Page

```
<!DOCTYPE HTML PUBLIC "-//IETF//DTD HTML//EN">
<HTML>
<HEAD>
  <TITLE>Home Page</TITLE>
  <META NAME="GENERATOR" content="Microsoft FrontPage 1.1">
</HEAD>
<BODY BGCOLOR="#F9E1A4">
  <H1 ALIGN=CENTER><FONT SIZE=7><EM><IMG SRC="images/title.gif"
    ALIGN=BOTTOM WIDTH=615 HEIGHT=100><BR></EM></FONT>
    <FONT SIZE=6><EM>&quot;The exciting way to
      go!&quot;</EM></FONT></H1>
  <P ALIGN=CENTER>For the latest fares, contact Julie Bergan at
    jmd@fantasytravel.com </P>
  <HR>
  <H2 ALIGN=LEFT><IMG SRC="images/firecrac.gif" ALIGN=BOTTOM
    WIDTH=59 HEIGHT=53>CURRENT SPECIALS</H2>
  <UL>
    <LI><P ALIGN=LEFT>Super airfare to San Francisco: $75, LA: $175,
      New York: $275, &amp; Miami: $375 </P></LI>
    <LI><P ALIGN=LEFT>London, air, 5 nights first-class hotel, breakfast,
      2 city tours, and more, $750 </P></LI></UL>
  <BLOCKQUOTE><BLOCKQUOTE>
    <P ALIGN=LEFT><FONT SIZE=2>(Some restrictions may apply to the above
      fares.)</FONT></P></BLOCKQUOTE></BLOCKQUOTE>
  <P ALIGN=CENTER> <IMG SRC="images/hrule.gif" ALIGN=BOTTOM
    WIDTH=480 HEIGHT=12></P>
  <H2 ALIGN=LEFT>AVAILABLE TRAVEL OPTIONS</H2>
  <OL>
    <LI><P ALIGN=LEFT><A HREF="air.htm">AIR TRAVEL</A>: Domestic, Canada,
      Europe, So. America, Africa, Asia, So. Pacific </P></LI>
    <LI><P ALIGN=LEFT>RAIL: Domestic, Canada, Europe, So. America,
      Africa, Asia, So. Pacific </P></LI></OL>
  <P ALIGN=LEFT> </P>
  <H5>Copyright 1996, Fantasy Travel, Inc. All rights reserved.<BR>
    Send comments on this web site to
    <A HREF="mailto:webmaster@fantasytravel.com">
    webmaster@fantasytravel.com</A>. Last revised 5/1/96.</H5>
</BODY>
</HTML>
```

9

There is not much difference whether you look at the Fantasy Travel Home Page HTML in FrontPage's View HTML window, or in either Microsoft Internet Explorer or Netscape Navigator. All three look like Listing 9-11 (with more or less formatting). Several items to observe in them are

- The use of the color value for the custom color you created. Without FrontPage to figure this out for you, you would have had to either be satisfied with one of the 16 color names, or get and work with one of the unwieldy color charts.

- The <FONT> and <EM> tags placed around the title graphic are left over from the original text title (which was replaced by the graphic).

- The replacement of the quote (") character in your text with """ because the quote is considered a reserved character. You can use it in text, unlike the other reserved characters.

- The appearance of the " " (a nonbreaking space) at the end of the contact section. This is an error—a space was left on the end of the line, causing the line not to be centered.

- The pair of Blockquote tags used to double indent the "Some restrictions" paragraph. While this looks awkward, it works—looks don't count.

Looking at Corporate Presence HTML

The Corporate Presence Wizard, and the web it creates (shown in Figure 9-10), is FrontPage's tour de force in that it uses most of the features available in FrontPage, including many of the WebBots. As a result the HTML looks very different depending on whether you look at it in the FrontPage View HTML window, shown in Listing 9-12, or in a browser where the web looks like Figure 9-11 and is based on the HTML shown in Listing 9-13. This difference is primarily caused by the bots used by the FrontPage Personal Web Server or FrontPage Server Extensions. In the server the HTML in the first listing is used to generate the HTML in the second listing. In Listings 9-12 and 9-13, significant repetition, for example, in the navbars, has been removed for brevity.

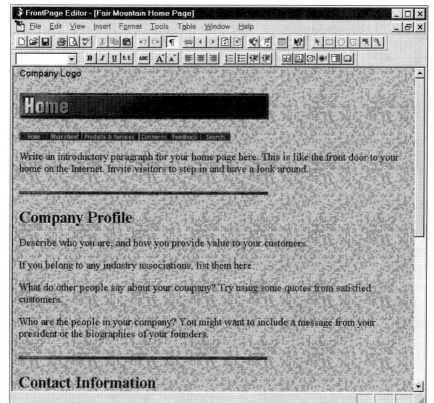

Corporate Presence web Home Page in the FrontPage Editor

FIGURE 9-10

Listing 9-12
Corporate
Presence
web Home
Page in the
FrontPage
Editor

```
<HTML>
<HEAD>
<TITLE>Fair Mountain Home Page</TITLE>
</HEAD>
<BODY STYLESRC="_private/style.htm">
  <!--VERMEER BOT=Include TAG="BODY" U-Include="_private/logo.htm"-->
  <P><IMG SRC="images/hhome.gif" ALT="[Page Banner Image]" BORDER=0
    WIDTH=472 HEIGHT=48></P>
  <!--VERMEER BOT=Include TAG="BODY" U-Include="_private/navbar.htm"-->
  <P><!--VERMEER BOT=PurpleText PREVIEW="Write an introductory..."
    S-Viewable=" "--></P>
  <P> </P>
  <P><IMG SRC="images/div.gif" ALT="[HRule Image]" BORDER=0 WIDTH=471
    HEIGHT=6></P>
  <P> </P>
  <H2>Company Profile</H2>
  <P><!--VERMEER BOT=PurpleText PREVIEW="Describe who you are, and how
    you provide value to your customers." S-Viewable=" "--></P>
  <P> </P>
  <P><IMG SRC="images/div.gif" ALT="[HRule Image]" BORDER=0 WIDTH=471
    HEIGHT=6></P>
  <P> </P>
  <H2>Contact Information</H2>
  <P><!--VERMEER BOT=PurpleText PREVIEW="Tell readers how to get in...
    ...support. " S-Viewable=" "--></P>
  <DL>
    <DT><STRONG>Telephone</STRONG>
      <DD><!--VERMEER BOT=Substitution S-Variable="CompanyPhone"-->
    <DT><STRONG>Electronic mail</STRONG>
      <DD>General Information: <A HREF="mailto:info@fairmountain.com">
        <!--VERMEER BOT=Substitution
          S-Variable="CompanyEmail"--></A><BR>
        Sales: <BR>
        Customer Support: <BR>
        Webmaster: <A HREF="mailto:webmaster@fairmountain.com">
          <!--VERMEER BOT=Substitution S-Variable="CompanyWebmaster"-->
          </A></DL>
  <!--VERMEER BOT=Include TAG="BODY" U-Include="_private/navbar.htm"-->
  <H5>Send mail to <A HREF="mailto:webmaster@fairmountain.com">
    <!--VERMEER BOT=Substitution S-Variable="CompanyWebmaster"--></A>
    Copyright &#169; 1996 <!--VERMEER BOT=Substitution
      S-Variable="CompanyLongName"--><BR>
    Last modified: <!--VERMEER BOT=TimeStamp S-Type="EDITED"
      S-Format="%B %d, %Y"--></H5>
</BODY>
</HTML>
```

Listing 9-13
Corporate
Presence
web Home
Page in a
browser

```html
<HTML>
<HEAD>
  <TITLE>Fair Mountain Home Page</TITLE>
  <META NAME="FORMATTER" content="Microsoft FrontPage 1.1">
</HEAD>
<BODY BACKGROUND="images/brntxtr1.jpg" BGCOLOR="#c5af8b">
  <P><IMG SRC="images/logo.gif" ALT="[Company Logo Image]"
    BORDER="0" WIDTH="120" HEIGHT="24">  </P>
  <P><IMG SRC="images/hhome.gif" ALT="[Page Banner Image]"
    Border="0" WIDTH="472" HEIGHT="48"> </P>
  <P><A HREF="index.htm"><IMG SRC="images/bhome.gif"
    Alt="[Home Icon]" BORDER="0" WIDTH="59" HEIGHT="15"></A>
   <A HREF="search.htm"><IMG SRC="images/bsrch.gif" ALT="[Search Icon]"
    BORDER="0" WIDTH="57" HEIGHT="15"></A></P>
  <P> </P>
  <P><IMG SRC="images/div.gif" ALT="[HRule Image]" BORDER="0"
   WIDTH="471" HEIGHT="6"> </P>
  <P></P>
  <H2>Company Profile</H2>
  <P><IMG SRC="images/div.gif" ALT="[HRule Image]" BORDER="0"
   WIDTH="471" HEIGHT="6"> </P>
  <H2>Contact Information</H2>
  <DL><DT><STRONG>Telephone</STRONG> </DT>
      <DD>206-555-1212</DD>
    <DT><STRONG>Electronic mail</STRONG> </DT>
      <DD>General Information:
         <A HREF="mailto:info@fairmountain.com">
           info@fairmountain.com</A><BR>
       Webmaster:
         <A HREF="mailto:webmaster@fairmountain.com">
           webmaster@fairmountain.com</A></DD></DL>
  <P> <A HREF="index.htm"><IMG SRC="images/bhome.gif"
     ALT="[Home Icon]" BORDER="0" width="59" height="15"></A>
   <A HREF="search.htm"><IMG SRC="images/bsrch.gif"
     ALT="[Search Icon]" BORDER="0" WIDTH="57" HEIGHT="15"></A></P>
  <H5> Send mail to <A HREF="mailto:webmaster@fairmountain.com">
   webmaster@fairmountain.com</A>
   Last modified: May 08, 1996</H5>
</BODY>
</HTML>
```

9

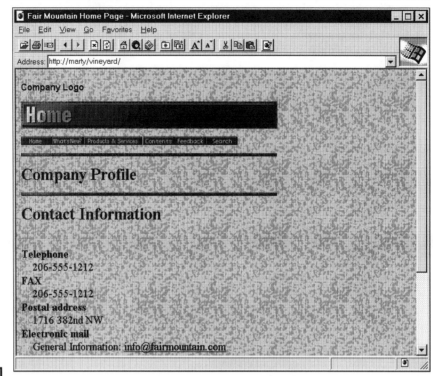

Corporate
Presence
web Home
Page in a
browser

FIGURE 9-11

The primary observation to make regarding Listings 9-12 and 9-13 is how the
WebBots in Listing 9-12 translate to straight HTML in Listing 9-13. Some of the
major points are

■ The internal FrontPage HTML in Listing 9-12 uses a unique-to-FrontPage
STYLESRC attribute to attach a background image and color as well as a
logo to each page in the web. This concept of a style sheet is being
discussed as a part of the HTML 3.2 specification and may become part
of the standard.

■ The Include bot for the navbar in Listing 9-12 is exploded into six Anchor
tags, only two of which were kept in Listing 9-13.

■ The "PurpleText" Annotation bots, which were sprinkled throughout the
original FrontPage listing (although only two remain in Listing 9-12), are

nowhere to be seen in the browser listing, as is intended. They provide text that the author only wants visible while authoring—not in the browser.

■ The Substitution bots also provide a useful and observable function by being a single source of information, like the company phone number, that can be used throughout the web.

If there is one feeling that you should come away with after looking at the HTML generated by FrontPage, it is a much greater sense of appreciation for FrontPage and what it saves you in creating web pages. Just the amount of reduced typing is mind boggling, but more important are all the automatic features, where you simply don't have to worry about some minutiae that is important to the browser, but to no one else. For example:

■ The hexadecimal triplet for the custom color you came up with

■ The height and width of your images

■ The particular font size for a piece of text

■ Making sure you have all the ending tags for all your beginning tags

■ Translating some characters into their escape sequence

Adding Capability to a FrontPage Web with HTML

Besides understanding the HTML that FrontPage generates, the other reason to learn about HTML is to be able to augment FrontPage when it doesn't provide an HTML-supported function. First look at how you'd add HTML to FrontPage, and then look at two examples of added features: one to add inline multimedia, and the other to add background color and a border color to a table.

How to Add HTML to FrontPage

There are three ways to add HTML to FrontPage:

■ Directly edit the HTML produced by FrontPage and resave it. This technique should be strongly discouraged, because it potentially removes the ability to maintain the web with FrontPage, and there are two other ways to add HTML within FrontPage.

■ Use the Extended Attributes dialog box, shown next, which is available from most properties dialog boxes by clicking on the Extended button.

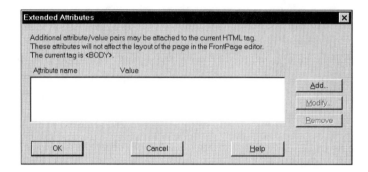

■ Use the HTML Markup bot, which is available anywhere on a page from the Insert menu Bot option.

In the two examples that follow you'll use both of the FrontPage approaches to adding HTML, and you can decide which you like best. As a general rule, the Extended Attributes dialog box is more finely tuned to precisely place an added tag or attribute within the generated HTML. The HTML Markup bot allows you to encapsulate the HTML you are adding and keep it separate from the FrontPage-generated and -checked HTML.

Adding HTML to Play Inline Multimedia

To use the HTML Markup bot to add inline audio to your Simple HTML web page:

1. If it isn't already, open the Simple HTML page in the FrontPage Editor, and move the insertion point to the upper-left corner, on the left end of the heading.

2. Open the Insert menu, choose Bot, and double-click on HTML Markup.

3. In the text window type

```
<bgsound src="all.wav">
```

so your dialog box looks like that shown next. (You can use any .WAV sound—you'll find a number of them in the \Windows\Media\ directory and on your Windows 95 CD.)

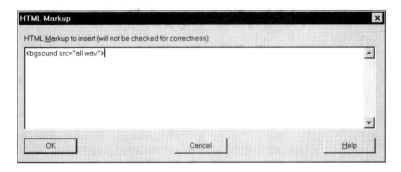

4. Close the dialog box, save the page, and then open it in the Microsoft Internet Explorer (Netscape Navigator 2.0 does not support inline sound). You should hear your sound played as the page loads.

5. Close your browser and the FrontPage Editor. Also close the Simple HTML web in the FrontPage Explorer.

Inserting HTML to Add Color to a Table

Next use the Extended Attributes dialog box to add background color and a border color to any simple table. For illustration purposes I am using the one created earlier in this chapter and shown in Figure 9-6, but you can use any table with these steps:

1. From the FrontPage Explorer either create a new web, or open an existing web with a table in it. In either the new page or the page with a table, open the FrontPage Editor.

2. If necessary, create a simple 4×4 table with some simple text in each cell (like "Cell 1," "Cell 2," and so on).

3. Right-click on the upper-left cell and choose Table Properties. In the Table Properties dialog box, click on Extended. The Extended Attributes dialog box that you saw earlier will open. Notice that the current tag is identified as <table>.

4. Click on Add to open the Set Attribute Value dialog box, click in the Name text box, type **bgcolor**, press TAB, type **yellow** for the Value, and click on OK.

5. Click on Add again, type **bordercolor**, press TAB, type **red**, and click on OK three times. As you are leaving the Extended Attributes dialog box, it should look like this:

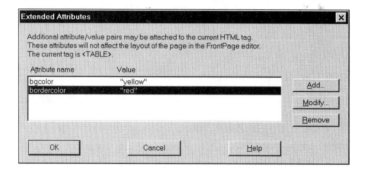

6. Save your page and then open it in a browser. Your result should look something like the table in Figure 9-12 (which appears, unfortunately, in black-and-white).

7. Close your browser, FrontPage Editor, and FrontPage Explorer.

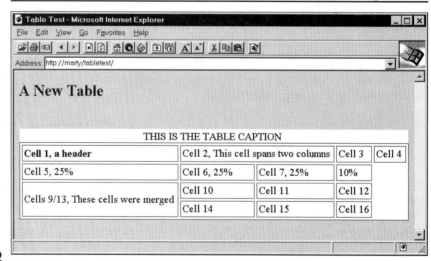

Table with a yellow background and red border (honestly)

FIGURE 9-12

With the two examples here and the HTML reference earlier in the chapter, you can see how easy it is to add significant capability to your FrontPage webs.

HTML Authoring Resources

There are a number of excellent resources on HTML authoring available on the Web. The following is a list of the ones that are most important.

n **OTE:** *URLs change very quickly. While every effort was made to get the following URLs correct when this book went to print, they probably will be incorrect by the time this book reaches the bookstores. If you are having trouble with a URL, drop off right-hand segments, delineated by slashes, until it works. Microsoft's site is changing faster than anybody's, so if one of their URLs isn't working, don't be surprised. The best workaround is to go to* http://www.microsoft.com *and work forward.*

A Beginner's Guide to HTML by NCSA (the National Center for Supercomputing Applications at the University of Illinois, original creators of Mosaic, the first of the web browsers from which Netscape Navigator, Microsoft Internet Explorer, and others have descended), last updated April 1996, available at:
http://www.ncsa.uiuc.edu/General/Internet/WWW/HTMLPrimer.html

Composing Good HTML by Eric Tilton, last updated December 8, 1995, available at: *http://www.cs.cmu.edu/~tilt/cgh/*

Style Guide for Online Hypertext by Tim Berners-Lee (the originator of the World Wide Web), last updated May 1995, available at:
http://www.w3.org/hypertext/WWW/Provider/Style/All.html

Web Etiquette by Tim Berners-Lee, last updated May 1995, available at:
http://www.w3.org/hypertext/WWW/Provider/Style/Etiquette

Style Guide for Online Hypertext by Alan Richmond (NASA GSFC), available at: *http://guinan.gsfc.nasa.gov/Style.html*

Elements of HTML Style by Jonathan Cohen, available at: *http://www.book.uci.edu/Staff/StyleGuide.html*

Microsoft offers a number of documents that provide support of HTML authoring for the Internet Explorer. Probably most valuable is **A Complete List of HTML Tags for Microsoft Internet Explorer 3.0**, available at: *http://microsoft.com/intdev/author/html30/ie30html.htm*

Netscape's HTML resources for use with the Navigator include a number of documents, some also referenced here, indexed at: *http://home.netscape.com/assist/net_sites/index.html*

World Wide Web Consortium's (W3C) **HTML 3.0 Specification** available at: *http://www.w3.org/hypertext/WWW/MarkUp/html3/CoverPage.html*

World Wide Web Consortium's (W3C) **HTML 3.2 overview** (full specification draft document expected in July 1996) available at: *http://www.w3.org/hypertext/WWW/MarkUp/Wilbur/*

One of the most valuable free HTML references on the Internet is **The HTML Reference Library** by Stephen Le Hunte. This is a very extensive Windows 3.1, or alternatively, Windows 95, Help System for HTML. It is a gold mine of information and is available for download from: *ftp://ftp.swan.ac.uk/pub/in.coming/htmlib*. You may also be placed on a mailing list to be notified of updates to the library by sending an e-mail request to: *cmlehune@swan.ac.uk*.

There are also a number of other good books on the Web and HTML authoring. Among them are

The World Wide Web Complete Reference by Rick Stout, published 1996 by Osborne/McGraw-Hill.

Beyond HTML by Richard Karpinski, published 1996 by Osborne/McGraw-Hill.

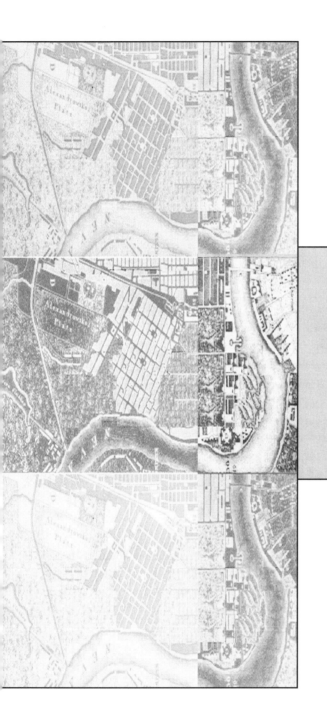

Creating Your Own FrontPage Templates

As you have been working with FrontPage, you have probably had some ideas for FrontPage templates that you wished were available. If you are setting up an intranet, this is especially true, because it makes excellent sense to have a template for each part of the organization to use to get a consistent web across the company. In any situation where several similar webs are needed, it makes sense to use a template to create them. If you are creating a large web with a number of pages that look alike—like the second-level and third-level pages in the Fantasy Travel web created earlier in this book—it makes sense to create a page template that will speed up the process. Finally, since there are no templates with tables or frames, it's possible that templates for these could be valuable to you.

In this chapter you'll look at the types of templates and their common characteristics, and then see how to build the different types. Building templates does not require programming, as does creating your own wizards, but templates do require considerable file manipulation—making sure the right files are in the right place. This chapter will spend some time making the file management clear and leading you through complete examples so you can see how templates are built.

Types of Templates

Templates are model or prototype webs or web pages, identical in every detail to an actual web or web page. The only thing that distinguishes them is that they are in a special directory or folder. You can view a template in a browser and use it as you can any other web or web page. In fact, a template is just a web or web page that has been set aside to serve as a model for other webs or web pages.

Because they are stored in different directories, think of web templates and page templates as two distinct types of templates, although there are many similarities. *Page templates* create a single page that becomes part of a separately created web. A page template is a single .HTM file. A *web template* creates one or more interconnected pages within a full FrontPage web, which means that it includes all of the directory structure that is a part of FrontPage. In both cases, though, you create

the web or the page in the same way that you would create any other web or page. When the web or page is the way you want it, you then place it in a special directory set up for templates with the extension .TEM. For example, Test.tem is a directory or folder containing the files for a template named "Test." The files within the template folder are just the normal .HTM HTML web files plus an .INF template information file.

FrontPage Directory Structure

The .TEM template folders are stored in different directories depending on whether they are pages or webs. Where these directories are depends on how you installed FrontPage and requires an understanding of the FrontPage directory structure.

FrontPage has two primary directories. One is called the FrontPage *root* directory and has the name "Microsoft FrontPage." The other directory is called the FrontPage *server* directory and has the name "FrontPage Webs." During installation you are asked where you want to place these directories. The default is to place the FrontPage root directory under the Program Files directory so it has the path:

C:\Program Files\Microsoft FrontPage

Also, by default, the server directory is placed directly under your drive's root directory and so has the path:

C:\FrontPage Webs

The FrontPage server directory contains the Content subdirectory, which stores all of the FrontPage webs that you create. It is *not* used to store templates, but comes into play when you create them, as you'll see later in this chapter. The FrontPage root directory is used to store templates and is central to the current discussion.

If you don't remember where you or someone else placed the FrontPage root directory during installation, you can find that information in the Frontpg.ini file, which is in your Windows directory. You can use Notepad to open this file. When you do that, look for the [FrontPage 1.1] section. In the line immediately under that heading you should see something like

FrontPageRoot=C:\Program Files\Microsoft FrontPage

as shown in Figure 10-1. Of course, your path may be different.

10

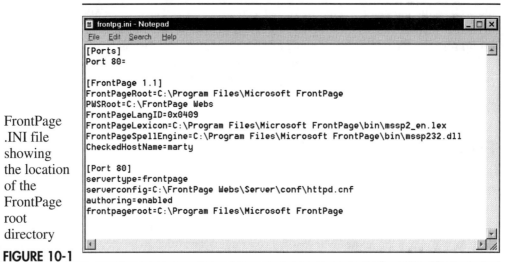

FrontPage
.INI file
showing
the location
of the
FrontPage
root
directory

FIGURE 10-1

Within the FrontPage root directory are two subdirectories named "Pages" and "Webs." The Pages subdirectory is used to contain all of the page templates and wizards, as you can see in Figure 10-2, and the Webs subdirectory contains all of the web templates and wizards.

Open your Pages subdirectory now, and then open one of the .TEM template folders. Within the template folder you should see two files. One of these files is an .HTM web file that, if you double-click on it, will open your default browser and display a normal web page. In any other directory, this file would be considered just another web page; there is nothing to distinguish it except the directory it is in. The other file within the template folder is an .INF template information file. Look at it next.

The .INF Information File

The .INF template information file is used to hold descriptive information about the template. It is similar to a Windows .INI file and is read by the FrontPage Editor and FrontPage Explorer when they are working with templates. The .INF file must have the same name as the .TEM folder it is in, so the Test.tem folder will contain the Test.inf file.

In the Pages directory, open the Agenda.tem folder, and then double-click on the Agenda.inf file. If the .INF file type is not associated with an application that can

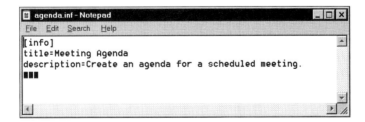

Microsoft
FrontPage
directory
and its
Pages
subdirectory
containing
templates

■ FIGURE 10-2

read it on your computer, select the Windows Notepad as that application. Notepad will open and display the file's short contents, like this:

The Information File [info] Section

The .INF information file will always have an [info] section with at least two items in it—the title of the template and its description—as you just saw. These items are used in the New Web or New Page dialog boxes to provide the name of the template and its description (as you can see next).

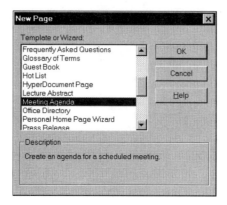

The three black boxes at the bottom are an end-of-file mark and are not important. If you look at a number of the template files, you'll see several that don't have them and they work fine. If the .INF file is not there, FrontPage uses the base name of the template folder ("Test" if the template folder is Test.tem) as the title and leaves the description blank.

The format of the .INF file is important and must match what you saw earlier. There must be a section named [info], and it must contain the title and description lines spelled correctly and with the equal signs. Whatever is on the right of the equal sign is data and will appear in the New dialog box. Each of the fields in the [info] section can be up to 255 characters long, including the attribute name ("title" and "description") and equal sign. As a practical matter, though, to be completely visible within the New Page dialog box, the title should be fewer than 30 characters, and the description should be fewer than 100 characters. Under most circumstances, this file will automatically be created for you, as you will see in later sections of this chapter.

IP: *If you do have to create an .INF file, the easiest way is to copy an existing file and change the name, title, and description.*

For page templates, which are displayed in the FrontPage Editor, only the [info] section of the .INF file is used. For web templates, which are displayed in the FrontPage Explorer, the .INF file can have three additional sections that are used

when the template is loaded into a server. These sections are a [FileList] section, a [MetaInfo] section, and a [TaskList] section.

The Information File [FileList] Section

The [FileList] section, which is shown in Figure 10-3, allows you to tell the FrontPage Explorer how you want the files in the template stored in a web. If you do not include a [FileList], the FrontPage Explorer loads all of the files in the .TEM directory, but does nothing with any subdirectories. The filenames in the .TEM directory are converted to all lowercase and become URLs in the web. Also, any .JPG or .GIF files in the .TEM directory are placed in the Images subdirectory of the web. You need to include the [FileList] section if you have any of the following situations:

- You have subdirectories to the .TEM directory containing files you want in the web.

- You want to specify the URL and/or the case it uses.

- You want to specify the specific files in the .TEM directory to be placed in the web (files in the .TEM directory and not in [FileList] are ignored).

```
custsupp.inf - Notepad                                          _ □ ✕
File  Edit  Search  Help
[info]
title=Customer Support Web
description=Create a web to improve your customer support services, parti◁
[FileList]
buglist.htm=
bugrep.htm=
cusuaftr.htm=
cusuahdr.htm=
cusucfrm.htm=
cusufoot.htm=
cusuhead.htm=
cusupost.htm=
cususrch.htm=
cusutoc.htm=
discuss.htm=
download.htm=
faq.htm=
feedback.htm=
footer.htm=
header.htm=
images\scrnshot.gif=images/scrnshot.gif
images\undercon.gif=images/undercon.gif
index.htm=
```

An .INF information file with a [FileList]

FIGURE 10-3

■ You want the files to go to directories in the web other than the root directory for the .HTM files and the images subdirectory for the .JPG and .GIF files. The other available subdirectories are _private and cgi-bin.

When you use the [FileList], you must list all of the files you want transferred. If you do not want to change the filename or the path, list just the filename with an equal sign after it, as you saw in Figure 10-3. If you want to specify the path, you need to switch from the MS-DOS/Windows use of the backslash between subdirectories on the left of the file list to the URL use of a slash between subdirectories on the right side, again, as shown in Figure 10-3.

 OTE: *While all of the examples of page templates that have images with them in FrontPage 1.1 have an Images subdirectory, the subdirectory is not required. It is recommended that web templates use the Images subdirectory for any image files.*

The Information File [MetaInfo] Section

The [MetaInfo] section can be used to store configuration variables used in the Substitution bot (see the discussion of the Substitution bot in Chapter 7). In this way the [MetaFile] section supplies the custom configuration variables that would otherwise have to be manually loaded into the Parameters tab of the Web Settings dialog box for each web. For example, you might provide the following company information for all users of a template:

```
[MetaInfo]
CompanyName=Fantasy Travel
CompanyAddress=1234 West Bayside Drive, Seattle, WA 98123
CompanyPhone=(206) 555-1234 or (800) 555-1234
```

The Information File [TaskList] Section

The [TaskList] section is used to provide a list of tasks to be placed in the FrontPage To Do List for a web template. The tasks in the list have the following format:

```
Number=Task|Priority|Template|URL|Bookmark|Description
```

The elements in the task list are separated by a vertical bar and are described in Table 10-1. Figure 10-4 shows a To Do List Task Details dialog box in which you can see how the elements are used.

 IP: *Adding the To Do tasks to a web template adds significantly to its value and can reduce the amount of support that is needed to help organizations use your template.*

Home Page Renaming

As a default, FrontPage names the home page in its webs Index.htm. On an NCSA server, the name "Index.htm" is implied and can be left off the URL for a web. For example, the URL *http:www.fairmountain.com/wine* opens the Index.htm page in the Wine web on the Fairmountain server. Depending on the server to which the web

Element	Description	Comments
Number	A unique number or a key	For example, "t01," "t02," "t03," and so on
Task	A short task description	A 3- or 4-word phrase used as the Task name
Priority	An integer describing relative importance	1 = High, 2 = Medium, 3 = Low
Template	Name of template	Used in the Created By field
URL	The URL for the task	The page or image that the task refers to
Bookmark	The bookmark for the task	The location on the page where work is required, in the form *#bookmark*
Description	Description of task	A longer description of what needs to be done (*cannot* contain new-line characters)

Description of [TaskList] Elements

TABLE 10-1

10

Task Details ✕

Task Name: Replace Logo Image

Priority
◉ High
○ Medium
○ Low

Assign To: Marty

Created By: Marty (Corporate Presence Web Wizard) on 05/08/96 at 14:34:20
Modified By: (Has not been modified)
Completed: No
Linked To: _private/logo.htm

Description:

replace the image on this page with your logo image

OK   Cancel   Help

To Do List
Task
Details
dialog box

FIGURE 10-4

is eventually uploaded, the implied name for a home page can differ. On a CERN server it normally is Welcome.htm, and on a Windows NT server it is Default.htm. When the FrontPage Explorer creates a web from a web template, it will automatically rename any file named "Index.htm" to the name appropriate for the current server. The FrontPage Explorer, though, *does* not *change any links to the home page.* To use the automatic renaming feature, you can make all links to the home page be a special ./ (period-slash) link that will force the server to locate the correct home page. If you do not want to use the automatic renaming feature, put the following line in the [info] section of the .INF information file:

```
NoIndexRenaming=1
```

Building Templates

Depending on whether you are building a single page template or a web template, the procedures vary. Therefore, to get a feeling for both of these, build one of each in the following sections.

Creating Single Page Templates

Building a single page template is simplicity itself. All you do is create a normal web page with the material you want on it, and then save it as a template. That's all there is to it! Before you go on to the next section, though, try it for yourself:

1. If they aren't already, load the FrontPage Personal Web Server and the FrontPage Explorer.

2. In the FrontPage Explorer, open the Fantasy Travel web, and open the Second-Level page in the FrontPage Editor.

3. Look at the existing page, and ask yourself what is standard about this page that should go on a template that will make creating a number of similar pages as easy as possible.

   The header, navbar, and footer are obvious. The line and the "Outside Sources" heading are pretty good bets. The page title ("CRUISES") and section titles (the first of which is "ALASKA") and a sample section would help preserve a consistent style.

4. From the Edit menu choose Select All to select all of the contents of the Second-Level page. You are getting more than you want, but it will be easier to delete what you don't want than to select just what you do want.

5. Click on Copy, click on New page, and click on Paste. Remove the image of the ship, change the word "CRUISES" to "TITLE," the word "ALASKA" to "DESTINATION 1," and the three lines that were under "ALASKA" to "Option 1," "Option 2," and "Option 3." Copy the "DESTINATION" heading and the three Option lines and paste them over "SOUTH PACIFIC" and its two option lines (you'll be replacing two option lines with three). Renumber the second "DESTINATION" to "2." Leave the word "Note:" but delete the rest of that line. Finally, delete the three graphics that were used as external links. When you are done, the top part of your page should look like Figure 10-5.

6. If you want your template to have a background image like the Second-Level page that already exists, open the File menu, choose Page Properties, click on Background Image, select **images/blutxtr1.jpg**, and click on OK twice.

10

7. From the File menu, click on Save As, type **Second-Level Template** for the Page Title, type **sectem.htm** for the Page URL, and click on As Template. The Save As Template dialog box will open as shown here:

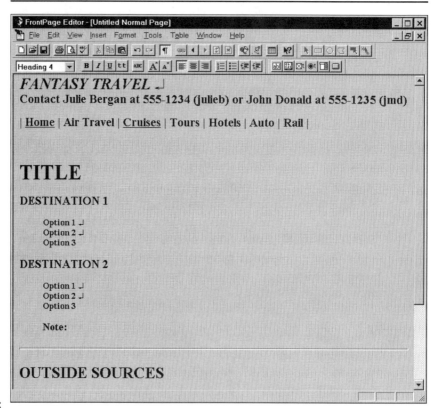

Page prepared for a template

FIGURE 10-5

8. Copy the Title to the Name box, type **Create a second-level page where the options of a type of travel are listed**, and click on OK.

9. You'll be asked if you want to save to a particular directory. This should be the Pages directory discussed earlier. If so, click on Yes. Otherwise, use Browse to find the correct directory and then click on Yes.

10. Close the template file in the FrontPage Editor, open the Windows Explorer, and locate the new template. If you used the default directory structure, it will be in **C:\Program Files\Microsoft FrontPage\pages**, like this:

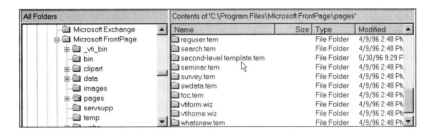

11. Open the Second-Level Template.tem. You should see three files: the Blutxtr1.jpg background image file, the .HTM web file, and the .INF information file. Double-click on the .INF file. It should open as you see here:

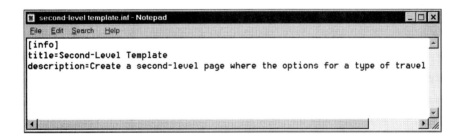

12. Close Notepad and return to the FrontPage Editor. Open the File menu, choose New, and scroll the Template Or Wizard list box until you can see the Second-Level Template, as shown here:

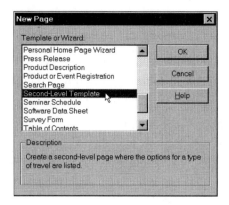

13. Double-click on Second-Level Template, and a new page based on your template will open ready for you to customize. When you are ready, save the page with a unique name and by clicking on OK to save it as a part of your web. When asked if you want the background image file to replace or be replaced by the existing file of the same name, allow it to be replaced so the existing file which is referred to by the original Second-Level page will also be used by your new page.

14. Close the FrontPage Editor, and then close the Fantasy Travel web.

With your template you should be able to substantially reduce the time it will take to create additional Second-Level pages, and all of the pages created that way will be very consistent.

Constructing Web Templates

Constructing a web template, while inherently more complex than a single page template, is not much more difficult to create. Basically you create and save a web as you normally would. You can then either use a special program to copy the new web to a web template, or you can manually copy the files. The next exercise will show you how to use both the manual steps and the special program to build a web template based on a table for displaying budgeting information.

1. From the FrontPage Explorer create a new web based on the Normal Web template. Name it **BudgetTemplate**. When it opens, double-click on the Normal Page to open the FrontPage Editor.

2. In the FrontPage Editor, type **BUDGETING HOME PAGE**, format it as a Heading 1, place a clipart image on the left of the heading, as you can see in Figure 10-6, and then use Save As to save the page. For the Page Title, type **Budget Home**, leave the Page URL as Index.htm, and then click on OK. Answer Yes to save the image in the web.

3. Click on New page, type **DEPARTMENTAL BUDGET**, format it as a Heading 2, press DOWN ARROW to go to the next line, type | **Home** | **Department 1** | **Department 2** |, format it as Heading 4, select the word "Home," and link it to the Budget Home page. Save the page with a page title of **Included Header** and a URL of **Inclhead.htm** and click on OK. Your Included Header page should look like this:

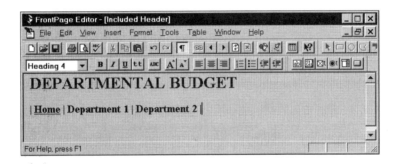

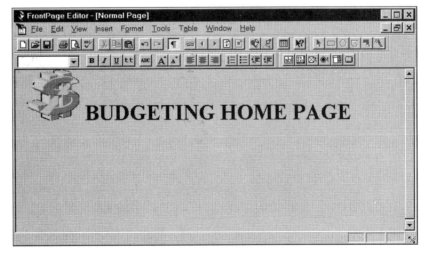

Home page
for
budgeting
template

FIGURE 10-6

4. Open a new page, open the Insert menu, choose Bot, and double-click on Include. In the Include Bot properties dialog box, browse to find and double-click on the Included Header, and then click on OK. The Included Header should appear on your new page.

5. On the line immediately following the header, type **DEPARTMENT 1**, format it as Heading 1, and center it.

6. Move down to the next line and insert an 8-row by 6-column table. Make the Border Size **3**, the Cell Padding **3**, and leave the Cell Spacing 2. Turn off (uncheck) Width and click on OK.

7. Type in the top row and left column as shown in Figure 10-7, and then save the page with a Page Title of **Department 1** and a page URL of **Depart1.htm**.

8. From the Edit menu choose Select All, click on Copy, open a new page, click on Paste, change the title to **Department 2**, and then save the page with the title of **Department 2** and URL of **Depart2.htm**.

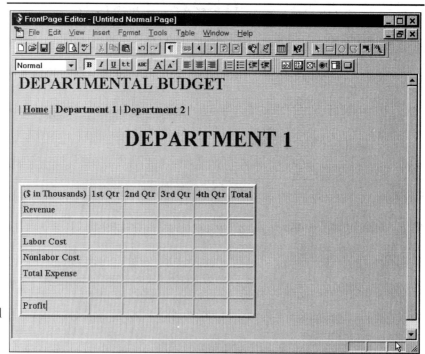

Departmental budget page

FIGURE 10-7

9. Open the Included Header page, and set the links to both the Department 1 and Department 2 references in the navbar. Resave this page.

10. Open the Budget Home page, and insert the Table of Contents bot under the title. Accept the defaults and click on OK. Save the Budget Home page and close the FrontPage Editor.

11. Try the web in a browser to make sure all is well. When you are done, close the browser.

At this point, you have completed a fairly complex web, as shown in Figure 10-8. It is important to have several pages, two bots, and an image in this example to see how all of these elements are handled. In two later sections you'll turn that web into a web template, using manual procedures in one section, and using a program in the FrontPage Developer's Kit in the other section. First, look at the file structure and see what files are in which directory.

A Web's Directory and File Structure

Figure 10-9 shows the directories created for a web by FrontPage and the files in the "root" directory. All four page (.HTM) files are there plus an access control file (#haccess.ctl). Also, there are eight directories. The use of each directory is shown in Table 10-2. Open each directory as you read through the table.

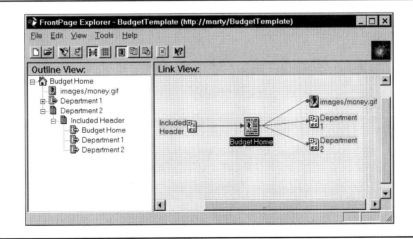

Completed
Budget web

FIGURE 10-8

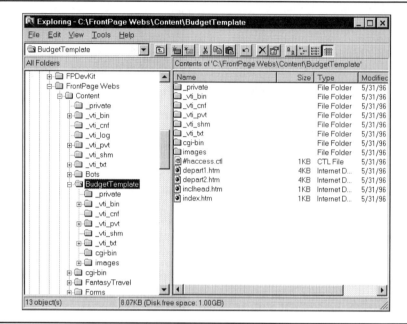

Web
directory
structure

FIGURE 10-9

Since you need to make copies of some of these files when you are creating a template, you need to have an understanding of this directory structure. Fortunately, you only need to worry about what is in _private, _vti_shm, cgi-bin, images, and the web's root directory (but that's still five of the nine possibilities).

Manually Creating a Web Template

Manually creating a web template means creating the necessary directories, copying the correct files to them, and then manually creating the .INF file. Do that as explained in the following steps.

> **OTE:**   *The instructions given here for manually creating a web template, while referencing the specific files in the current example, are all the steps needed in the general case to create a web template. Some of the steps are not needed in this example, but are included for reference.*

1. Using the Windows Explorer, locate the Webs subdirectory with the FrontPage root directory. By default this is C:\Program Files\Microsoft

Directory	Contents
_private	Pages that you don't want available to a browser or to searches; for example, included pages
_vti_bin	FrontPage-created common gateway interface (CGI) programs for controlling browse time behavior, administrator, and author operations on the server
_vti_cnf	A configuration page for every page in the web, containing the name of the page, the created-by and modified-by names, and the creation and modification dates, among other variables
_vti_pvt	Several subdirectories with both the current and historical To Do List files, meta-information for the web, and the dependency database
_vti_shm	The source page for every page in the web that contains bots; the source is the page *without* the bots
_vti_txt	Text indexes for use by the Search bot
cgi-bin	Custom CGI scripts and other executable pages
images	All images associated with a web

FrontPage
Web
Directory
Structure

TABLE 10-2

FrontPage\webs. Open the Webs directory so its contents are displayed in the right pane of the Windows Explorer.

2. Right-click in the right pane, choose New, and then select Folder. Type **Budget.tem** and press ENTER.

3. Still in the Windows Explorer, locate the new BudgetTemplate subdirectory within the FrontPage Webs\Content directory (by default this is C:\FrontPage Webs\Content\BudgetTemplate), and open it in the right pane.

4. Select the Images subdirectory and all the .HTM files (do not copy the #haccess.ctl). While holding down CTRL, drag the files and directory to the new Budget.tem directory. Holding down CTRL is important, because otherwise you will move the files and not copy them.

5. Locate and open the _vti_shm subdirectory within the original BudgetTemplate directory (by default C:\FrontPage Webs\Content\BudgetTemplate_vti_shm). Select all the .HTM files, and while holding down CTRL, drag the files to the new Budget.tem directory. When asked if you would like to replace an existing file, click on Yes in response to all such queries in this step.

OTE: *The web's root directory holds the expanded version of all page files (the version used in a browser), while the _vti_shm subdirectory holds the source version of all pages that have bots. For templates, you want only the source version. So the pages on which you use bots will have their source version copied over the expanded version.*

6. Open the Custsupp.tem subdirectory within the Webs directory (C:\Program Files\Microsoft FrontPage\webs\custsupp.tem). Select the Custsupp.inf file, and while holding down CTRL, drag it to the Budget.tem directory to copy the file there.

7. In the Budget.tem directory, select the Custsupp.inf file and rename it **Budget.inf**.

8. Double-click on Custsupp.inf to open it in Windows Notepad. Change the title to **Budgeting Web**. Change the description to **Create a quarterly departmental budget**. Replace all of the .HTM files in the FileList with the depart1.htm, depart2.htm, inclhead.htm, and index.htm files that are in the budgeting web. Finally, on *both* sides of the equal sign, replace the image file named "scrnshot.gif" with the name of the image file that you used. When you are done, your Budget.inf file should look like Figure 10-10. Save and close your .INF file.

OTE: *You only need a [FileList] section in the .INF file if you have files in one or more of the images, cgi-bin, or _private subdirectory.*

9. Although it isn't necessary in this example, if you use either the _private or cgi-bin subdirectory, you will need to copy it to the template directory. It is possible that you can have bots on the pages in the _private subdirectory, in which case there will be a _vti_shm subdirectory under it with the source files that you want to place in the _private subdirectory

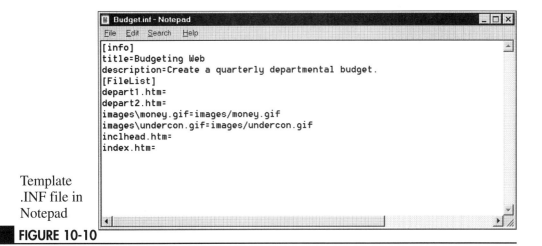

Template
.INF file in
Notepad

FIGURE 10-10

(*not* _vti_shm) of your template. The easiest way to do this, if it is
necessary, is to copy the _private and cgi-bin subdirectories to your
template directory. If there is a _vti_shm subdirectory under _private,
copy its contents to _private, accept any replacement, and delete
_viti_shm.

10. Open the FrontPage Explorer, select New Web from the File menu, and
you should see your Budgeting Web displayed in the New Web dialog
box, like this:

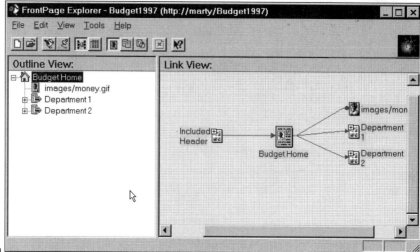

Budget
web
created
from the
template

FIGURE 10-11

11. Click on OK to create a new web based on the template. Give the new web some name like "Budget 1997," and it will open in the Explorer as shown in Figure 10-11 (shown above). Open the home page in the FrontPage Editor. Everything should be there, just as you originally created it.

12. Close the FrontPage Editor, open the new web in a browser, and click on one of the department links in the table of contents to see if it works. It should appear as shown in Figure 10-12.

13. Close the browser and delete the new web you just created.

If your new web does not work as you would expect, look at the files in the template, and make sure that all your files are placed where they should be and that the .INF file is as shown earlier. Those are about the only things that can go wrong.

Automatically Creating a Web Template

The FrontPage Developer's Kit includes a program, Webtmpl.exe, that automatically does most of the work you just did in the last section. Before you burn this book, there are at least two good reasons for doing the manual approach first. One, it familiarizes you with the web structure of FrontPage and how webs and web templates are stored, so that you are in a position to check what the program does.

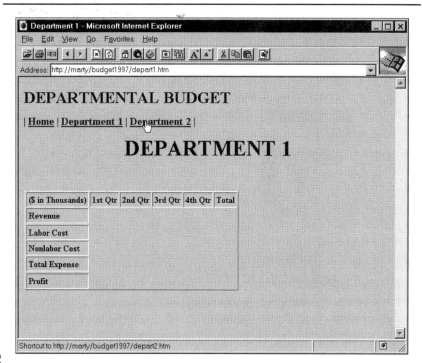

New
budget web
in a browser

FIGURE 10-12

Two, the Webtmpl.exe program is just a simple utility that requires the web from which you want to make a template to be on your computer in MS-DOS/Windows format (not UNIX). In other words, you need to check that what the utility does is correct.

The Webtmpl.exe program lets you select an existing web on your computer from which a web will be made. It then creates the template web in the correct directory; copies all the .HTM files in the original web's root directory plus the images, cgi-bin, and _private subdirectories; properly handles bots; and creates the .INF file including any configuration variables and active To Do List tasks. So while you do need to check it, the program does a lot for you.

This program is in the FrontPage Developer's Kit, which is available as a free download from *http://microsoft.com/frontpage/freestuff/fs_fp_sdk.htm*. Download it now so it is available with the following steps.

1. After downloading Fpdevkit.zip, unzip it with PKUnzip, WinZip, or some other program, being sure to use whatever your unzip program requires to

have it create the directories that are included in the zip file (-d for PKUnzip).

2. When the file has been unzipped, open the directories so you can see the Utility and Webtmpl directories and the Webtmpl.exe program, like this:

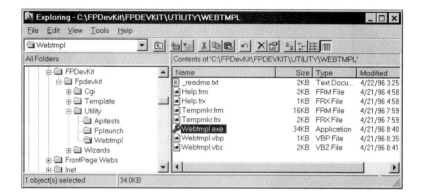

3. Double-click on Webtmpl.exe to start the program. The FrontPage Web Template Maker will open, as you can see in Figure 10-13.

4. Click on BudgetTemplate, change the title to **Budgeting Web**, the name to **Budgeting**, and the Description to **Create a departmental budgeting web**.

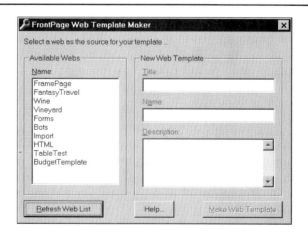

FrontPage
Web
Template
Maker

FIGURE 10-13

5. Click on Make Web Template. In about the time it takes you to remove your hand from the mouse, the program will be done. Click on the Close button to get rid of it.

6. Open the Windows Explorer and under Webs, you should see the Budgeting.tem directory immediately beneath the Budget.tem directory you created earlier, as shown next. Notice how the _private and cgi-bin directories were copied in this case, although there is nothing in them.

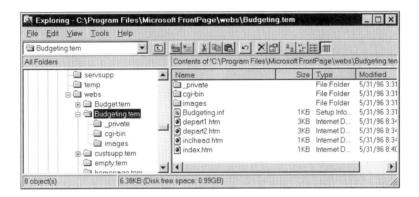

7. Double-click on Budgeting.inf to open it in Notepad. Except for the different wording for the title and description and the fact that the filenames are repeated (which is not necessary), it is the same as the .INF file that you created.

8. Open the FrontPage Explorer and click on New web. The New Web dialog box will now show two Budgeting Web templates. If you wish, create a new web based on this template, and then open it in a browser. You should see that the results are the same as you saw earlier.

Creating your own templates is another very significant bit of leverage that FrontPage gives you to quickly and effectively create webs.

10

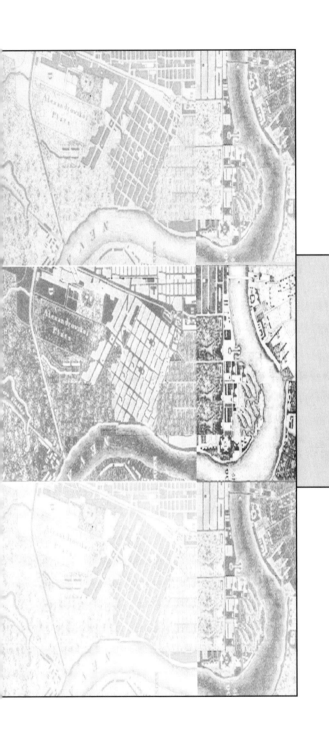

Setting Up an Intranet Web Site

Just as the Internet and the World Wide Web are an exploding phenomenon, so are LANs and intranets. And as this growth increases, many expect the use of intranets to exceed the Internet. The competitive success of a company often depends on internal communication and the ability to quickly share information—two major benefits of intranets. But like any new technology, and to some degree philosophy, there are and will be many opportunities to stumble. How a company implements an intranet may be even more important than the decision to do so.

This chapter will look at intranets—what they are, why they are needed, and how to set them up—both in terms of the hardware and software needed to make them function, and the content they should provide. You will learn about intranets, how they can help your business or organization, and how to create an intranet by using FrontPage. This chapter is meant to be an introduction to a subject on which numerous books will be written.

What Is an Intranet Site?

With the focus on the World Wide Web and connecting to the world over the Internet (a wide area network, or WAN), the fact that the same protocols and technology can be used over a local area network (LAN) can be overlooked. With the FrontPage Personal Web Server and a LAN, you can create your own web to link computers in an office, between buildings, or even among company sites around the world. FrontPage, with its Personal Web Server, offers some real advantages over other means of implementing an intranet.

While the *Internet* is a network that provides access to information outside an organization, an *intranet* is a network that does exactly the same thing within an organization. An intranet may be as simple as two computers networked in a home office, or as complex as a network linking the offices of a global corporation. In the latter case, an intranet could link the computers within the organization, while the Internet could be used to connect the various intranets (or private lines could be used).

Networking computers to share information is, of course, not a new concept. Networked computers can be found in virtually every medium-to-large business today and in many smaller ones. When networked, the resources on any computer can be shared by any other computer on the network. With Windows 95, the addition of a network interface card can turn any PC into either a network server or a workstation. For larger networks, specialized software, such Novell's NetWare, has traditionally been required to effectively allow computers to share information.

Classical networking involves the sharing of files and some hardware devices such as printers, and more recently the use of e-mail. An intranet with FrontPage and the technology of the Web significantly enhances the functionality of a LAN or a corporate WAN by adding the ability to read and interact with a large set of documents that are easily created and kept up to date.

As was explained in Chapter 1, the Internet and the World Wide Web are built upon three software technologies:

- **TCP/IP** (Transfer Control Protocol/Internet Protocol), which is the underlying technology of the Internet for the exchange of information and the identification of parts of the network

- **HTTP** (HyperText Transfer Protocol), which handles the actual transmission of Web documents

- **HTML** (HyperText Markup Language), which is the programming language of the Web

These same technologies are used to implement an intranet, and they must be added to the networking software that is already in place. HTTP and HTML are used only by the web server and the browser, and do not affect the classical networking software. TCP/IP, on the other hand, is in direct competition with classical networking protocols such as IPX/SPX or NetBEUI on Intel-based computers. TCP/IP can be used instead of or in addition to other protocols, and setting it up can be one of the major pitfalls. The objective, of course, is to have the protocols operate in harmony to perform all of the necessary networking functions.

One of the problem areas with classical networking was linking different types of computers, such as PCs or Macintosh, Hewlett-Packard, or UNIX computers. Each operating system (or platform) requires its own specialized software, which isn't always compatible between systems. An intranet built with TCP/IP, HTTP, and HTML doesn't have the compatibility problems of other networking systems. The early support of the federal government ensured the widespread adoption of TCP/IP as a network protocol, and HTTP servers and HTML browsers are available for virtually every platform. For organizations that have acquired a variety of computer hardware, creating an intranet has never been easier. While a simple file-sharing network allows files to be accessed between computers, the three Internet

11

technologies allow much greater interactivity by use of hypertext links, searches, and forms. Some of these features are available with products such as NetWare, but at greater cost and complexity. A FrontPage intranet presents a middle course of power and economy.

 OTE: *For an example of an intranet that uses Microsoft's Office family, visit the Volcano Coffee Company at* http://www.microsoft.com/msoffice /intranet/volcano/index.htm.

Why Have an Intranet?

The reasons for an intranet are as varied as the organizations creating it, but the common purposes are to communicate with and involve the members of the organization. The communication aspect is obvious. The intranet can replace newsletters, reports, lists of job openings, manuals, procedures, employee guidelines, meeting schedules, details of benefit plans, and lunch menus. Almost anything that is written or graphic and has an audience of more than a couple people is a candidate for the intranet. The benefits of using the intranet are substantial:

- An intranet document can be put up when convenient for the creator, and read when convenient for the reader.

- Readers can keep and conveniently file an intranet document, or they can just read it and discard it, knowing the source document will be there for some time.

- The documents can be simple text or full multimedia. By including multimedia, documents can be more inviting to open and read.

- The communication can be one-way, from the creator to the reader, or it can include forms and discussion groups to let the reader communicate back to the creator.

- The documents can be easily indexed and searched, making the information they contain easier to find and use.

- The cost of printing, distributing, and maintaining manuals, procedures, and guidelines is reduced, as are some fax and express delivery expenses.

■ Information can be shared over many different computers and workstations, not just PCs. The Internet protocols and technology have been implemented on most computers, giving them the ability to attach to an intranet.

One of the biggest benefits, though, and the second major reason for using an intranet, is that it facilitates the involvement of more members of the organization in the organization's activities. The reasoning is that if you make it easier to locate, read, excerpt, file, and dispose of documents, more people will use them and acquire the knowledge they contain. If you make it easier to comment on and participate in the creation of something that can be put on an intranet, more people will. If you provide easy access and use of indexing and search capabilities, more archival information will be directly sought by end users. If you add multimedia and color graphics and thereby make a document more fun and interesting, more people will read it. If you allow many different types of computers and workstations to connect to an intranet, more people will be able to participate.

Simply stated, an intranet greatly facilitates the dissemination of information within, the communication among, and the involvement of members of an organization.

What to Put on an Intranet

The decision on what to put on an intranet is one of the most difficult involving the intranet and very much depends on the character and philosophy of the organization. How open does your organization want to be, and how much security do you need? What does the company want to do with their intranet? Disseminating relatively simple information, such as newsletters, administrative manuals and procedures, and lunch menus, is not a problem. On the other hand, disseminating financial information, marketing reports, and corporate plans may well be more difficult.

Therefore, the answers to these questions can be found beginning at the top of a company. Here a policy needs to be set on how open the company wants to be with its employees. This broad policy then needs to be translated into specific examples of documents in each of the major areas of the company (marketing, production, finance, and so on) that are allowed on the intranet and those that are not. It is very easy to gloss over this issue in the crush of all the other issues, but unless this is clearly thought through and then delineated, problems can occur.

Once the policy is established, specific documents and their priority have to be identified. This is best done by a committee of users and providers. The users can

11

set out their needs and desires, and the providers can respond with their ability and willingness to satisfy the requests. Either group alone is liable to create an intranet that is not as effective as it might be.

With the committee constituted, they should look at all the documents the company produces that fit within the policy guidelines. For each document, the following questions should be answered:

- How wide an audience does it have?

- How often is it produced, and is that schedule supportable on the intranet?

- Do the layout and graphics lend themselves to the document being easily placed on the intranet?

- Does the addition of intranet features such as searching, forms, and hyperlinks make it a particularly attractive candidate?

- Are there any pressing needs to get the document up on the intranet?

- Is the document going to be revised soon?

Based on the answers to these questions, a prioritized list of documents to go on the intranet should be drawn up, and the documents created and placed on the intranet in their designated order. The review process should be repeated periodically to make sure the documents on the intranet should stay there and determine what new documents should be added.

Building a FrontPage Intranet

Building a FrontPage intranet is fairly simple. The first requirement is that you have a local area network (LAN) that supports the TCP/IP protocol. The specifics of setting up such a network are beyond the scope of this book. Two excellent sources of information on setting up LANs and networking are Tom Sheldon's *Encyclopedia of Networking,* and *The Windows NT Web Server Handbook*, which contains an excellent section on intranets (both published by Osborne/McGraw-Hill).

Once your LAN is functioning, you can use FrontPage as the basis for an intranet as small as two computers in the same office, or use it to link a number of computers in several remote locations. The limits on growth for your intranet will be determined by the number of users and the amount of traffic on the LAN. For several computers in an office, you do not need a dedicated server. In other words, the computer running FrontPage Personal Server can still be used for other tasks. As the number of users and network traffic grow, a computer will need to be dedicated to running the FrontPage Personal Server. At that point you may also want to switch from Windows 95 to Windows NT for your server operating system.

For larger intranets you should consider using Microsoft's Internet Information Server (IIS) as your HTTP server software. IIS is more powerful than FrontPage Personal Server and is an integral part of Windows NT 4.0. FrontPage and the FrontPage IIS Server Extensions are completely compatible with Windows NT 4.0. *The Windows NT Web Server Handbook* (Osborne/McGraw-Hill, 1996) mentioned previously is an excellent reference for creating an NT and Internet Information Server intranet or Internet Web server.

Installing TCP/IP on Your Network

The first step in building a FrontPage intranet on your local area network is to install the TCP/IP protocol. If you have a connection to the Internet, either through a dial-up or network connection, TCP/IP will already be installed and configured on your computer. If you need to install TCP/IP, follow these steps:

OTE: *If you are using a dial-up connection for the Internet, you may still need to install TCP/IP for your LAN, so you should go through the next set of steps just to check it out.*

1. Open the Start menu, click on Settings, and then select Control Panel.

2. When the Control Panel opens, double-click on the Network icon.

3. In the Network dialog box select the Configuration tab, if it's not already selected. Your Network dialog box should appear similar to Figure 11-1.

   In Figure 11-1 the NetBUI protocol is bound to both the network interface card and the Dial-Up Adapter (modem). Multiple protocols can be bound to these cards, so TCP/IP can be added without removing any existing protocols.

11

Network
dialog box
before
installing
TCP/IP

FIGURE 11-1

4. Click on Add. In the Select Network Component Type dialog box select Protocol, and click on Add again.

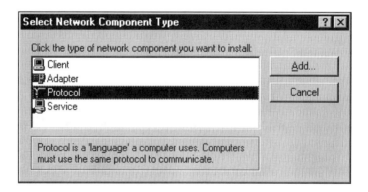

5. In the Select Network Protocol dialog box select Microsoft from the Manufacturers list box, and then select TCP/IP from the Network Protocols list box. Click on OK.

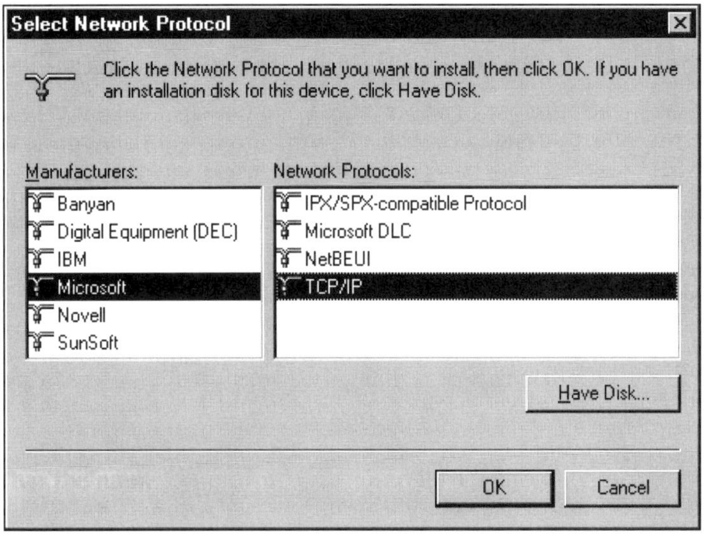

In a moment the Network dialog box will be redisplayed, showing that the TCP/IP protocol has been installed and bound to your installed adapters, as you can see in Figure 11-2.

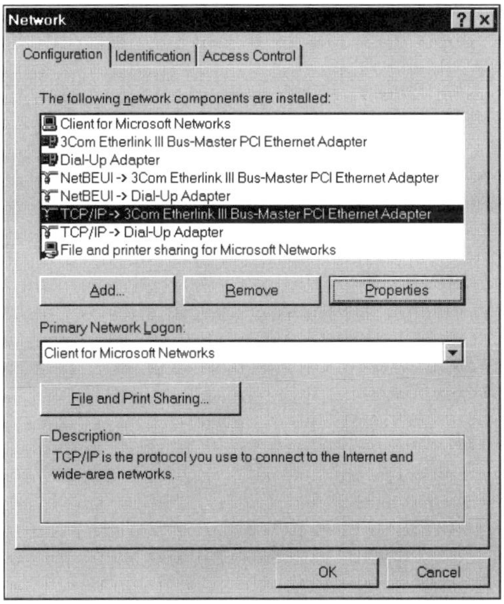

Network
dialog box
with
TCP/IP
installed

FIGURE 11-2

11

Configuring TCP/IP

You need to configure the TCP/IP protocol for each device it is bound to. For an intranet, the device is your network interface card. For a dial-up connection to the Internet, the device is the dial-up adapter. Configure your network card with these instructions:

1. In the Network dialog box, select the TCP/IP binding to your network card (in Figure 11-2 this is the line that reads "TCP/IP–>3Com Etherlink III…") and click on Properties. Your TCP/IP Properties dialog box will open, as shown in Figure 11-3.

2. In the TCP/IP Properties dialog box select the IP Address tab, if it's not already selected.

The IP (Internet Protocol) address is a group of four numbers that uniquely identify your computer on a TCP/IP network. For a dial-up connection to the Internet, your IP address will usually be assigned automatically by the server, as might be the case with large intranets using dedicated web servers. For small intranets using the FrontPage Personal Web Server, you need to specify an IP address. You should consult your network administrator to learn what IP address you should use. However, on a small TCP/IP network, you can basically make up your own number—*128.0.0.1,* for example. You could then increment the number for each computer—*128.0.0.2* for the next machine, and so on. As long as your computer does not try to use your IP addresses on the Internet (which it won't, if you use the dial-up adapter to connect to the Internet), you will not have a problem. The IP addresses you use for your network card will not affect your settings for your dial-up adapter.

An IP address is like a phone number. If you set up your own small phone system, you can use any phone numbers you want, but if you then connect your phone system to the outside world, you must use the phone numbers assigned by the outside authority.

OTE: *Do not use an IP address beginning with 127 (for example, 127.0.0.1), as this is reserved as a localhost, or loopback, address.*

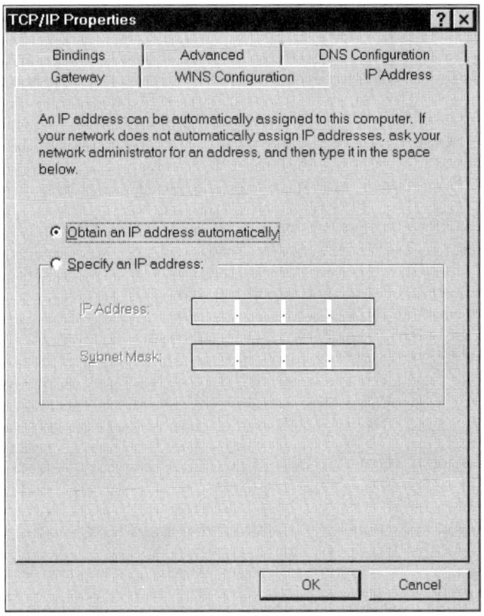

TCP/IP
Properties
dialog box

FIGURE 11-3

3. Click on Specify An IP Address, click on the left of the text box opposite IP Address, and type your IP address. If any number is fewer than three digits, you'll need to press RIGHT ARROW to move to the next block of numbers. If you don't have a normally assigned IP address, use the 128.0.0.n (n is a number between 1 and 255) set of numbers with 128.0.0.1 being the first. (Type **1280**, press RIGHT ARROW, type **0**, press RIGHT ARROW, and type **1** to get the address shown next.)

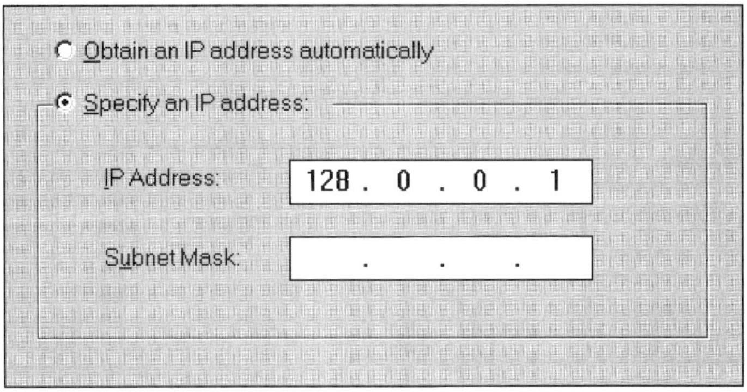

11

4. Select the Bindings tab. Client For Microsoft Networks should be selected, and File And Printer Sharing For Microsoft Networks should be selected, as you can see in Figure 11-4. Click on them if they are not.

5. Click on OK twice.

After changing your network settings, you must restart your computer for the changes to take effect. Make sure you save any open documents before restarting.

AUTION: *For TCP/IP on your dial-up adapter, you do not want to have File And Printer Sharing selected. This is for security. If you are connected to the Internet by use of your dial-up connection, it is possible, although unlikely, for others on the Internet to access your shared resources over the TCP/IP connection. You can still share resources with others on your network by using your LAN adapter.*

Using Your FrontPage Intranet

Once TCP/IP is configured properly on your network, accessing your FrontPage webs from any computer on the network is a simple process. First make sure the

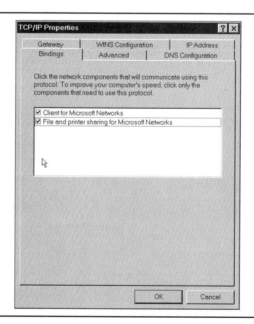

TCP/IP
Properties
bindings

FIGURE 11-4

FrontPage Personal Server is running on the computer that will be the server. Then start your web browser on one of the other computers on the network. To access a web, use the URL

http://computername/webname

where *computername* is the name of the computer running FrontPage Personal Server, and *webname* is the name of the web you want to open.

For example, I have two networked computers named "Marty" and "Marty2" using Windows 95 and Ethernet cards. Here are the steps I went through to bring up a FrontPage intranet:

1. Set up the TCP/IP protocol bound to the LAN adapters on both computers, as described earlier.

2. Restart both computers.

3. Start the FrontPage Personal Web Server on Marty.

4. Start a browser on Marty2, enter the address **marty/fantasytravel/**, and press ENTER. My Fantasy Travel Home page appears as shown in Figure 11-5.

Page received on an intranet

FIGURE 11-5

If your intranet doesn't immediately come up the first time you try, take heart, mine didn't either. Here is a list of troubleshooting questions:

- Does your network otherwise function normally between the two computers you are trying to use with an intranet? If not, you must solve your networking problems before trying to use an intranet. See your network administrator or other technical network reference.

- Has TCP/IP been successfully installed and bound to your LAN adapter (*not* just to your dial-up adapter)? Reopen your Network control panel to check this.

- Did you restart *both* computers after installing TCP/IP?

- Is the FrontPage Personal Web Server loaded on the machine where the webs are located? When you address this machine from the second machine, you should see the FrontPage Personal Web Server in the task bar momentarily go from "IDLE" to "BUSY."

- Have you entered the correct server name and web name in your browser? You can determine the server name by running the FrontPage TCP/IP Test. It will respond with the "Host name," as shown next, which is the server name to use in the address.

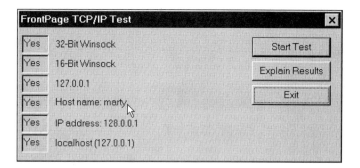

If you take a couple of minutes to make sure that each of the preceding questions is answered in the affirmative, your intranet will almost surely work. I made several errors, including forgetting to restart one of the computers and not spelling the web name correctly.

Security and Firewalls

Anytime you share resources over a network, the possibility exists that someone may access your files without your permission. The risk is greater when one or more computers on an intranet are also connected to the Internet. There are several things you can do to protect yourself and your files. One of the simplest, as mentioned previously, is to disable file and printer sharing for TCP/IP on your dial-up adapter. You can still share files over your LAN, but you have closed access to everyone on the Internet coming in through TCP/IP and your dial-up adapter.

Greater security can be achieved through the use of a firewall. A *firewall* is a computer that allows data to flow from an intranet to the Internet, but restricts the access from the Internet to the intranet. Firewalls fall into two main categories: proxy servers and packet filters.

Use of a *proxy server* means that every request and response must be examined by the proxy server. This can slow the response of your network, but the proxy server can also cache frequently requested information, thus speeding some responses. If the source of a request is a computer without permission to access your intranet, the proxy server will reject it.

Packet filtering passes or rejects IP packets based on the IP address that sent the packet. This allows you to configure your firewall to allow access from specific computers outside your intranet that you trust. This method isn't as secure as a proxy server, because it's possible for someone to duplicate a trusted IP address.

Books have been written on the subject of network security and how to implement it. If your intranet will be accessible to the outside world, you will need to take measures to protect your data. The books mentioned earlier in this chapter can provide a good place to start.

11

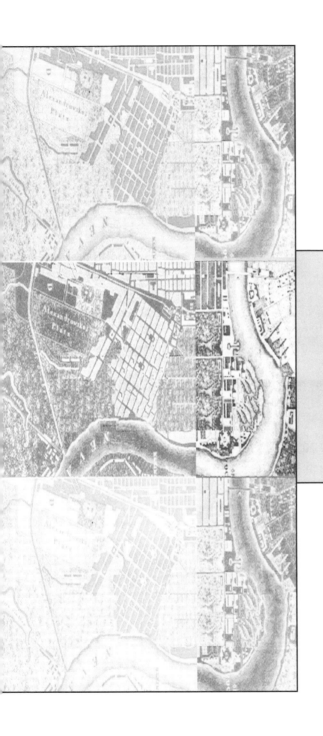

Publishing and Promoting Webs on the Internet

By now in this book, you have created your own webs with FrontPage and possibly put them on your intranet. Next you can make your efforts available to the millions of people worldwide who have access to the Internet. You do this by first publishing your web on a web server, a computer that is connected to the Internet. Then you promote your web site by using traditional and web-based advertising.

Publishing Your Web Pages

Unless you have your own server connected to the Internet, you will need to find an Internet service provider (ISP) who will rent you space on their web server for your web. Also, to get the full functionality of your web, your ISP should support the FrontPage Server Extensions.

Providing access to the Internet has become a very competitive field, and you should be able to find several ISPs in your area that you can choose from. You can find a local ISP by asking others, by looking in your regional newspapers and other periodicals, and even by looking in a recent phone book. You can also use the Internet. You can begin by using one of the many search engines available, such as Alta Vista (http://www.altavista.digital.com). Simply enter a search criterion such as "internet access providers [your state]" (include the quotes). Another Internet site with a list of providers is Yahoo (http://www.yahoo.com). Finally, Microsoft posts a list of ISPs with FrontPage Server Extensions at *http://www.microsoft.com/ frontpage/ispinfo/isphost.htm.* With a little searching, you should be able to locate several ISPs in your area. It is not necessary that your ISP be located close to you physically. Most of your transactions will occur over the Internet, and there are a number of national providers, such as Netcom (http://www.netcom.com) or AT&T's Easy World Wide Web Services (http://www.att.com), and AT&T offers the FrontPage Server Extensions as part of their service.

Generally an ISP will provide dial-up access to the Internet, as well as hard disk storage for webs. Many offer space for a personal (noncommercial) web as part of their basic package. The amount of hard disk space allowed for a personal web site varies. In many areas this basic service costs $20 to $30 a month with unlimited Internet access. (These rates are for 14.4 Kbps or 28.8 Kbps modems; rates for ISDN and cable modems are higher.)

Rates for commercial web sites can vary greatly, from \$30 to several hundred dollars a month, depending on the ISP, the amount of hard disk storage, and the bandwidth used. Bandwidth is the amount of data that is transferred from your web site over the ISP's Internet connection. For example, if your web is 1 megabyte (MB) in size and it was accessed 100 times in the course of a month, you would have used 100MB of bandwidth (or transfer bandwidth) in that month.

Another point to consider is whether you want to have your own domain name. Without your own domain name, your web's URL would begin with the ISP's domain name, such as *http://www.ispname.com/yourname*. With your own domain, your URL would be *http://www.yourname.com*. Your own domain is not really needed for a personal web site, but should be seriously considered for a commercial web. Your ISP can help you set up a domain name for your web site.

In deciding upon an ISP, you should be more concerned about the quality of the service than the price. The Internet is a little chaotic—new technologies (particularly in data transmission) are coming into play, and finding people who truly understand and can use these technologies is not always easy. Software doesn't always work as advertised, and keeping everything flowing smoothly sometimes requires a little "spit and baling wire." When evaluating an ISP, look at the design and features of their own web site, and contact others who have their webs on the ISP's server. Choosing the cheapest ISP could be an expensive decision in the long run if they don't provide the services you need, such as the FrontPage Server Extensions.

FrontPage Server Extensions

HTML used to be written by hand, by use of text editors such as Windows Notepad. When you wanted to include a form for the user to fill out, you had to make sure there was an application running on the server that would implement this. There were a number of applications that could do this, so you needed to know the syntax required by the particular application running on your server. If your web page was transferred to another server running a different application, your HTML will probably have to be modified.

With FrontPage those days are over. A great deal of the functionality and usefulness of FrontPage comes from the fact that it includes a standard set of server extensions that can run on virtually any HTTP server platform with any major server software. This means your FrontPage-created web can be placed on any Web server running the FrontPage Server Extensions and will function correctly.

As a content creator, you simply need to know that the FrontPage Server Extensions are installed on your ISP's Web server. (When you installed FrontPage on your local computer, the server extensions for the FrontPage Personal Web Server

12

were also installed.) Then you are assured that any WebBots, forms, or discussion groups you've included in your web will function on your ISP's server.

IP: *Microsoft maintains a list of ISPs who support the FrontPage Server Extensions at* http://www.microsoft.com/frontpage/ispinfo/isphost.htm. *Given the vast improvement in creating web content enabled by FrontPage, you should expect this list to grow considerably.*

Installing the FrontPage Server Extensions

If you are maintaining your own Web server (as distinct from your FrontPage Personal Web Server), you need to install the FrontPage Server Extensions on it. Alternatively, you may have to work with your ISP to install the FrontPage Server Extensions on their server. (For a variety of reasons, including security, ISPs can be reluctant to install every piece of software a client suggests.) Therefore, the next several paragraphs provide some of the reasoning behind the FrontPage Server Extensions, and an overview of the installation process.

For the most part, the FrontPage Server Extensions use the standard common gateway interface (CGI) found on all web servers. The CGI provides a standard protocol for the transfer and processing of data between a client (a web browser, for example) and a server. On an Internet Information Server, the server extensions are implemented as dynamic link libraries (DLLs). This allows the server extensions to take up less room and to execute faster. In any case, data is transferred to the FrontPage Server Extensions from the web server software. The server extensions then process the data and hand the output back to the server software. For example, in the case of a text search, the search criteria would be passed from the HTTP server to the appropriate FrontPage Server Extension. The database would then be searched using the specified criteria, and the results of the search handed back to the HTTP server. It would then be formatted with the specified HTML code and sent back to the client (web browser) that initiated the search.

Adding the FrontPage Server Extensions to an existing web server is a relatively simple process. The first step is to get a copy of the FrontPage Server Extensions for your web server. These are available at no charge from Microsoft's web site (http://www.microsoft.com/frontpage/freestuff/fs_fp_extensions.htm).

Microsoft currently provides FrontPage Server Extensions for:

■ Intel-based computers running Windows 95 using the FrontPage Personal Web Server or the O'Reilly WebSite 1.1

■ Intel-based computers running Windows NT 3.51 or 4.0 Beta 2 using the FrontPage Personal Web Server, the O'Reilly WebSite 1.1, Netscape Communications Server v1.12, Netscape Commerce Server, or Microsoft Internet Information Server

■ Sun workstations SPARC architecture running Solaris 2.4 or SunOS 4.1.3 using Netscape Communications Server v1.12, NCSA, CERN, Apache, or Open Market Web Server

■ Silicon Graphics computers running IRIX 5.3 using Netscape Communications Server v1.12, NCSA, CERN, Apache, or Open Market Web Server

■ Hewlett-Packard computers running HP/UX 9.03 using Netscape Communications Server v1.12, NCSA, CERN, Apache, or Open Market Web Server

■ Intel-based computers running BSDi UNIX /OS 2.1 using Netscape Communications Server v1.12, NCSA, CERN, Apache, or Open Market Web Server

As you can see, the FrontPage Server Extensions are available for the majority of web server platforms and HTTP server software.

Installation of the FrontPage Server Extensions varies depending on the platform, but complete instructions are included with the server extension files from Microsoft and are relatively simple. The only time FrontPage has to be installed on the web server running the server extensions is when you're using Windows NT and Microsoft Internet Information Server.

The primary issue with an ISP over installing the FrontPage Server Extensions (besides being one more thing to learn) will be security. When someone accesses a web page on a server, they are given certain permissions. Normally these are limited to reading data on the server. The user is usually not allowed to write to the server's hard disk or to change any of the files on the server. The reason is obvious: if a user is allowed to place a file on a server, that file, through malicious intent or simple ignorance, could wreak havoc on the server. Network administrators protect their

12

servers by restricting the type of access users are allowed (and some people make a hobby of beating the administrator's best efforts).

The FrontPage Server Extensions, like virtually every CGI application and script, need to allow the user to write to a file or directory on the server. The server's security is maintained by cordoning-off these specific areas. Depending on the operating system and HTTP server software, the FrontPage Server Extensions generally require the same permissions as other CGI applications and do not represent an increased security risk.

The last word may simply be that FrontPage fills a tremendous gap in the quality of tools available for creating web content. If you remember the days of creating HTML in a text editor, you know how much more efficiently your time is used with FrontPage (if you don't remember, fire up Notepad and review Chapter 9).

It is possible to re-create the interactive functions of your web on a web server that is not using the FrontPage Server Extensions. Rather than the integrated set of functions that FrontPage Server Extensions provide, the web server may have a number of individual applications and scripts that provide the same functions. It may be, however, that if your ISP can't be convinced to install the FrontPage Server Extensions, you need to find another ISP.

Posting to a Host with FrontPage Server Extensions

Once your FrontPage web is completed and tested on your FrontPage Personal Web Server, it's ready for the Big Time: the World Wide Web. Hopefully your ISP has the FrontPage Server Extensions installed and has created a directory for your creation on the web server. (Posting your web to a server without the FrontPage Server Extensions is covered in the next section.)

To post a FrontPage web to a server with FrontPage Server Extensions, you must first have permission to write files to the server. Your webmaster or server administrator will be able to assign the proper permission to your account. Your webmaster or administrator may have you post your web to a temporary directory as an additional security measure. Once you have the proper permissions and location on the server for your web, you would use these steps to post your web:

1. Start the FrontPage Personal Web Server and then the FrontPage Explorer, if necessary.

2. If you use a dial-up account to access the Internet, activate your Internet connection.

3. In the FrontPage Explorer open the web you will place on the web server.

4. Open the File menu and select Copy Web. The Copy Web dialog box will be displayed, as shown here:

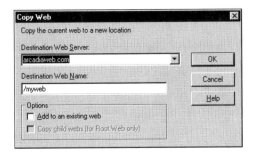

5. Select or type in the name of the destination server in the Destination Web Server drop-down list box.

6. The current name for the web is displayed in the Destination Web Name text box. If you want to use a different name for the web, type it there.

7. If you are adding to or replacing pages in an existing web, select the Add To An Existing Web check box. If you are copying the root web of the server, select the Copy Child Webs (For Root Web Only) check box to have the child webs of the root web copied also.

8. Click on OK. Since you need administrator permission to copy a web, the Name And Password Required dialog box will be displayed.

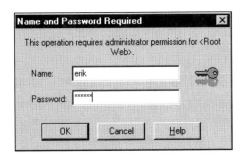

> *n* **OTE:** *The "Administrator" permission and password that you need here are the administrator of the server, not the administrator name and password that you are used to entering on your own computer.*

9. Enter the name and password, and then click on OK.

10. After the web files are successfully copied to the destination web, a message stating that will be displayed. Click on OK.

You can now open your favorite browser and open your web on the destination server to make sure that it still functions correctly. In most cases posting your web to the server will be this simple. There is, however, the possibility that one or more of the files may not transfer correctly or become corrupted, particularly if your web contains a number of large files. If you think this has happened, the easiest way to correct the problem is to delete the web from the server and copy it again. To delete your web:

1. In FrontPage Explorer, with your Internet connection active, open the web by selecting Open Web from the File menu.

2. In the Open Web dialog box select the correct web server in the Web Server drop-down list box.

3. Click on the List Webs button, and select the web from the Webs list box.

4. When the web has opened in the FrontPage Explorer, select Delete Web from the File menu.

Once the web is deleted, repeat the steps given previously to again copy the web to the web server. If you continue to have problems copying your web to the web server, contact the webmaster or server administrator. It is possible to delete individual files from the web server, by using Dial-up Networking and Windows Explorer (provided, once again, you have the correct permissions), but this can confuse FrontPage. FrontPage keeps track of all the components of your web; if you change any of the components outside of FrontPage, then FrontPage may end up looking for files that no longer exist or are in a different place.

If you successfully copy your web to the server, but find that some elements don't function correctly, first make sure that the web works correctly on your Personal Web Server. Then contact your webmaster or server administrator and explain the problem. If other webs using the same feature function correctly on the web server, the odds are that the problem is in your web. If the problem is common to other webs on the web server, then the FrontPage Server Extensions might not be installed correctly.

Posting to a Host Without FrontPage Server Extensions

You can also post a web created in FrontPage to a web server that isn't running FrontPage Server Extensions. While any features relying on the server extensions (forms, and so on) will not function, all the standard HTML functions, such as hyperlinks, will be unaffected.

Microsoft separately provides the FrontPage Publishing Wizard, which assists you in posting your web to a web server that does not support the FrontPage Server Extensions. The FrontPage Publishing Wizard can be found at *http://www.microsoft.com/frontpage/freestuff/fs_fp_pbwiz.htm*. The FrontPage Publishing Wizard copies the web pages you select to the destination web server and notifies you of which pages require the FrontPage Server Extensions to function correctly. The FrontPage Publishing Wizard posts your web pages to an FTP (file transfer protocol) server, rather than a web server. An FTP server is usually just a separate directory on the ISP's web server. However, your web pages will not be able to be opened by a web browser until they are placed on the web server. The webmaster or server administrator will have to do that once the pages are uploaded to the FTP server. You will also need permission to write to the destination FTP server. Your webmaster or server administrator will be able to assign the proper permission to your account.

The following instructions can be used with the FrontPage Publishing Wizard to post a FrontPage web to a server without the FrontPage Server Extensions:

1. After downloading and installing the FrontPage Publishing Wizard, open the Windows 95 Start menu, select Programs, Microsoft FrontPage, and

12

then FrontPage Publishing Wizard. The Publishing Wizard will open, as shown here:

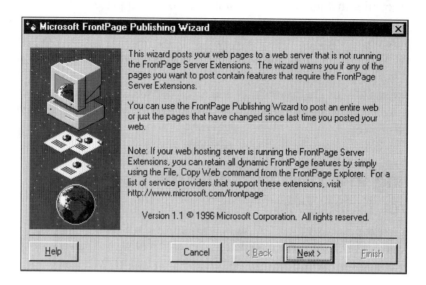

2. Click on Next. You will be prompted for the name of the destination FTP server and directory to copy your web, your user name, and your password to write to the server.

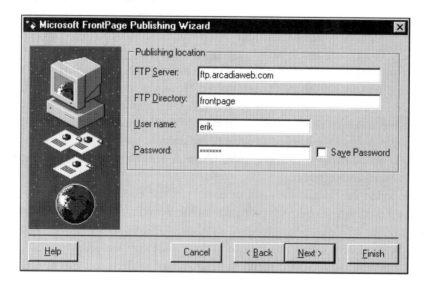

3. Next, the FrontPage Publishing Wizard will display the webs that are on your computer.

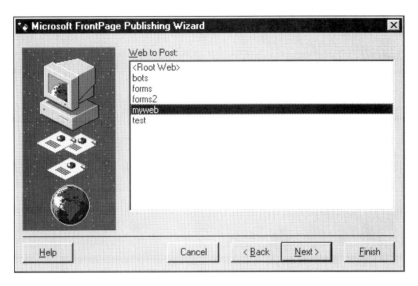

4. Select the web or webs you want copied and click on Next.

5. Next, the FrontPage Publishing Wizard will identify which pages contain elements that require the FrontPage Server Extensions to work correctly. Click on Next.

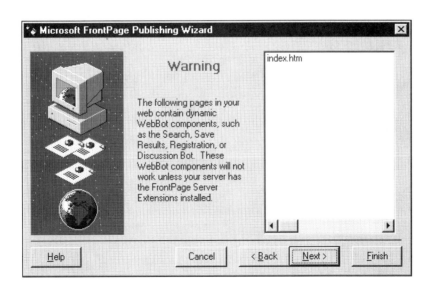

12

6. You are then asked to select which web files to post. You can post all the files or only the files that have changed since you last posted the web, including or excluding the pages that require the FrontPage Server Extensions to work correctly. You can also manually select which pages to post.

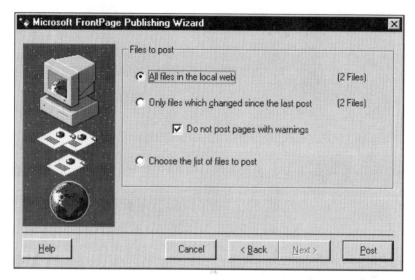

7. If you select the Choose The List Of Files To Post option, an additional screen is displayed. Select the files you want by double-clicking on them, or select them and click on Add. After selecting the web pages to post, click on Post.

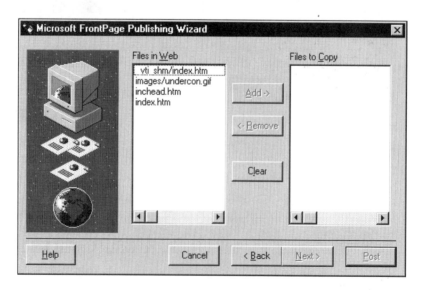

Even if the web server that will host your web pages does not have the FrontPage Server Extensions, you may still be able to have the same functionality. For example, most servers will have an application or script for handling form input. You would need to ask your webmaster or server administrator how to access the application and then incorporate it into your web page by editing the HTML. Of course, it would be much easier if the server hosting your web supported the FrontPage Server Extensions.

Promoting Your Web Site

Once your web site has been posted to a web server, you need to let people know that it is there. If your web site is business related, the first step is to tell your existing customers about it. You might include an announcement with your regular invoicing, for example. You should also include your URL in all your conventional advertising, including your business cards, invoices, statements, purchase orders, drawings, reports, and any other document you produce. It's not uncommon to see URLs on everything from television commercials to billboards.

You also need to make sure you can be found on the Web by anyone looking for the products and services you offer. A number of search engines for the Web have been developed. Some, like Digital's Alta Vista, actively search the Web for information. Others, like Yahoo, depend more on having web sites submitted to them. Figure 12-1 shows part of the online form used to submit web sites to Yahoo. You can also submit your web site to virtually all the search engines. A simple way to reach a number of search engines is to use the Submit It web site (http://www.submit-it.com/), where your single entry is submitted to over 15 search engines.

Since many search engines are actively searching the Web for sites, it helps to have an introductory paragraph on your home page that gives a concise description of your site. This paragraph should include the keywords that apply to your site.

The following are search engines that you should make sure you are correctly listed on:

Alta Vista	http://www.altavista.digital.com/
Excite	http://www.excite.com/
Hot Bot	http://www.hotbot.com/
Lycos	http://lycos.cs.cmu.edu/
Switchboard	http://www2.switchboard.com/
Web Crawler	http://webcrawler.com/
Yahoo	http://www.yahoo.com/search.html

12

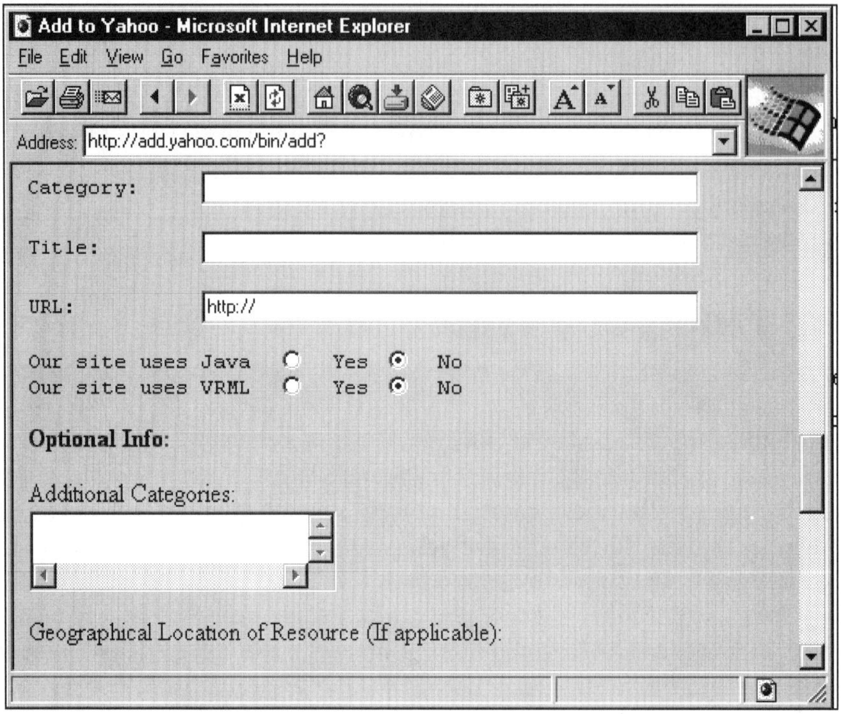

Yahoo
submission
form

FIGURE 12-1

Another useful tool for promoting your web site is *reciprocal links.* These are simply hyperlinks on your web page that point to someone who has a link to your site. Say you sell mountain-climbing equipment. You could do a search of the Web for climbing clubs and other groups with web sites relating to climbing. You then contact the owners of the sites, offering to put a link on your site to theirs if they will return the favor. This way anyone who finds any of the sites you're linked to has a direct link to your site. If you gather enough links on your site, it may become a starting point for people "surfing the Net."

You shouldn't overlook a press release, either. When your web site goes online, or you make a major addition, let the press and publications related to your business know about it. What you should *not* do is advertise your web site or business in newsgroups, unless the newsgroup is specifically run for that purpose. Say you decide to have a sale on climbing equipment. In your zeal to let the world know, you post a message on a recreational climbing newsgroup. The one result you can count on is that you will be flooded with "flames," and, frankly, you will deserve them.

A surefire way to get your web site widely known is to simply produce an outstanding web site. Today, there are over 30 million sites on the World Wide Web. Aim to be in the top 5 percent of that group. In the era of conventional marketing that goal would be virtually impossible for a small business, but the web is a new paradigm. Creativity and content count more than advertising budgets. Give people a reason to visit your site by providing content that is unique and useful to them. Then package it in an effective, pleasing design. Take the time to explore the Web and gather ideas for your own site. (Gathering ideas is fine, gathering graphics or other actual content, no matter how easy it is, is a violation of copyright laws.)

The World Wide Web, whether you use it for business or pleasure, is having an effect on society as fundamental as the invention of the printing press. With FrontPage you have the tools to participate in this new world.

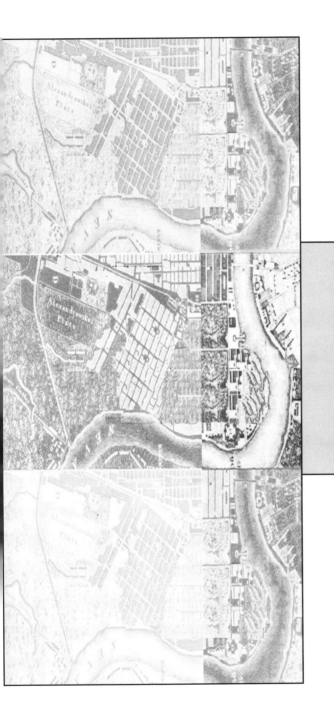

Installing FrontPage

Installing FrontPage is an easy task, as you'll discover in this appendix. The onscreen instructions are clear, and with the information in this appendix, you will soon have FrontPage ready to use.

What System Requirements Are Needed

To install FrontPage you'll need the following software and hardware:

- Windows 95 or Windows NT (version 3.51 or higher)

- PC with a 486DX-66 or higher or a Pentium

- 16MB of memory

- At least 20MB of disk space

To access the Internet or an intranet network where FrontPage will be used, you also must have installed the TCP/IP protocols (see Chapter 1 for a discussion of this) on either or both a dial-up network and/or a local area network (LAN). If you are using a network browser with Windows 95 or Windows NT, you probably have already installed and correctly configured TCP/IP. If you are just now coming up on the Internet or a network, you need to install TCP/IP. For the Internet, the best source is Microsoft Plus for Windows 95, which provides all the necessary programs, as well as installation wizards and lots of instruction. For an intranet you need to work with your network administrator or other source of technical information to set up your network for TCP/IP. One of the best references is Tom Sheldon's *Encyclopedia of Networking,* published by Osborne/McGraw-Hill (1994).

What Components You'll Find in FrontPage

FrontPage is delivered with a number of components, which are described in detail in Chapter 2. Among these are

- **FrontPage client software** This allows you to create and edit webs (documents that you can deliver over the Internet or an intranet). It includes the FrontPage Explorer, the FrontPage Editor, the To Do List,

and the FrontPage wizards. Most of this book discusses how to use this software.

■ **FrontPage web server software**   This allows you to maintain and deliver webs to creators and users of them. It includes the FrontPage Personal Web Server, which is a full 32-bit web server for your PC that uses the HyperText Transfer Protocol (HTTP) and common gateway interface (CGI) standards; and the FrontPage Server Extensions, which provide additional programs and tools to use with the Personal Web Server. Chapters 11 and 12 discuss the server software in depth.

■ **FrontPage utility software**   This includes FrontPage TCP/IP Test, which will verify if your system is correctly configured with TCP/IP, and a FrontPage Server Administrator, to assist in working with passwords, updating web sites, and installing and uninstalling features.

How to Install FrontPage

You may install FrontPage with either a Typical or a Custom installation procedure. If you choose Typical, recommended for most users, all FrontPage components will be installed. This is the choice assumed in this book and reflected in its examples and illustrations. If you choose Custom, you may choose which components to install. Be wary of using the Custom installation if you are not knowledgeable about FrontPage and its internal structure.

Before you start, be prepared to specify two directory paths: one for installing FrontPage client software, and another for the web server programs and the webs that you will create. FrontPage will create default directories for you if you have no other preferences, and that is the assumption and recommendation of this book. Throughout the book you'll see the statement "if you followed the default installation procedure," which identifies the default directories that the FrontPage Setup program will create for you.

OTE: *It is strongly recommended that you choose the Typical installation and that you let the Setup program create the default directories where FrontPage will be installed.*

Performing a Typical Installation

Follow these steps for a Typical installation:

1. Exit all programs before installing FrontPage. Nothing should be running but Windows.

2. If you are installing FrontPage from disk, insert Disk 1 into your drive. If you are installing FrontPage from a network, connect to the source of the Setup program.

3. On Windows 95, choose Run from the Start menu, and type the path to the disk containing FrontPage Setup; then type **setup**, as shown next. If you are using Windows NT, select Run from the File menu, and type the same path and name to load the setup program.

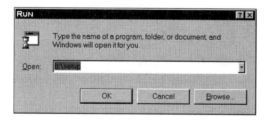

4. After a minute you will see the "Welcome" message. After you have read it, click on Next to continue.

5. In the Destination Path dialog box that opens next, you will see the Destination Directory where FrontPage client software will be placed, as shown in Figure A-1. The default is C:\Program Files\Microsoft FrontPage.

6. If you want to install FrontPage into a different directory, choose Browse and select the Path to the destination directory you want. Do this by selecting the drive in the Drives field, and choosing the directory in the Directories field. If you want to install FrontPage on another computer, click on Network and find the drive and directory on your network where FrontPage is to be installed. Choose OK (twice if you have selected a Network directory) when you have displayed the destination directory you want in the Path field. If the directory does not exist, Setup will create it for you.

The
Destination
Path dialog
box shows
the
directory
for
FrontPage
installation

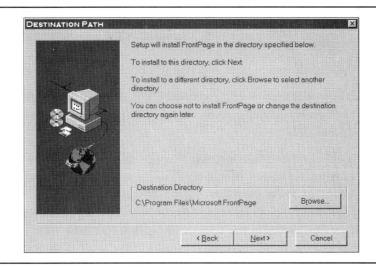

■ FIGURE A-1

7. Click on Next to accept the Destination Directory and continue.

8. The Setup Type dialog box, shown in Figure A-2, allows you to select the type of installation, Typical or Custom, to perform. If it is not already selected, click on Typical to select it, and then click on Next to continue. (A Custom installation will be looked at later in this appendix.)

The Setup
Type dialog
box allows
you to
select the
type of
installation

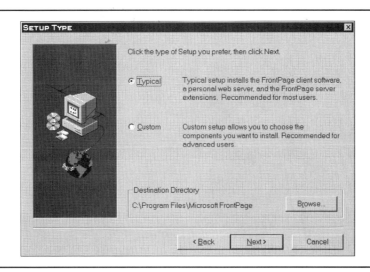

■ FIGURE A-2

9. The default directory for the FrontPage server software as well as the webs that you create will be displayed in the Choose Personal Web Server Directory dialog box. The default directory is C:\FrontPage Webs and is the recommendation assumed in this book.

10. If you choose another directory, click on Browse and select that directory as discussed in step 6. When the directory is what you want, click on Next to continue.

11. The Select Program Folder dialog box will add FrontPage shortcuts to a program folder for easier access, as shown in Figure A-3. If the default folder in the Program Folders box, Microsoft FrontPage, is not what you want, either select another from the list found under Existing Folders, or type the name you want. Click on Next to continue.

12. The Start Copying Files dialog box will display your selections for directories and components that will be installed. The default selections are shown in Figure A-4. If you agree with the selections, click on Next to begin copying the program files. If you see something you want to change, click on Back as necessary to return to the original dialog box of the item that needs attention, change it, and then click on Next as necessary to return and begin the copying.

13. You will see a summary of resources being used as the copying proceeds. The three bars represent the percentage of the current file being copied,

The Select Program Folder dialog box adds program icons to the stated folders

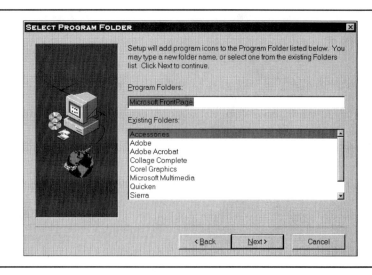

FIGURE A-3

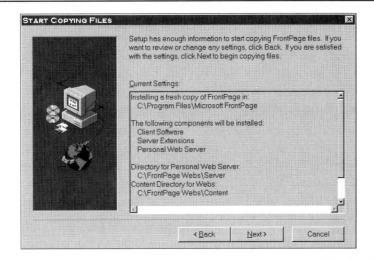

Display of
selected
directories
and
components

FIGURE A-4

the percentage of the current disk copied, and the percentage of your
computer's disk space used. After a bit, you'll be asked for additional
disks in the Setup Needs The Next Disk dialog box, shown here:

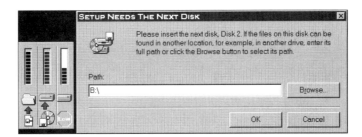

14. If you are installing FrontPage from disks, remove the current disk and
insert the requested disk. If you are installing from another source, use
Browse to find the next disk sequence. Click OK to continue with the copy.

15. When the copying is complete, the Administrator Setup For Personal Web
Server dialog box will be displayed, as you can see in Figure A-5. Type a
name that you will use with the web server, press TAB, and type in a
password. This will be the name and password by which authorized persons
can request access in order to edit the web site. Press TAB and retype the
password to confirm it. Click on OK to complete the installation.

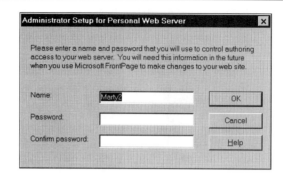

Selecting a name and password to use with the web server

FIGURE A-5

16. The "Setup Complete" message allows you to immediately start up the FrontPage Explorer. If you do not want to do that at this time, click on Start The FrontPage Explorer Now to uncheck it. In either case, click on Finish to complete the installation.

17. FrontPage will now determine your computer's hostname and TCP/IP address. Click on OK to initiate this procedure.

FrontPage is now installed. If you selected it, the FrontPage Explorer will now be displayed. Otherwise you will be returned to your normal environment.

Performing a Custom Installation

Use the Custom installation when you want to install only some of the three FrontPage component programs, for instance, if you are only interested in the FrontPage Client Software and not the Personal Web Server, or vice versa. You also may use Custom installation if you are upgrading a previous copy of FrontPage. If you are installing FrontPage over a previous copy, you will want to use the same directory structure you used originally in order to preserve access to your webs. If you want to use a different directory, you will first have to uninstall the first copy and reinstall it to the desired directory.

To perform a Custom installation, follow these steps:

1. Exit all Windows programs before installing FrontPage.

2. If you are installing FrontPage from disk, insert Disk 1 into your drive. If you are installing FrontPage from a network, connect to the source of the setup program.

3. On Windows 95, choose Run from the Start menu, type the path to the disk containing FrontPage, and then type **setup**, as shown next. If you are using Windows NT, select Run from the File menu, and type the same path and name.

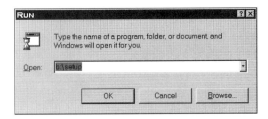

4. After a minute you will see the "Welcome" message. After you have read it, click on Next to continue.

5. When the Destination Path dialog box is displayed and you are upgrading an existing copy, you will be informed that a previous copy of FrontPage has been detected, as shown in Figure A-6. If you want to upgrade or install programs over the current copy, click on Next. If you want to

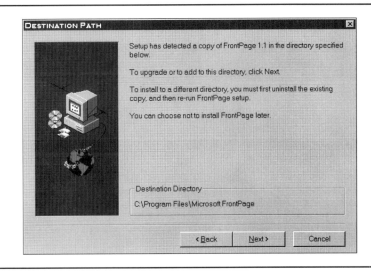

The Destination Path dialog box requires a unique directory name

FIGURE A-6

install to a different copy, you will first have to uninstall FrontPage and reinstall it into the desired directory. Choose Cancel to install to a different directory, open the Control Panel, choose Add/Remove Programs, select Microsoft FrontPage, click on Add/Remove, and follow the instructions.

Due to the complex directory structure that Setup builds, you should probably use the default directories. The rest of this book, in its references and graphics, assumes that you have chosen the defaults.

6. In the Setup Type area, click on Custom and then click on Next.

7. The Select Components dialog box, displayed in Figure A-7, allows you to select the FrontPage components to be installed. To not install any of the components, click on the check box to clear it. (However, if you want to install the Personal Web Server, you also should install the Server Extensions.)

8. If you find that your disk space is limited, you can search for additional space by clicking on Disk Space. As shown next, Available shows the disk space available on the selected disk drive. Required shows the disk space required for your selected components. Click on OK to close the Available Disk Space dialog box, and then click on Next.

The Select Components dialog box specifies which components will be installed

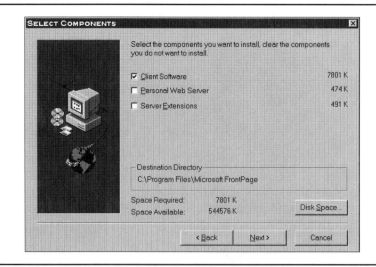

FIGURE A-7

9. The default directory for the FrontPage server software as well as the webs that you create will be displayed in the Choose Personal Web Server Directory dialog box. The default directory is C:\FrontPage Webs and is the recommendation assumed in this book. Click on Next to select it, or first use Browse to choose a new directory.

10. The Select Program Folder dialog box will add FrontPage shortcuts to a program folder for easier access, as shown in Figure A-8. If the default folder, Microsoft FrontPage, is not what you want, either select another from the list found under Existing Folders, or type the name you want. Click on Next to continue.

11. The Start Copying Files dialog box will display your own selections for directories and components that will be installed. The defaults are shown in Figure A-9. If you agree with the selections, click on Next to copy the programs from the source to the destination directories. If you see something you want to change, click on Back as necessary to return to the

The Select Program Folder dialog box adds program icons to the stated folders

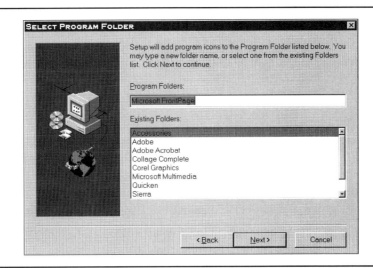

FIGURE A-8

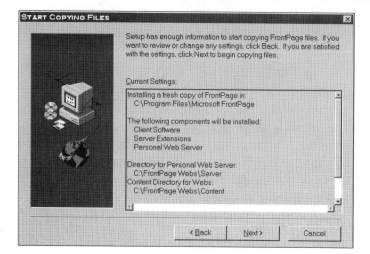

Display of
selected
directories
and
components

FIGURE A-9

original dialog box of the item that needs attention, change it, and then click on Next as necessary to return and begin the copying.

12. You will see a summary of resources being used as the copying proceeds. The three bars represent the percentage of the current file being copied, the percentage of the current disk copied, and the percentage of your computer's disk space used. After a bit, you'll be asked for additional disks, as shown here:

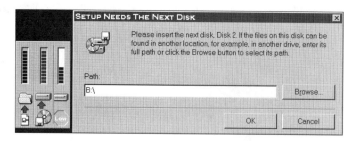

13. If you are installing FrontPage from disks, remove the current disk and insert the requested disk. If you are installing from another source, use Browse to find the next disk sequence. Click OK to continue with the copy.

14. When you are finished, click Finish on the Setup Complete message to complete the installation.

FrontPage Explorer will be displayed, ready for you to begin working with the updated programs.

Checking Your Network Setup

The FrontPage package includes a program that tests whether you are properly set up on a network with the TCP/IP protocol, and what your host name and IP address are. Run that test as follows:

1. Open the Start menu, choose Programs, Microsoft FrontPage, and FrontPage TCP_IP Test. (If, during installation, you choose a program file different from Microsoft FrontPage, choose that name in the Programs menu.) The FrontPage TCP/IP Test dialog box will open.

2. Click on Start Test. You may be asked if you want to connect to your Internet service provider (ISP). If you want to use your FrontPage Personal Web Server for the local creation of your webs, click on Cancel in the Connect To dialog box. (Using your FrontPage Personal Web Server is assumed and recommended in this book.)

3. Your test results will appear. If all is well, they will look like those shown in Figure A-10. In any case, click on Explain Results. The Results Explanation dialog box will open with a detailed explanation of what was found and how to solve or work around any problems. If you are having problems, this is an excellent resource.

4. Click on OK to close the Results Explanation dialog box, and then click on Exit to close the FrontPage TCP/IP Test.

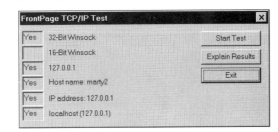

Results of
TCP/IP test

FIGURE A-10

If the suggestions in the Results Explanation dialog box did not solve your problems, here are some ideas of where to look for solutions:

■ Is FrontPage installed properly? Uninstall and reinstall it using nothing but defaults and make absolutely sure *nothing* but Windows is running during installation.

■ If you are on a network, make sure that the TCP/IP protocol has been set up. Do that by opening your Control Panel (Start menu, Settings, Control Panel) and double-clicking on Network. There you should see TCP/IP as a protocol, as you can see in Figure A-11 (you may only need it on either your LAN or your dial-up network, and not necessarily on both, as shown in Figure A-11).

If you don't have TCP/IP as one of your protocols, click on Add in the Network control panel, double-click on Protocol, click on Microsoft in the left list, and then click on TCP/IP on the right. Click on OK twice, and answer Yes to restarting your computer.

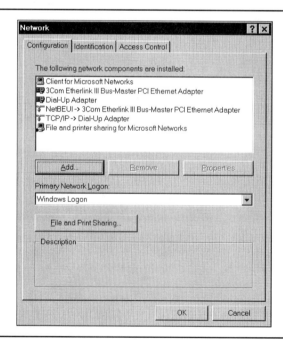

Network control panel showing TCP/IP protocol

FIGURE A-11

■ If you are only using the Internet over phone lines, you still need to have dial-up networking installed and the TCP/IP protocol assigned to it. The easiest way to do all that is to install Microsoft Plus for Windows 95 and to use that to install Internet capability.

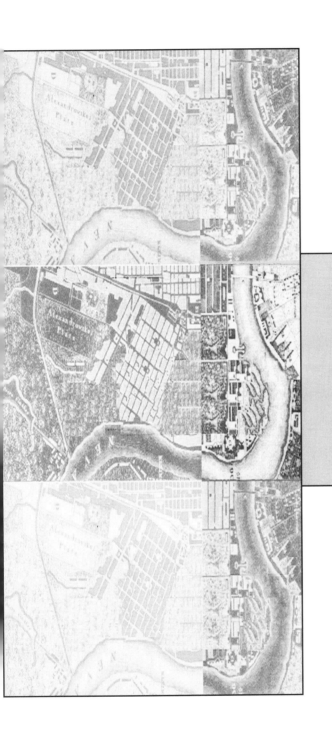

FrontPage on the Web

Web Sites Created with FrontPage

As FrontPage gains popularity, an increasing number of FrontPage-created sites are appearing on the Web. This appendix presents four examples of FrontPage pioneers who began by using FrontPage 1.0 in early 1996 or before. You are encouraged to look at these sites and possibly correspond with the webmasters. They have done what you are setting out to do.

Wisconsin Bankers Association

URL: *http://www.wisbank.com*
Webmaster: Kurt R. Bauer, Assistant Director-Communications
E-mail: kbauer@wisbank.com

One East Main Street, Suite 200
Madison, Wisconsin 53703
(608)256-0673
(608)256-7162 (fax)

About WBA OnLine

The Wisconsin Bankers Association (WBA) created its web site, WBA OnLine, to provide an Internet link to news and information about the Wisconsin banking industry. WBA, founded in 1892, represents nearly 380 banks of all sizes—99 percent of all Wisconsin banks. Their home page, shown in Figure B-1, has a definite bank feel with a marble look to the name plate and a parchment background. The site is broken into two major areas: one, a password-protected area, shown in Figure B-2, that provides information on WBA member services, and another that provides bank-related information to consumers, shown in Figure B-3.

When webmaster Kurt Bauer was asked what he likes about FrontPage, he responded that it was being able to do WYSIWYG (what-you-see-is-what-you-get) web creation and editing. He did not want to go through the process of learning HTML only to have it become a forgotten art, much like DOS commands have become. Kurt said, "Windows has replaced the need to know DOS just as FrontPage and other programs like it will undoubtedly replace the need for raw HTML programming."

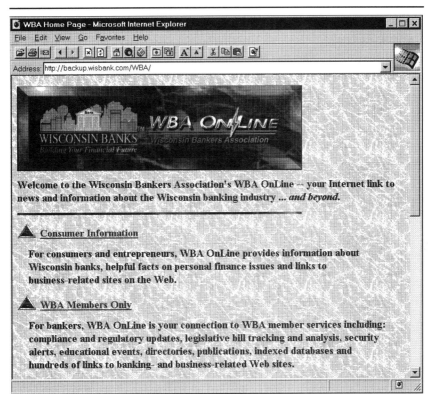

Wisconsin
Bankers
Association
home page

Figures B-1 through B-3 used with permission of the Wisconsin Bankers Association.

FIGURE B-1

Kurt believes that FrontPage's best feature is its very short learning curve. He taught himself the basics on a Saturday and picked up the more advanced features as he went along. What he doesn't like is the skimpy manual. It should be more comprehensive. He says, "I am also running the first version of Vermeer FrontPage, so the software is a bit buggy at times. But, overall, I think it is a fun and easy software package that takes the mystery out of web authoring. With FrontPage, anyone who knows how to point and click can become a webmaster!"

WBA OnLine went "live" in late January 1996 after roughly one month of construction. Kurt became the webmaster because of his communications and writing background, and because he saw the World Wide Web's potential as a means for the WBA to communicate timely and critical information to its membership. He also wanted to use WBA OnLine to deliver information about banks and personal

B

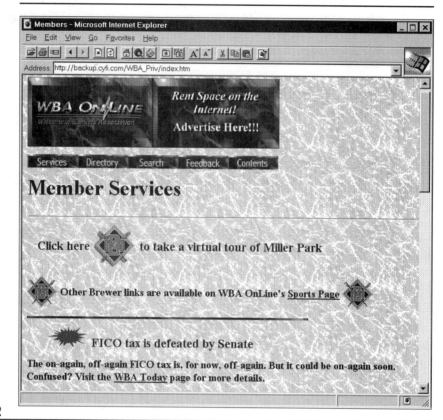

WBA
OnLine
Member
Services
page

FIGURE B-2

finance to the surfing public who are, according to demographic studies, the best potential new customers for banks.

FrontPage Tips

Kurt's tips on using FrontPage are

- "Don't accidentally delete your web! This recently happened to me. While trying to do two things at once, I meant to delete a file under the Edit menu. However, under the File menu is a "delete web" option which I hit instead. Both options ask you if you really want to do it and the messages are similar."

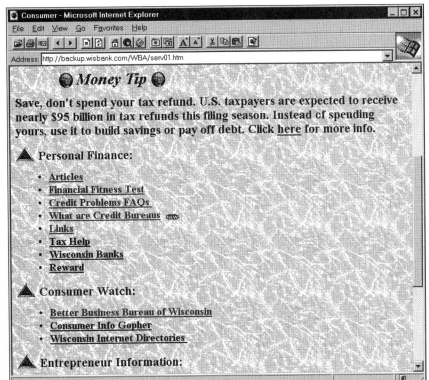

WBA
OnLine
Consumer
Information
page

FIGURE B-3

- "I also recommend saving your work often, and close pages as soon as they have been updated or constructed."

- "Finally, ask for frequent input from your target audience and make changes accordingly. I have created a users group for WBA OnLine to help make it user friendly. Feedback is very important. Sometimes what the webmaster thinks makes sense doesn't to the end user."

B

The Pennsylvania Chamber of Business and Industry

URL: *http://www.pachamber.org*
Webmaster: Renee Loomis, Manager, Communications Technology
E-mail: rloomis@pachamber.org

One Commerce Square
417 Walnut Street
Harrisburg, PA 17101
(717)255-3252
(800)225-7224
(717)255-3298 (fax)

About the PAChamber Web

The Pennsylvania Chamber of Business and Industry created its web site to provide information to and about Pennsylvania businesses and the Pennsylvania economic climate. The Pennsylvania Chamber represents over 5,000 member businesses employing half of Pennsylvania's private work force. It is the fastest growing state chamber in the United States. The PAChamber's home page has a stylish flair, as you can see in Figure B-4, and was created with a table. (Since the PAChamber's web was created with FrontPage 1.0, which did not have tables, the home page was created outside of FrontPage, although it could now be created in FrontPage 1.1.) Of the many pages at this site, two of the most interesting are Committees OnLine, which provides password-protected information and discussion groups for committee members, as shown in Figure B-5, and the PaBiznet page, which provides news and information for Pennsylvania businesses, as you can see in Figure B-6.

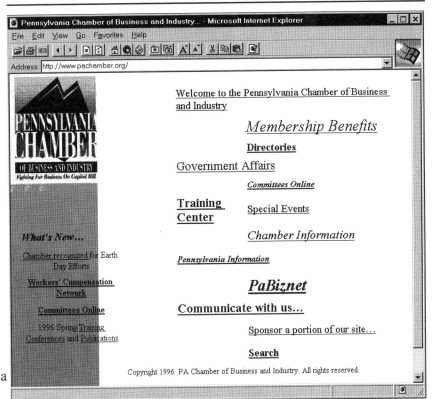

Pennsylvania
Chamber's
home page

FIGURE B-4

Webmaster Renee Loomis said that the PAChamber started using FrontPage because it was part of an AT&T pilot project on the Web and they were asked by AT&T to use FrontPage. She had been using Microsoft's Internet Assistant for Microsoft Word. After a very short time, though, FrontPage became her preferred way to produce pages. Her favorite features in FrontPage are the Include bot and the image mapping capability because of the time they save and their power. She also likes how the FrontPage Explorer and FrontPage Editor work together, and likes the Verify Links command. Since she has been using FrontPage 1.0, she is very anxious to get 1.1 and use the tables and frames features.

B

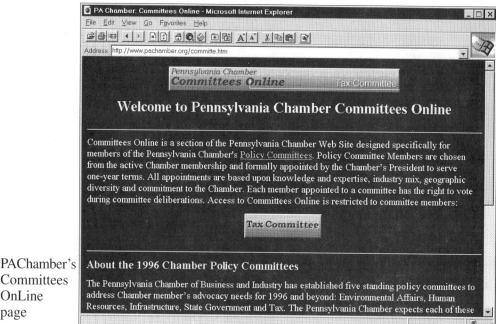

PAChamber's
Committees
OnLine
page

FIGURE B-5

The PAChamber site started out as a bulletin board for members to track legislation in the state and in Washington D.C. In an effort to find a quicker way of informing and involving members, the PAChamber put up their first pages on the Web in September, 1995 using Internet Assistant and Microsoft Word. In January 1996, most of their pages were converted to FrontPage and employed image mapping, the Include and Timestamp bots, and new backgrounds. Since the conversion to FrontPage, the PAChamber has gotten a lot of positive feedback on their site. Renee has been involved with this since the bulletin board days and has really enjoyed the switch to the Web and FrontPage. She says, "Unfortunately, I also have a number of other duties and cannot spend a large percentage of my time creating web pages—all the more reason why FrontPage is such an important tool for me."

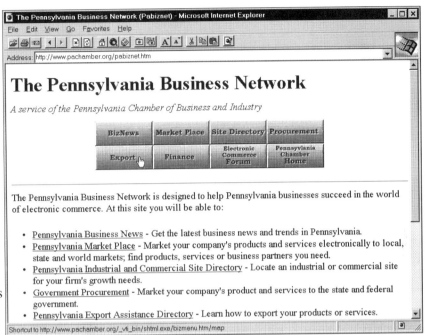

PAChamber's
PaBiznet
page

FIGURE B-6

FrontPage Tip

Renee says that her best tip on using FrontPage is to "Make heavy use of the Include bot. It can save you a tremendous amount of time creating and maintaining a set of pages with repetitive features."

ComBase Communications

URL: *http://www.combase.com*
Webmaster: Alex Kiwerski, Senior Systems Administrator
E-mail: alex@combase.com

148 N. Parsons Avenue
Brandon, FL 33510
(813)681-9020
(813)681-9180 (fax)

About the ComBase Web

ComBase Communications created its web site as a service to their users and to promote their services. ComBase is an independent Internet service provider (ISP) located in Brandon, Florida, and sponsored by Upgrade Computers. From their home page, shown in Figure B-7, you can get information on Internet access, Upgrade Computers, their User and Businesses home pages, and can search the Web. Of particular interest is the ComBase search page, which you can see in Figure B-8, where you can use any one of a number of search engines. Also, the ComBase service rates page that is shown in Figure B-9 has a particularly attractive design.

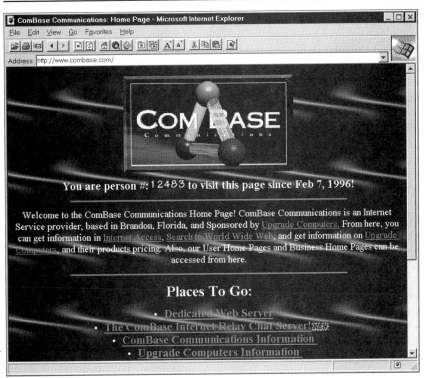

You are person #: 12483 to visit this page since Feb 7, 1996!

Welcome to the ComBase Communications Home Page! ComBase Communications is an Internet Service provider, based in Brandon, Florida, and Sponsored by Upgrade Computers. From here, you can get information in Internet Access, Search to World Wide Web, and get information on Upgrade Computers, and their products pricing. Also, our User Home Pages and Business Home Pages can be accessed from here.

Places To Go:

- Dedicated Web Server
- The ComBase Internet Relay Chat Server! NEW
- ComBase Communications Information
- Upgrade Computers Information

ComBase Communica- tion's home page

Figures B-7 through B-9 are used with the permission of ComBase Communications.

▉ FIGURE B-7

Webmaster Alex Kiwerski said that after using several other products, including Hot Metal Pro and Live Markup, he ran across FrontPage and started working with it in November, 1995. In his mind it really stood out for its WYSIWYG characteristics and the automation provided by its wizards and WebBots. He likes the ability to see what he's designing while he's designing it. He also likes the ability to copy directly to the web server instead of having to FTP to it. His primary dislike is that bots, which represent so much of the power of FrontPage, require the FrontPage Server Extensions, and there is no easy way to replace the bots with custom CGI when you need to run off of a server without the Extensions.

B

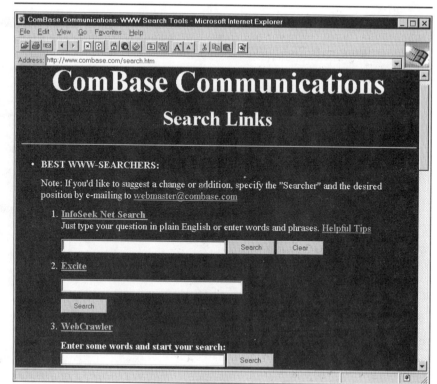

ComBase's
search page

FIGURE B-8

ComBase Communications is a provider of all forms of computer networking, WANs (wide area networks) as well as LANS. As Alex said, "If it has to do with networking, we do it." It was therefore natural that they get involved with both the Internet and World Wide Web, as well as intranets. They have had a Web presence since the fall of 1995. The Web, and especially intranets, are a growing part of their business.

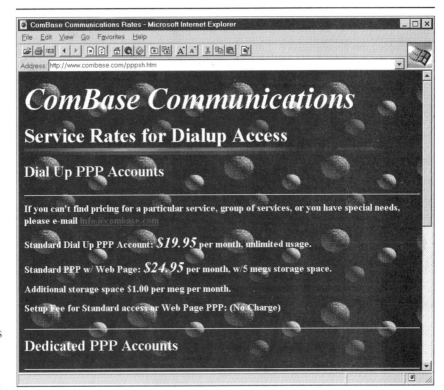

ComBase's
service
rates page

FIGURE B-9

FrontPage Tip

Alex's tip on using FrontPage is that, "You should not rely 100 percent on FrontPage. Figure you'll have to write some HTML by hand."

Realacom and Tourismo

URL: *http://www.realacom.com*
Webmaster: Rob Rawson, Site Manager
E-mail: realacom@www.realacom.com

> 258 Riverside Drive
> Holly Hill, FL 32117
> (904)258-9500
> (904)253-8042 (fax: call first)

About the Realacom Web

Realacom created their web site as a service to their customers and, most importantly, to people trying to use FrontPage. The site also is used to promote their services. Realacom is an independent Internet service provider (ISP) based in a suburb of Daytona Beach, Florida. From the Realacom home page, shown in Figure B-10, you can get information on Internet access, make use of a vehicles for sale database (Figure B-11), and view their User and Businesses home pages (and a graphical ranking of usage of those pages with a dynamic table shown in Figure B-12). You can also go to a test page where you can upload your FrontPage webs and try them out with an NT server and the FrontPage Server Extensions for free (they are not committing to how long this will last!).

Webmaster Rob Rawson says that FrontPage is the most powerful tool he has seen to create or edit a web page without destroying any existing HTML if some of the page was designed manually. He further says that, "FrontPage takes hours out

Realacom's home page

Figures B-10 through B-12 are used by permission of Realacom and Tourismo.

FIGURE B-10

of designing a page or web site compared to conventional methods. Take for example, the table of contents on our home page. That was made in five seconds. It took another 10 to 15 minutes to correct our site because FrontPage showed our mistakes. If I did that manually, it might take up to a half a day. If I change a page in my site, then I would have to change the table of contents, but FrontPage does that automatically." Also Rob likes the ease with which you an create forms, as seen

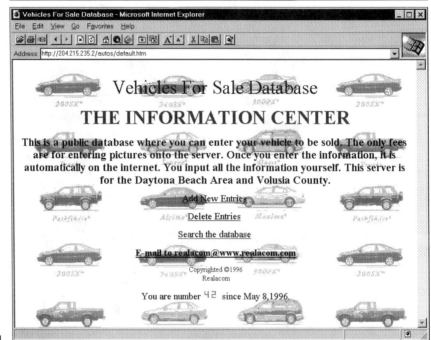

Realacom's
Vehicles
for Sale
Database
page

FIGURE B-11

in his autos database. He dislikes the </P> FrontPage puts in the HTML because Netscape reads it as a <P>, and he designs his pages for both Netscape and Microsoft browsers. Another dislike is the high CPU consumption, but that is balanced by FrontPage being such a powerful tool.

Realacom's web site came up in February, 1996. It previously existed as a BBS that was on an prototype Internet platform. Rob says that most or all Internet providers got their start as a BBS, which is a crude platform compared to the Internet and the World Wide Web today. Rob has been involved with Realacom since its BBS days and is mostly involved in the programming side of the business.

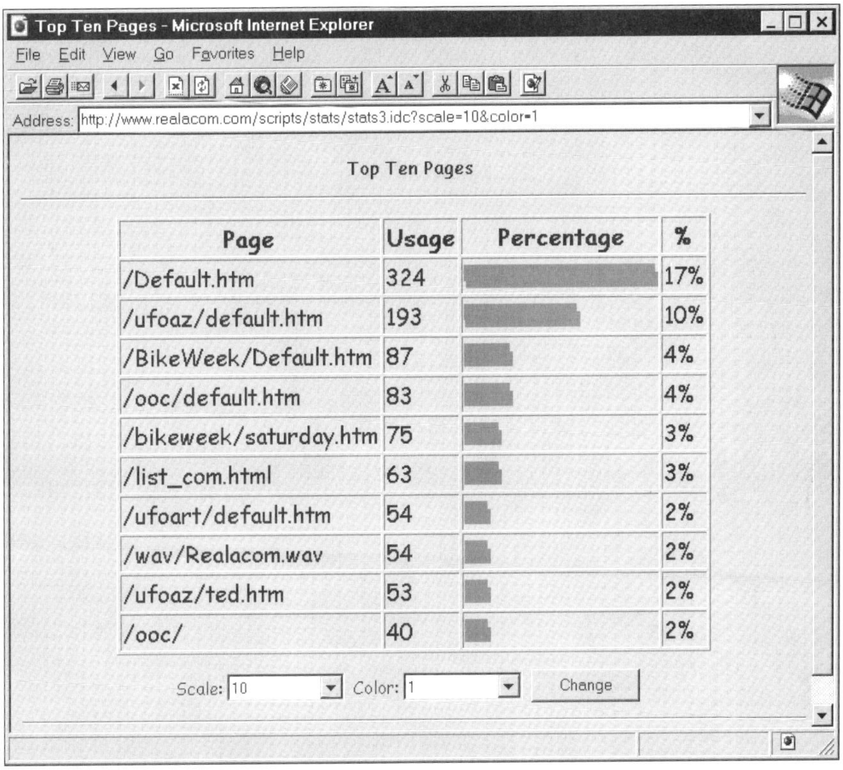

Realacom's
Top Ten
Pages page

FIGURE B-12

FrontPage Tip

Rob's best FrontPage tip is to "Read the help files and practice with the tutorial wizard."

A

INDEX

D

G

I

N

Y

DIGITAL DESIGN
FOR THE
21ST CENTURY

You can count on Osborne/McGraw-Hill and its expert authors to bring you the inside scoop on digital design, production, and the best-selling graphics software.

Digital Images: A Practical Guide
by Adele Droblas Greenberg
and Seth Greenberg
$26.95 U.S.A.
ISBN 0-07-882113-4

Scanning the Professional Way
by Sybil Ihrig and Emil Ihrig
$21.95 U.S.A.
ISBN 0-07-882145-2

Preparing Digital Images for Print
by Sybil Ihrig and Emil Ihrig
$21.95 U.S.A.
ISBN 0-07-882146-0

**Fundamental Photoshop:
A Complete Introduction,
Second Edition**
by Adele Droblas Greenberg
and Seth Greenberg
$29.95 U.S.A.
ISBN 0-07-882093-6

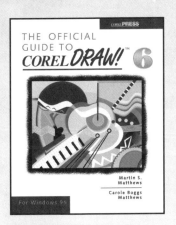

**The Official Guide to
CorelDRAW!™6 for Windows 95**
by Martin S. Matthews and Carole Boggs Matthews
$34.95 U.S.A.
ISBN 0-07-882168-1

**The Official Guide to Corel
PHOTO-PAINT 6**
by David Huss
$34.95 U.S.A.
ISBN 0-07-882207-6

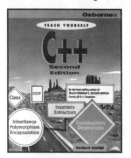

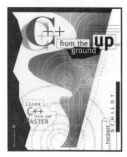

ORDER BOOKS DIRECTLY FROM OSBORNE/McGRAW-HILL

For a complete catalog of Osborne's books, call 510-549-6600 or write to us at 2600 Tenth Street, Berkeley, CA 94710

Call Toll-Free, *24 hours a day, 7 days a week, in the U.S.A.*
U.S.A.: 1-800-262-4729   **Canada: 1-800-565-5758**

Mail *in the U.S.A. to:*   **Canada**

McGraw-Hill, Inc.   McGraw-Hill Ryerson
Customer Service Dept.   Customer Service
P.O. Box 182607   300 Water Street
Columbus, OH 43218-2607   Whitby, Ontario L1N 9B6

Fax *in the U.S.A. to:*   **Canada**
1-614-759-3644   **1-800-463-5885**
                               Canada
                               orders@mcgrawhill.ca

SHIP TO:

Name _____

Company _____

Address _____

City / State / Zip _____

Daytime Telephone *(We'll contact you if there's a question about your order.)*

ISBN #	BOOK TITLE	Quantity	Price	Total
0-07-88				
0-07-88				
0-07-88				
0-07-88				
0-07-88				
0-07088				
0-07-88				
0-07-88				
0-07-88				
0-07-88				
0-07-88				
0-07-88				
0-07-88				
0-07-88				
	Shipping & Handling Charge from Chart Below			
	Subtotal			
	Please Add Applicable State & Local Sales Tax			
	TOTAL			

Shipping & Handling Charges

Order Amount	U.S.	Outside U.S.
$15.00 - $24.99	$4.00	$6.00
$25.00 - $49.99	$5.00	$7.00
$50.00 - $74.99	$6.00	$8.00
$75.00 - and up	$7.00	$9.00
$100.00 - and up	$8.00	$10.00

Occasionally we allow other selected companies to use our mailing list. If you would prefer that we not include you in these extra mailings, please check here: ❑

METHOD OF PAYMENT

❑ Check or money order enclosed (payable to Osborne/McGraw-Hill)

❑ AMERICAN EXPRESS   ❑ DISCOVER   ❑ MasterCard   ❑ VISA

Account No. ☐☐☐☐☐☐☐☐☐☐☐☐☐☐☐☐

Expiration Date _____

Signature _____

In a hurry? Call with your order anytime, day or night, or visit your local bookstore.

Thank you for your order

Code BC640SL